# Analysing Sentences
## An Introduction to English Syntax

## Learning About Language

General Editors: Geoffrey Leech and Mick Short,
Lancaster University

# Analysing Sentences
## An Introduction to English Syntax

Noel Burton-Roberts

Longman
London and New York

**Longman Group Limited**
Longman House, Burnt Mill, Harlow
Essex CM20 2JE, England
*and Associated Companies throughout the world*

*Published in the United States of America*
*by Longman Inc., New York*

First published 1986
Eleventh impression 1995

**British Library Cataloguing in Publication Data**

Burton-Roberts, Noel
  Analysing sentences: an introduction to
  English syntax.
  I. English language——Syntax
  I. Title
  425     PE1361
  **ISBN 0-582-29136-4**

**Library of Congress Cataloging in Publication Data**

Burton-Roberts, Noel, 1948-
  Analysing sentences.

  Bibliography: p.
  Includes index.
  I. English language——Sentences.    2. English language—
  Syntax.    I. Title.
  PE1375.B87    1986    425    84-29699
ISBN 0-582-29136-4

Produced through Longman Malaysia, CL

# Contents

# Acknowledgements

This book grew out of a longish pamphlet used with first year undergraduates in the University of Newcastle upon Tyne, which I wrote in 1979. I'd like to acknowledge the late Barbara Strang's encouragement when I wrote that pamphlet. Thanks, too, to Geoff Leech and Mick Short (the series editors) for their help and encouragement in producing the book as it now stands. Valerie Adams, painstakingly and to good effect, went through each chapter as it was completed and for this I am very grateful. This book has also benefited from comments made by Ewan Klein, Maggie Cooper, Rodney Huddleston, Michael Anthony, Phil Carr, Liz Smith, and Lesley Milroy. Herman Moisl's arbitrations between myself and the word processor are gratefully acknowledged. I owe a general debt of gratitude to Sir Randolph Quirk, who introduced me to the study of the English language in the first place. Finally, my thanks to Tessa for her support and patience.

# Introduction

Attempting to describe the language you speak is about as difficult as attempting to describe yourself as a person. Your language is very much part of you and your thinking. You use your language so instinctively that it is difficult to stand outside yourself and think of it as something that is independent of you, something which you know and which can be described. You may even feel inclined to say that your language is not something you know, you just speak it, and that's all there is to it. But as the native speaker of a language, there is an important sense in which you do know all that there is to know about that language. This is not to deny that there are almost certainly words with which you are not familiar. Perhaps you don't know the meaning of the word *lagophthalmic*. If so, your (understandable) ignorance of this is more medical ignorance than ignorance about the English language, and is anyway quickly remedied with the help of a dictionary. But there is much more to a language than its words. There is much more that you do know about your language which cannot so conveniently be looked up, and which you were never explicitly taught. And this is knowledge of a more fundamental and systematic kind than knowledge of the meanings of individual words. The more fundamental such knowledge is, the more difficult it is to become consciously aware of it.

We are brought up sharply against our own knowledge of the language when, for example, we hear a foreigner make a mistake. You may have had the frustrating experience of knowing that something is wrong but not being able to say precisely what it is, beyond saying 'We just don't say it like that.' The very deep-seated character of a speaker's knowledge of his language makes it extremely difficult for him to explain what it is that he knows in knowing the language.

Here are some examples to illustrate the point. As a speaker of

English, you will agree that [1] and [2] are good English sentences:

[1]  Dick believes himself to be a genius.
[2]  Dick believes he is a genius.

but that there is something wrong with [3] and [4]:

[3]  Dick believes he to be a genius.
[4]  Dick believes himself is a genius.

It is interesting that, simply on the basis of assuming you speak English, and knowing nothing else about you, I can predict that you will judge [1] and [2] to be good and [3] and [4] to be odd, even though these sentences are something you may never have considered before.

In attempting to answer the question 'Is this an example of a good English sentence or not?' we are obliged to go to speakers of the language and ask them whether they would accept it as such. (If we ourselves speak the language, then we may ask ourselves.) It is difficult to see how else we could decide what is and what is not a sentence of English. Yet, if this is so, our agreement about [1]–[4] constitutes a fact about the English language. In a real sense, then, all the facts about the language lie inside the heads of its speakers.

But can you give an explanation for the oddity of [3] and [4] – beyond saying that we just don't say it like that?

Here is another example. If the negative of [5] is [6],

[5]  They were jumping on it.
[6]  They weren't jumping on it.

why isn't [8] the negative of [7]?

[7]  They tried jumping on it.
[8]  They triedn't jumping on it.

And another example: Since [9] is a good English sentence, why aren't [10] and [11]?

[9]  Bevis mended his car in the garage and Max did so in the lay-by.
[10]  Bevis put his car in the garage and Max did so in the lay-by.
[11]  Bevis went to the circus and Max did so to the zoo.

Finally, we can say [12]

[12]  Those charming atomic scientists called round again.

but [13] sounds odd:

[13] Those atomic charming scientists called round again.

These are just a tiny sample of a large body of facts, mysteries, and puzzles offered by the English language. Some of the puzzles have been solved (to our present satisfaction, at least). Others remain puzzles, or there is disagreement as to what the most appropriate explanation might be. And, as we find out more about the language, we should expect to discover further puzzles, and perhaps even find things puzzling which we thought we had understood.

The aim of this book is to encourage you to stand outside yourself and confront just one aspect of your largely unconscious knowledge of English. It does not discuss, let alone offer solutions to, all the puzzles known to exist, nor even to give very detailed accounts of intricacies like those above. But it will introduce you to a method of describing the language, and provide you with a vocabulary with which to start thinking about the language in terms of which the puzzles can be identified and solutions sought.

The chapters that follow are concerned with English SYNTAX. *Syntax* is traditionally the name given to the study of the form, positioning, and grouping, of the elements that go to make up sentences. In a word, it is about the STRUCTURE of sentences. In studying a language, there is of course a lot else to talk about besides its syntax. For example, we can investigate the form and grouping of the elements within words themselves. The systematic study of word–structure is called MORPHOLOGY. Or we can concentrate on the meaning of sentences and how their meaning is related to the meaning of the words they contain. This is called SEMANTICS. Or we can concentrate on what they can sound like when spoken. This is called PHONOLOGY.

I shall say nothing about the phonology of English, and not much about meaning, but it should become clear just how closely the form (syntax) and the meaning (semantics) of English sentences are related. Occasionally, it will be necessary to look at the form of words themselves (morphology), but the book does not pretend to offer a systematic introduction to morphology.

The book is an introduction to the practical analysis of English sentences rather than an introduction to linguistic theory. But since we will be concerned with a language and its syntax, some of the concepts, aims and methods of linguistics are relevant. For anyone who is interested in discovering more about linguistic theory, finding out something of the syntax of a language he knows well seems an appropriate (indeed indispensible) way to start. Chapter 11 is included with such readers in mind. It is designed to place the description of English offered in the previous chapters in a wider context and raise some questions about the general aims and principles of syntactic analysis.

Finally, a word or two about the description offered here. In a book of this length, it hardly needs pointing out that the description is not exhaustive. Nevertheless, the range of structures covered is intended to be comprehensive enough for the book to serve not only as the basis for more exhaustive and specialised study but as a self-contained description for non-specialists who need a practical, and appliable, system of analysis for the major structures.

Since this last aim is important, I have concentrated on presenting a single, more or less traditional, analysis of each structure considered, without overburdening the reader with too much discussion of how that analysis might or might not be justified in the light of further evidence. This might give the misleading impression that there is just one possible analysis and that there is universal agreement that it is the one in this book! This is far from being the case. But sometimes the evidence that might support an alternative analysis is complex and indirect and its discussion would be inappropriate in such an introduction. The reader should bear in mind, then, that we are never irrevocably committed to a particular analysis but are free to amend it in the light of further evidence. Finding that evidence, and deciding between competing analyses on the basis of such evidence is, in the end, what 'doing syntax' is all about.

## The organisation of the chapters

Chapters 1, 2, and 3 have a dual purpose: they introduce general ideas relevant to the analysis of sentences while simultaneously beginning the analysis itself.

Chapters 4 and 5 complete the general overview of the simple sentence.

Chapters 6 and 7 each go into more detail on certain aspects of the structure of simple sentences.

Chapters 8, 9, and 10 deal with different kinds of subordinate clause in the complex sentence.

Chapter 11 is a more general discussion of the background to and purpose of the kind of analysis presented in Chapters 1 to 10.

## A note on how to read this book

There are end-of-chapter exercises which are followed immediately by answer/discussion sections. Some of them recapitulate material discussed in the Chapter, but others develop that material. These exercises, then, should be considered as an important part of each Chapter and not just an optional extra. In addition, there are small exercises within the text of each chapter, forming an integral part of its discussion. Try doing these exercises as and when they occur before reading further. As often as not, the discussion that follows depends on your having done the exercise. A line has been ruled at the point where it is suggested you stop and do the exercise. (You may find it helpful to have pencil and paper to hand.) Doing these should make your reading of the book more productive and interesting than attempting to absorb the material passively.

# CHAPTER 1

# Sentence Structure: Constituents

## Structure

The concept of STRUCTURE is fundamental to the study of syntax. But it is a very general concept that can be applied to any complex thing, whether it be a bicycle, a commercial company, or a carbon molecule. When we say of a thing that it is COMPLEX we mean, not that it is complicated (though of course it may be), but that

(a) it is divisible into parts (called CONSTITUENTS),
(b) there are different kinds of parts (different CATEGORIES of constituents),
(c) the constituents are ARRANGED in a specifiable way,
(d) that each constituent has a certain specifiable FUNCTION in the structure of the thing as a whole.

When anything can be analysed in this way, we say that it has structure. And in considering structure it is important to note that, more often than not, the constituents of a complex thing are themselves complex. In other words, the parts themselves consist of parts which may in turn consist of further parts. When this is so we may speak of a HIERARCHY of parts and HIERARCHICAL STRUCTURE.

It is obvious, for example, that a complex thing like a bicycle is not just a collection of randomly assembled bits and pieces. Suppose you gathered together all the components of a bicycle: metal tubes, hubs, spokes, chain, cable, and so on. Now try to imagine all the possible objects you could construct by fixing these components together. Would they all be bicycles? Surely not. Some of them would no doubt be excellent bicycles, while others wouldn't remotely resemble a bicycle (though they might make interesting sculptures). And, of course, there would be intermediate cases, things which we would probably want to say were bicycles, if only because they resembled bicycles more than anything else. So, only some of the possible ways of fitting bicycle components together produce a bicycle. A bicycle consists not just of its components but, much more importantly, in **the STRUCTURE that results from fitting them together in a particular way.** When we turn to linguistic expressions, we find a similar state of affairs. Suppose you have a collection of words, say all the words in a dictionary. Can you imagine all the possible word–sequences you could construct by putting these words together? The possibilities are endless. Clearly not all the sequences would be acceptable expressions or sentences of English. And again, some would be odder than others. When a sequence of words fails to constitute a good expression in the language, I shall describe it as being UNGRAMMATICAL (or ILL-FORMED) and mark it with an asterisk (*). Here are some examples:

[1a] *the nevertheless procrastinate in foxtrot
[1b] *and and if
[1c] *disappears none girls of the students
[1d] *put Mary
[1e] *Max will bought a frying pans.

More subtle examples of ungrammatical sentences were given in the introduction.

Ultimately, a full syntactic description of the English language (indeed, of any language) consists in explaining why some strings of words of the language are well-formed expressions and why others are not. Just how this ultimate (and very ambitious) goal might be attempted is discussed in Chapter 11. For the moment it is enough to say that it could not be achieved without recognising the importance of structure. Just as the concept of structure was required in distinguishing between the bicycles and the would-be bicycles, so the concept of structure is essential in distinguishing between the strings of words that are well-formed expressions in the language and those that are not.

We can use diagrams to show how things can be analysed into their constituent parts. For instance, [2] says that a bicycle can be analysed into two wheels, a frame, a chain, handlebars, among other things (the dots mean 'and other things'):

[2]                            Bicycle

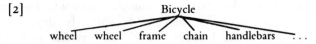

wheel    wheel    frame    chain    handlebars    . . .

Such diagrams are called TREE-DIAGRAMS; as conventionally represented, however, the trees are upside-down.

I have mentioned that the constituents of a complex thing can themselves be complex. An example of this is a bicycle wheel. It is itself a constituent of the bicycle, but in turn consists of hub, spokes, rim, tyre, etc. Although it is true that spokes are constituents of bicycles, it is more important to note that they are constituents of bicycles only because they are constituents of the wheel which, in turn, is a constituent of the bicycle. The relation between spoke and bicycle is indirect, mediated by wheel. We might express this by saying that, though the spoke is a constituent of the bicycle, it is not an IMMEDIATE CONSTITUENT of it. It is important to recognise the indirectness of the relationship between bicycle and spoke because, in giving a description of the structure of bicycles, we need to be able to say that wheels are parts of bicycles. But if we were to allow that spokes were immediate constituents of bicycles rather than of wheels this would leave wheels rather out of the picture. It would imply that bicycles could have spokes independently of the fact that they have wheels, and that spokes were not a necessary part of the structure of wheels.

As mentioned, specifying the FUNCTION of constituents is an important part of structural analysis. Notice that if we were to represent spokes as immediate constituents of bicycles, it would be impossible to specify correctly what the function of the spokes is – for the spokes don't have a function in respect of the bicycle directly, but only in respect of the wheels of which they are part. In talking of the function of the spokes, then, we are going to have to mention the wheels anyway.

Which of the following tree-diagrams best represents the structural relationship between bicycle and spoke just discussed?

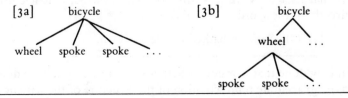

[3a]    bicycle

wheel    spoke    spoke    . . .

[3b]    bicycle

wheel    . . .

spoke    spoke    . . .

Although each tree-diagram is incomplete, [3b] more accurately reflects the structural relationship between bicycle and spoke, since it says that spokes are constituents of wheel which, in turn, is a constituent of bicycle. It correctly describes the relationship between bicycle, wheel, and spoke as being a hierarchical relation. [3a], on the other hand, in having a line directly joining spoke to bicycle, says that spokes are immediate constituents of bicycles, independently of the fact that wheels are constituents of bicycles.

This book is concerned with SYNTACTIC STRUCTURE, that is, with analysing linguistic expressions into their constituent parts, identifying the categories of those constituents, and determining their functions. But what kind of expressions should we begin with? I shall take the SENTENCE as the starting point for analysis. I shall assume (and in fact already have assumed) that you have an intuitive idea of what counts as a sentence of English.

The first question to be asked is 'What do sentences consist of?' The answer might appear to be blindingly obvious: 'Sentences consist of words.' In the rest of this chapter (and, for that matter, the rest of the book) I shall try to convince you that this apparently natural answer is not the most appropriate one. In fact, the discussion of hierarchical structure and the importance of recognising that sentences have such structure forces us very quickly to abandon the idea that sentences consist, in any simple way, of words.

This can be shown by asking whether the relationship between a sentence and its words is direct, or whether it is indirect, mediated by parts of intermediate complexity. This amounts to asking the question 'Are words the IMMEDIATE CONSTITUENTS of the sentences that contain them?' It is only if the words contained in a sentence are its immediate constituents that we can allow that sentences actually consist of words. As an aid to thinking about this question – and to gain practice in getting such diagrams to say what you want them to say – draw a tree-diagram, starting with 'Sentence' at the top, which says of sentence [4] that its words are its immediate constituents, that it consists directly of the words it contains.

[4]   Old Sam sunbathed beside a stream.

---

Having done that, consider whether the diagram you have drawn gives an accurate representation of the structure of the sentence as you feel it to be.

---

The diagram that says of sentence [4] that its words are its immediate constituents looks like this:

[5]
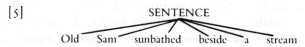

Do you feel that the diagram is wrong or unhelpful as a description of sentence [4]? How much does it tell us? Certainly it tells us what words appear in the sentence. And it tells us in what order they appear.[1] But it tells us nothing more. In addition to being uninformative the diagram is actually wrong as a description of the structure of the sentence. In essence, it says of sentence [4] that it has no structure – or no more structure than a sequence of numbers (1–2–3–4–5) or an ordered string of beads. This is surely wrong.

In not allowing that the sentence has constituents that mediate between it and its words, the diagram does not allow that certain of the words seem to belong with others, that the words seem to work in groups. It says that the words have no relationship to each other except the relationship of being in a certain order in the same sentence. And, although the diagram tells us in what order the words occur, in failing to assign any but the simplest possible structure to the sentence, it fails to give any explanation of why they occur in that order to form a sentence, and why the orders in [6] and [7], for example, do not form sentences of English.

[6] *Stream old Sam sunbathed beside a
[7] *Sunbathed old beside stream a Sam[2]

We need to say that sentence [4] is more highly structured

---

1. In this respect such diagrams are especially appropriate for the representation of linguistic structure – more appropriate than they are for the representation of the structure of a physical three-dimensional object like a bicycle – since they cannot be relied on to express information about physical arrangement in space but only about a rather abstract kind of organisation. Both bicycles and sentences have abstract organisation but, since bicycles are physical objects as well, such diagrams only give part of the story on bicycles.

2. You may be interested to know that, mathematically, there are seven hundred and twenty ways of stringing six words together. And yet, if the six words are those that appear in sentence [4], very few (well under twenty) of these strings would make grammatical sentences of the English language.

than [5] says it is. After all, as we saw in the discussion of bicycles earlier, what position a spoke occupies in the structure of a bicycle is determined by its being a constituent of wheel, which itself has a certain specifiable position within the bicycle. If you attempt to reposition the spokes from out of their structural position within the wheel, you land up with an unworkable bicycle. A very similar thing has happened in [6] and [7]. The arrangement of words in a sentence is largely determined by the fact that the words are not immediate constituents of the sentence, but belong with other words to form groups which have their own specifiable position in the structure of the sentence. It is these groups (or further groups made up of these groups) that function as immediate constituents of the sentence.

In addition, we need to be able to say what KINDS (or CATEGORIES) of words can combine to form structural groups. What is wrong with [6] and [7] is that words have been displaced from positions in which they are capable of forming groups with the words next to them to positions where they are not, given the kinds of words they are. But the diagram gives no information of this sort. Such information is not only needed to account for the ungrammaticality of [6] and [7]; it is also needed if we want to explain why replacing *stream* with *road* yields another good sentence of English:

[8]  Old Sam sunbathed beside a road.

but replacing *stream* with *laughing* or *surreptitiously* does not.

[9a]  *Old Sam sunbathed beside a laughing.
[9b]  *Old Sam sunbathed beside a surreptitiously.

*road* can replace *stream* in [4] because *road* and *stream* belong to the same CATEGORY: they are both NOUNS. *laughing* (a VERB) and *surreptitiously* (an ADVERB) cannot replace *stream* because they belong to different categories.

So we need to include information about GRAMMATICAL CATEGORIES in our diagrams and this is something I shall consider in later chapters. This, together with information on how the words group together to form intermediate constituents, will help to explain not only the facts about [6]–[9], but also facts about the functions of words (and groups of words) in sentences.

The discussion so far suggests that diagram [5] is not just unhelpful, but actually wrong as a structural description of sentence [4]. As soon as we want to explain even the simplest things about sentences, it becomes necessary to go beyond the idea that sentences simply consist of words strung together in a line. We need to acknowledge that sentences have hierarchical structure.

## Establishing constituents

I have been complaining in a rather general way about diagram [5]. What is needed now is a more specific demonstration of just how it is wrong. This will help us work towards a more appropriate representation of its structure. I shall not attempt here to give a comprehensive or systematic analysis of sentence [4], but to give a general introduction to the identification of constituents larger than the word.

One way of clearly establishing that [5] is wrong is as follows. If the sentence had the same (lack of) structure as an ordered sequence of numbers, we should be able to lop words off the end of the sentence and still be left with a good sentence every time we did so. We can lop numbers off the end of a number sequence and still be left with a good (though shorter) number sequence: 1–2–3–4–5, 1–2–3–4, 1–2–3, 1–2, 1. Begin by removing first one word and then another from the end of sentence [4] until you are left with just one word. Each time write down the string that remains. In front of every string of words that seems to you not to constitute a COMPLETE AND GRAMMATICAL SENTENCE, put an asterisk.

Assuming we all speak the same language, you should have a list of five strings marked in the following way:

[10]  *Old Sam sunbathed beside a
[11]  *Old Sam sunbathed beside
[12]   Old Sam sunbathed
[13]  *Old Sam
[14]  *Old

Of the strings, only [12] could stand as a complete and well-formed sentence. [13] may not seem quite as odd as [10], [11] and [14] do, for reasons which will become apparent shortly. Nevertheless, it should still be asterisked since it is not a complete sentence. What needs to be explained is why string [12] is a good sentence while none of the others are.

In the first place, you should note that not all parts of a

sentence are necessary in order for that sentence to be complete and well-formed. For simplicity, consider [15].

[15]  Martha smiled.

[15] is a good sentence as it stands. But notice that we could add to it. For example, we could add the word *invitingly*, to produce another good sentence [16]:

[16]  Martha smiled invitingly.

In [16], then, we may say that *invitingly* is an OPTIONAL part of the sentence: leaving it out gives us another complete and perfectly grammatical sentence, namely [15]. (By contrast, *Martha*, and *smiled* are OBLIGATORY.)

The importance of this in the present context is that I have referred to *invitingly* as a PART, as a CONSTITUENT, of sentence [16]; I have said that it is an optional part. Now it is obvious that *invitingly* must be a constituent part (a structural unit) in sentence [16], since it is a single word. Now, to go back to sentence [4], we saw in [10]–[14] that we could omit the SEQUENCE OF WORDS *beside* plus *a* plus *stream* and be left with a good sentence. In other words, that SEQUENCE is optional. Notice, however, that it is only the sequence as a whole, as a single unit, that is optional. None of the words in the sequence can be omitted individually. So, just as I needed to refer to the single word *invitingly* and say that it was an optional constituent in the structure of sentence [16], so I need to be able to refer to the sequence of words *beside* plus *a* plus *stream* as a unit, and say of it that, as a unit, it is optional in the structure of sentence [4]. In doing so, I acknowledge that word-sequence as an identifiable part, as a consituent, of that sentence.

**Sequences of words that can function as constituents in the structure of sentences are called PHRASES.** And since our tree diagrams are intended to represent structure by marking which sequences of words in a sentence are its constituent phrases, such diagrams are called PHRASE-MARKERS.

I have shown that the sequence of words *beside a stream* is a constituent of sentence [4]. It is, therefore, a phrase. And once we have recognised it as a phrase, we must treat the words within it as parts, not so much of the sentence, but of the phrase itself. This phrase is intermediate between the sentence and the words, rather in the way that wheel is intermediate between bicycle and spoke. Since we cannot omit any of the words individually, it appears that, while the phrase as a whole is optional in the structure of the sentence, the words themselves are not optional, but necessary in the structure of the phrase.

In sentence [17] below, there are two separate sequences of words which can be omitted without affecting the grammaticality of the sentence. Can you identify them?

[17]  The very muscular gentleman next to me lit a cigar.

---

Since [18], [19], and [20] are all perfectly good, complete sentences

[18]  The (. . .) gentleman next to me lit a cigar
[19]  The very muscular gentleman (. . .) lit a cigar
[20]  The (. . .) gentleman (. . .) lit a cigar

we need to be able to say that *very muscular* (omitted in [18] and [20]) and *next to me* (omitted in [19] and [20]) are PHRASES which are optional constituents in the structure of sentence [17]. In saying this, I am not necessarily saying that they are immediate constituents of the sentence itself: we may (and in this case will) find that they are immediate constituents, not of the sentence, but of yet further phrases within the sentence.

**If a sequence of words can be omitted from a sentence leaving another good sentence, this is a good indication that the sequence is a phrase functioning as a constituent in the structure of the sentence. However, not all phrases are omissible.** We must therefore find a more general and systematic way of demonstrating that a given sequence of words is a phrase.

There are several different ways of doing this. You will recall that we were never in doubt that *invitingly* was a constituent in [15]: it is a single word, after all. And we wanted to say of the sequence of words *beside a stream* that it had the same unitary character as a single word. This suggests that **if you can replace a SEQUENCE OF WORDS in a sentence with a SINGLE WORD without changing the overall structure of the sentence, then that sequence functions as a constituent of the sentence and is therefore a phrase.** This test will confirm that *beside a stream* is functioning as a constituent in sentence [4]. For example, if the speaker of sentence [4] were in a position to point to the spot where Sam sunbathed, he could quite easily replace *beside a stream* by *here* or *there*:

[21a]  Old Sam sunbathed here.
[21b]  Old Sam sunbathed there.

Or he could be vague about where Sam sunbathed, replacing *beside a stream* with *somewhere*.

[22]  Old Sam sunbathed somewhere.

If we consider questions and their answers, we find a very clear example of this. We can form a question from sentence [4] by replacing *beside a stream* with the single question word *where* as in [23] and [24]:

[23]  Old Sam sunbathed where?
[24]  Where did old Sam sunbathe?

Since we have used *where* to replace *beside a stream*, it is natural that *beside a stream* should be a possible answer to the question, since answering such questions is a matter of replacing the question word with an informative phrase. So, **answers to 'WH' questions (that is, questions that contain one of the question words *who*, *which*, *what*, *why*, *where*, *when*, *whose*, and *how*) are phrases.**

So, it seems that we are justified in taking *beside a stream* as a phrase. The question that arises now is, How should we represent this phrase in terms of a phrase-marker? As with the whole sentence, we need to know whether the words of the phrase are its immediate constituents, or whether it contains further phrases. There are just three phrase-markers that could possibly represent the structure of *beside a stream*:

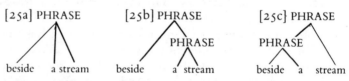

Each gives a different analysis. Which do you think is the best representation of the structure of the phrase? In coming to a decision on this, you should ask yourself whether *a* belongs more with *beside* than with *stream*, more with *stream* than with *beside*, or whether it doesn't seem to belong more with one than the other. It may be useful to note that if it seems very definitely not to belong with one (i.e. if [b] or [c] seems more definitely wrong than the other), then it will almost certainly belong with the other. [a] is right, therefore, only if [b] and [c] seem equally bad.

---

Now check that the tests mentioned above, replacement by a single word and the question test, confirm the analysis you have chosen.

---

Phrase-marker [25a] says that the phrase does not contain any further phrases. It says that *a* does not belong more with either of the other words, that the words themselves are the immediate constituents of the phrase. As mentioned, if [25a] is correct, then [b] and [c] should seem equally bad as representations of the structure. But [c] is surely much worse than [b]. [c] suggests that we should be able to find a single word to replace the supposed phrase *beside a*. It is difficult to start thinking of what kind of word could replace that sequence. Not only does it seem incomplete as it stands, but it is impossible to say what it is supposed to mean. On the other hand, *a stream* does seem complete, it is fairly clear what it means, and we don't have to rack our brains too much to discover that there are several single words that we could use to replace it. For example, *it, something*, or *one*, yield perfectly good phrases: *beside it, beside something*, and *beside one*.

Notice, too, that if we were to change the singular *stream* to the plural *streams*, we would get the ungrammatical word-sequence *\*beside a streams* – unless we also omit *a* (to give *beside streams*). This suggests rather strongly that *a* belongs definitely with *stream* rather than with *beside*, that *a* is DEPENDENT on *stream*. This piece of evidence is similar to that produced by the test of replacement by a single word, since it shows that we are obliged to use the single word *streams* to replace the sequence *a stream*.

The question test confirms that *a stream* is a phrase:

[26] Question: [a] Old Sam sunbathed beside what?
              [b] What did old Sam sunbathe beside?
Answer: A stream.

And notice that there is no question to which *\*beside a* would be a suitable answer.

[27] provides further evidence that *a stream* forms a phrase, since it has been moved as a unit in forming a new construction.

[27] *A stream* is what old Sam sunbathed *beside*.

It is worth noting, then, that **the MOVEMENT of a sequence of words in forming a construction indicates that the sequence is a phrase.** As a further example, not the acceptability of moving *beside a stream* to the beginning of sentence [4]:

[28] Beside a stream, old Sam sunbathed.

In short, the various kinds of evidence discussed confirm that [25b] is the correct representation of the structure of our phrase.

As an exercise, think of some other possible answers to the question represented in [26]. They can be as different as you like from the answer already given, and they can be as long as you like. Provided they do not sound ungrammatical, every sequence of words you choose will be a phrase.

---

Here are some suggestions:

[29a]  his magnolia bush
[29b]  a large pile of Bokhara rugs
[29c]  the most beautiful olive grove I've ever laid eyes on
[29d]  an unreliable alsatian that was taking the occasional nip at his toes.

All these are phrases. They could all serve as answers to the question, and they are all replaceable by a single word. Furthermore, they all contain further phrases.

Earlier, when we were considering whether there was a single word that could be used to replace the sequence *beside a*, I mentioned meaning and implied that **phrases form not only SYNTACTIC UNITS (constituents in the structural form of sentences) but also SEMANTIC UNITS. By this I mean that they form identifiable parts of the MEANING of sentences; they form coherent units of sense.** While it may be reasonable to ask what *beside a stream* and *a stream* mean, it does not seem reasonable to ask what *beside a* means; it would be impossible to answer such a question.

Does the discussion so far suggest any explanation why the sequence of words in [13] on page 13 seems more acceptable than those in [10], [11] and [14]? How, exactly?

---

I put an asterisk in front of [13] because it was not a complete sentence. However, it is a complete phrase, and in this it contrasts with the other strings. *Old Sam* could be replaced by a single word – *he, someone,* or even just *Sam* – making no difference to the overall structure of the sentence. Furthermore, *old Sam* could be used as an answer to the question *Who sunbathed beside a stream?*, where I have replaced the sequence *old Sam* with the single 'WH' word *who*.

## A difference between 'phrase' and 'constituent'

I have said that a PHRASE is a sequence of words that can function as a CONSTITUENT in the structure of sentences. The important word here is 'can'. We have seen that *beside a stream, a stream*, and *old Sam* can function as constituents in sentence-structure (and do function as constituents in sentence [4]). They are therefore phrases. The fact that those word-sequences are constituents in sentence [4], however, does not mean that they function as constituents of every sentence in which they appear. Here, as an obvious example of this, is a sentence in which the sequence consisting of *old* and *Sam* is not a constituent:

[30]   Though he was old Sam did regular press-ups.

This is immediately clear when we try to replace that sequence with a single word:

[31]   *Though he was *someone* did regular press-ups.

and when we apply the question test:

[32a]   *Though he was who did regular press-ups?
[32b]   *Who though he was did regular press-ups?

Out of the context of any particular sentence, *old Sam* is a phrase. It is a phrase because it can be a constituent of a sentence – but it does not have to be. *old Sam* is not a constituent of sentence [30] and therefore, in the context of that particular sentence, is not functioning as a phrase.

Consider now sentence [33]:

[33]   Sam sunbathed beside a stream that had dried up.

and decide whether the sequence *a + stream + that + had + dried + up* is a constituent or not.

Since that sequence of words would constitute a perfectly good answer to the question 'What did old Sam sunbathe beside?' and since (like the sequence *a stream* in sentence [4]) it is replaceable by a single word while preserving the overall structure of the sentence, it is a constituent. And, just as with *a stream* in sentence [4], it forms a further phrase with *beside*. This further phrase can be represented as in [34]:

[34]    PHRASE–a

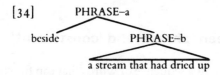

In [34] I have adopted the useful convention of using a TRIANGLE to represent a constituent when I am not concerned with its internal structure. And for ease of reference I have distinguished the phrases by letter.

The question I want you to consider now is this: Do the words *beside*, and *a* and *stream*, which formed a constituent in sentence [4], form a constituent in sentence [33]? And if not, why not?

---

You have probably guessed that the answer is 'No'. But why not? Well, we agreed that in [33]/[34] *a + stream* is part of a larger phrase, but that larger phrase is not *beside a stream* but *a stream that had dried up*. *Beside* forms a phrase, not with *a stream*, but with the whole sequence *a stream that had dried up*. The words *a* and *stream* are part of PHRASE–b. If an element is part of a phrase, it can only relate to other elements within that same phrase. If we wanted to say that *beside a stream* formed a phrase in [33], we would be forced to represent the complete phrase *beside a stream that had dried up* as in [35]:

[35]    *PHRASE–a

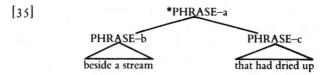

But [35] is wrong, since it does not represent *a stream that had dried up* as a phrase. The moral is that an element can belong directly only to one phrase at a time. I say 'directly' since in [34], for example, *a stream* belongs both to PHRASE–b (directly) and to PHRASE–a (indirectly). It is, in fact, impossible to draw a phrase-marker that says of *a stream* that it simultaneously forms a phrase directly with *beside* AND with *that had dried up*.

In case you are uncertain whether or not a given sequence of elements is represented as a phrase or not by a phrase-marker, the following discussion should help to clarify matters. Any point in a phrase-marker that could branch and bear a label is called a NODE. In phrase-marker [34] there are two nodes. I have labelled them 'PHRASE–a' and 'PHRASE–b'. A node is said to

DOMINATE everything that appears below it and joined to it by a line. Thus the node labelled 'PHRASE–a' DOMINATES all the following elements: *beside*, PHRASE–b, *a, stream, that, had, dried,* and *up*. A node is said to IMMEDIATELY DOMINATE another element when there are no intervening elements. Thus PHRASE–a IMMEDIATELY DOMINATES just *beside* and PHRASE–b; though PHRASE–a dominates *stream*, it does not immediately dominate it, because the node labelled 'PHRASE–b' intervenes.

Using this convenient terminology, I can now show how to decide whether a sequence of elements is represented as a constituent in a phrase-marker. **A sequence of elements is represented as a constituent in a phrase-marker if there is a node that dominates all those elements and no others.** In other words, if you can trace just the elements under consideration (i.e. all those elements and only those elements) back to a single node, then those elements are represented as a constituent.

Look at the phrase-marker given in [34]. The sequence *a + stream + that + had + dried + up* is represented as a constituent because the elements (words, in this case) can all be traced back to a single node that does not dominate any other element, namely, PHRASE–b. The sequence *beside + a*, on the other hand, is not represented as a constituent because the only node that dominates both of the elements within that sequence (PHRASE–a) dominates other elements as well (namely, *stream, that, had, dried,* and *up*). Similarly, in the incorrect phrase-marker [35], *a stream that had dried up* is not represented as a constituent because there is no node that dominates all and only those words. The only node that dominates all of them is PHRASE–a, but PHRASE–a does not dominate only those words, it also dominates *beside*.

I have given two examples in which a sequence of words functioning as a constituent in one sentence does not function as a constituent in another. Here, as a final example, is an AMBIGUOUS sentence (a sentence with two meanings). On one interpretation, the sequence *old + Sam* does function as a constituent, while on the other interpretation it doesn't:

[36] Hazeltine asked how old Sam was.

Try to identify the two meanings of [36]. A good way of doing this is to decide on the exact question which Hazeltine is reported in [36] to have asked. You may find it helpful to make a written note of the two questions.

---

Having identified the two meanings in the way suggested, you should not have much difficulty in deciding which interpretation demands that the sequence does form a constituent and which demands that it does not.

---

The two quite different questions that could have been asked by Hazeltine are [a] 'How old is Sam?' and [b] 'How is old Sam?'. As the different questions show, on the first interpretation [a] *old* belongs with *how* to form the phrase *how old*. In this question, the phrase as a unit has been moved from its position at the end of the sentence (*Sam is how old?*). On this interpretation, since *old* forms a constituent with *how*, it cannot also form a constituent with *Sam*. It is on the second interpretation [b] that *old* and *Sam* go together to form a phrase. This example illustrates how deciding what phrases there are in the sentence is necessary in order to decide what the sentence actually means.

Most people, when presented with a sequence of words out of the context of any sentence, have quite definite feelings as to whether that sequence could function as a constituent in a sentence (i.e. whether it is a phrase). As mentioned, it is usually simply a matter of deciding whether it seems to form a unit of sense. In the main, this is a reliable guide as to whether that sequence actually is a constituent in a given sentence to be analysed, though, as we have seen from the last three examples, not one hundred per cent reliable. And, even in the context of a sentence, you will find that you do have an intuitive feeling as to which sequences are functioning as its constituents. In this chapter I have considered various kinds of evidence for constituents – omission, replacement by a single word, the question test, movement, the sense test. These are useful in confirming your intuitions, and in checking on cases where you are in doubt – one's first intuitions are not always strong and not always reliable.

## Exercises

1. On the basis of tree-diagram (a) below, say which of the following sequences are CONSTITUENTS of A.
   (i) c + d   (ii) a + b + c   (iii) c + d + e + f   (iv) e + f   (v) e + f + g + h   (vi) g + h   (vii) E + C   (viii) D + E   (ix) F + g + h.

(a)

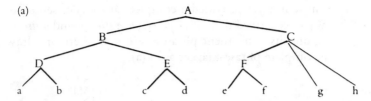

2. In tree-diagram (a) above, what are the IMMEDIATE CONSTITUENTS of: (i) A? (ii) B? (iii) C?

3. (a) If *from the Ministry* is a phrase and *the Ministry* is a phrase, draw a phrase-marker that shows all the constituents of the phrase *men from the Ministry*.

(b) If *rather dubious jokes* is a phrase and *rather dubious* is a phrase, draw a phrase-marker that shows all the constituents of the phrase *their rather dubious jokes*.

4. Decide whether the italicised strings in the following sentences are constituents of those sentences or not. N.B. one of the sentences is ambiguous; as with the ambiguous example discussed in this chapter, you should identify the two interpretations and be quite clear in your mind on which interpretation the italicised sequence forms a constituent.

(a) John considered *visiting his great aunt*.
(b) Maria retreated from *the bollard she had just demolished*.
(c) Maria retreated *from the bollard* she had just demolished.
(d) *In the machine* the gremlin could be heard juggling with ball-bearings.
(e) *In the machine the gremlin* could be heard juggling with ball-bearings.
(f) Sam managed to touch *the man with the umbrella*.
(g) Rory put *a silencer on the gun*.

5. In the light of the discussion of this chapter, how many constituents can you identify in sentence (a) given that the much shorter (b) is a grammatical sentence? (Do not attempt a complete analysis of sentence (a) – the fact that sentence (b) is well-formed does not provide enough information for this.)

(a) Being of a cautious disposition, Timothy very wisely avoided the heavily built man whenever he drank at the Wrestler's Arms.
(b) Timothy avoided the man.

**6.**    I have not yet provided a complete analysis of sentence [4]. We have agreed that *old Sam*, *beside a stream*, and *a stream* are among its constituent phrases. We may therefore draw an incomplete phrase-marker as in (a):

(a)

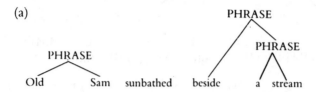

We know that the complete string constitutes a sentence. In order to complete the phrase-marker, then, all the elements must finally be joined up to a single (SENTENCE) node in some way. The question is How? There are three ways in which this could be done. Each way offers a different analysis of the sentence (in particular, each way offers a different analysis of how *sunbathed* fits into the structure). Draw the three complete phrase-markers and explain in words what different claims are made about the structure of the sentence by each phrase-marker. (You should take care that the phrases we have already acknowledged remain represented as phrases in your complete phrase-markers.) You are not asked here to choose which you think is the most appropriate phrase-marker (though you will almost certainly have views on the matter). In fact, all three analyses have been proposed at one time or another, though one of them is more common than the others, and it is this that I shall adopt in the next chapter.

## Discussion of exercises

**1.**    (i) Yes. Both c and d (and only c and d) can be traced back to the node labelled E.    (ii) No. D dominates a and b but it does not dominate c; and while node B dominates a and b and c, it also dominates d; so there is no node that dominates all of a and b and c, and only a and b and c.    (iii) No. There is no single node that dominates all of c, d, e, and f and only them. Only A dominates them all, but A dominates a, b, g, and h too.    (iv) Yes. e and f (and only e and f) can be traced back to the single node F.    (v) Yes. They alone can be traced back to C.    (vi) No.    (vii) No.    (viii) Yes.    (ix) Yes.

**2.** (i) B and C.   (ii) D and E.   (iii) F, g, and h.

**3.** (a)                                    (b)

```
        PHRASE                            PHRASE
         /\                               /\
        / PHRASE                         / PHRASE
       /   /\                           /   /\
      /   / PHRASE                     /   PHRASE \
     /   /   /\                       /    /\      \
   men from the ministry           their rather dubious jokes
```

**4.**(a) Yes. It could be replaced by *it* and by *what* in forming the question *What did he consider?*, to which *visiting his great aunt* is a possible answer. (Note also that the sequence needs to be treated as a unit in forming the construction *visiting his great aunt is what he considered.*)

(b) Yes. (cf. *she retreated from it; what did she retreat from?* Answer: *the bollard she had just demolished.*)

(c) No, In (b) the sequence *the + bollard* was shown to be part of the phrase *the bollard she had just demolished*; it cannot then form a constituent with *from*. (See the discussion of *beside a stream that had dried up* [33] in the chapter, pp. 19–20.)

(d) Yes. It could be replaced by *there* or *somewhere; in the machine* is a good answer to the question *Where could the gremlin be heard juggling with ball-bearings?* Notice that the sequence could be omitted leaving a well-formed sentence.

(e) No. This is most easily demonstrated by trying to imagine what question *In the machine the gremlin* could be an answer to. There is no single question word that would cover the sequence. *Who/What could be heard . . .?* could receive *the gremlin* as a possible answer; *Where could the gremlin be heard . . .* could receive *In the machine.* Each of these, then, are phrases. But there is no single question word that covers both *where* and *what.* So here we have a sequence of phrases that do not between them form a larger phrase. Replacement by a single word as a test of constituency must be treated with caution here. You might have decided that the sequence was a constituent since if we had used *it* to replace the sequence we would have derived the perfectly good sentence *it could be heard . . . .* But here *it* (as noted in (d) above) just replaces the *the gremlin*, while *in the machine*, being an optional constituent (as noted above), has simply been omitted.

(f) This is the ambiguous sentence. On one interpretation the sequence is a constituent, cf. *Sam managed to touch HIM and*

*WHO did Sam manage to touch?* (Answer: *The man with the umbrella*). On the other interpretation, it is not a single phrase but a sequence of two phrases. Cf. *Sam managed to touch HIM with an umbrella, WHO did Sam manage to touch with an umbrella?* (Answer: *the man*). Notice that, on this second interpretation, there is another possible question, namely, *HOW did Sam manage to touch him/the man?* (Answer: *with an umbrella*).

(g)    No. Consider the oddity of *\*Rory put IT/\*Rory put SOMETHING, \*What did Rory put?* (Answer: *\*A silencer on the gun*).

5.    The fact that (b) is a well-formed sentence allows us to infer that every sequence of words omitted from (a) in order to form (b) can be counted as a constituent of (a), viz.

Being of a cautious disposition
very wisely
heavily built
whenever he drank at the Wrestler's Arms.

There are other constituents, of course, and the constituents listed here themselves contain further phrases.

6.    The three complete phrase-markers are:

(a)

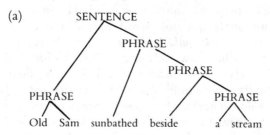

(b)

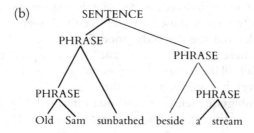

(c)

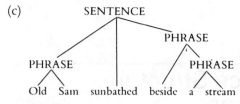

Phrase-marker (a) represents *sunbathed* as forming a constituent with *beside a stream*, and divides the sentence into just two immediate constituents: *Old Sam* and *sunbathed beside a stream*. Phrase-marker (b) again divides the sentence into two, but this time the two parts are *Old Sam sunbathed* and *beside a stream*. Phrase-marker (c) represents the sentence as having three immediate constituents, *Old Sam* and *sunbathed* and *beside a stream*; it says that *sunbathed* forms a constituent neither with *old Sam* nor with *beside a stream*.

In attempting to represent what phrase-marker (a) represents, you may have been tempted simply to draw an extra line out from the phrase node dominating *beside a stream* as in phrase-marker (d):

(d)

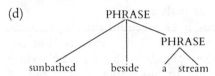

(d), in fact, is incorrect. Can you see why? (Check the discussion on page 21.) Although it associates *sunbathed* with *beside a stream*, it fails to represent *beside a stream* as a phrase in its own right, independently of *sunbathed*. It fails to do this because there is no node that dominates all and only *beside + a + stream*. (The only node that dominates them all dominates *sunbathed* as well). Check that you have not succumbed to a similar temptation in connection with (b).

# CHAPTER 2

# Sentence Structure: Functions

As I pointed out at the beginning of Chapter 1, understanding the structure of a sentence involves more than knowing what its CONSTITUENTS are. It involves being able to specify the CATEGORY and the FUNCTION of those constituents. As you will see in this and the next chapter, these three aspects of syntactic analysis are closely bound up with one another. This chapter is mainly about syntactic functions, and about how function relates to category and constituency. My aim is to show how an understanding of syntactic functions helps in identifying constituents in a systematic sentence analysis.

A systematic analysis is best begun, not by immediately considering the words contained in the sentence, but by first identifying the very largest phrases – those phrases which are immediate constituents, not of any other phrase, but of the sentence itself. So my first illustration of the relationship between constituents, their categories, and their functions, will concern **the immediate constituents of the sentence itself.**

## Subject and predicate

In order to be sure of identifying only the very largest (immediate) constituents of the sentence I shall, wherever possible, divide the sentence into the fewest possible parts, i.e. into two. Take the simplest possible complete sentence structure, as exemplified in [1]:

[1] Ducks paddle.

(*Blenkinsop coughed, Pigs fly, Empires decline,* and *Martha retaliated* would do just as well.) In this case, it is clear that we have no option but to analyse the sentence as consisting of two parts, as in [2]:

[2]                        Sentence

Ducks            paddle

But what about more complicated sentences? A speaker's ability to recognise the structure of the sentences of his language is largely a matter of being able to perceive a similar pattern across a wide range of apparently different sentences. Take [3] as an example:

[3]  The ducks are paddling away.

We want to say that [3] has **the same general structure** as [1]. By this I mean that **it is divisible into two CONSTITUENTS in exactly the same way, that the two constituents are of the same general kind (or CATEGORY) as the corresponding constituents of [1], and that they have the same syntactic FUNCTIONS as those in [1].**

Notice that, in asking which sequence of words in [3] corresponds to *ducks* in [1], I am again asking which sequence of words in [3] could be replaced by the single word *ducks* while leaving a grammatical sentence. The answer can only be *The ducks*. Replacing that sequence by *ducks* yields the well-formed sentence *Ducks are paddling away*. In each of their sentences, both *Ducks* and *The ducks* could be replaced by the same single word *They*. And the rest of [3] – *are paddling away* – can be replaced by the single word *paddle* (from [1]), giving the well-formed sentence *The ducks paddle*.

This exhaustively divides [3] into two parts, as in [4]:

[4]  [The ducks] [are paddling away].

The same division is shown in [5] and [6]:

[5]  [Those gigantic ducks] [were paddling away furiously].
[6]  [The mouth-watering duck on the table] [won't be paddling away again].

**In making this first division I have divided these sentences into two constituents, the first of which is traditionally said to function as SUBJECT, and the second as PREDICATE.** One way of thinking of these functions is to think of the subject as being used to mention something and the predicate as used to say something true or false about the subject. The general structure of [1], [3], [5], and [6] is identical. Those sentences only differ at a lower (more detailed) level in the hierarchical structure.

In exercise 6 of Chapter 1, I raised the question of how *sunbathed* fitted into the structure of *Old Sam sunbathed beside a stream*, and offered three alternative analyses. Each analysis makes a different claim as to what the immediate constituents of that sentence are. On the basis of the discussion so far, can you decide which of those analyses is being adopted here?

---

It is analysis (a): [*Old Sam*] (subject) and [*sunbathed beside a stream*] (predicate).

It will have occurred to you that sentences can be a good deal more complicated than those that we have looked at here. In fact, theoretically, there is no limit to the degree of complexity. If, when presented with a more complicated sentence, you are in doubt as to the correct subject-predicate division, a simple test can be applied:

### Question test for subject:
Turn the sentence into a question that can be answered by 'yes' or 'no' (a yes/no question). The phrase functioning as subject is the one that requires to change its position when the sentence is so changed.

You will recall from Chapter 1 that the MOVEMENT of a sequence of words in forming a construction shows that it is a constituent. This particular movement test will confirm not only that *the ducks*, *those gigantic ducks* and *that mouth-watering duck on the table* are constituents, but that those constituents are functioning as the subjects of the sentences in which they appear:

[7] Are [the ducks] paddling away?

Now form the yes/no questions that correspond to [5] and [6].

---

[8]  Were [those gigantic ducks] paddling away furiously?

[9]  Won't [the mouth-watering duck on the table] be paddling away again?

You may find that you intuitively know what the correct subject-predicate division is without having to apply the test. However, the question movement test is important because it is actually part of the definition of what a 'subject' is that it changes its position in such questions. The test is particularly useful in cases like the following:

[10] It is snowing again.

In [10] it is rather difficult to view the predicate (*is snowing again*) as being used to say something true or false of *It* (the subject). *It* does not mention anything. (Notice that [10] is not really an answer to the question 'What is snowing again?' which is itself an odd question.) Nevertheless, *It* is the subject of [10] precisely because it changes position in the yes/no question:

[11] Is [it] snowing again?

Using this test, identify the subjects of the following sentences:

[12]  Some nasty accident could have occurred.
[13]  The clown in the make-up room doesn't want to perform.
[14]  Elizabeth and Leicester are rowing on the river.
[15]  None of her attempts to give up chocolate were really serious.
[16]  As a matter of fact, the man you paid to do it has been arrested.

---

Examples [12]–[15] can be analysed as having a subject-predicate structure as follows:

[12]  [Some nasty accident] [could have occurred].
      (Could some nasty accident have occurred?)
[13]  [The clown in the make-up room] [doesn't want to perform].
      (Doesn't the clown in the make-up room want to perform?)
[14]  [Elizabeth and Leicester] [are rowing on the river].
      (Are Elizabeth and Leicester rowing on the river?)
[15]  [None of her attempts to give up chocolate] [were really serious].
      (Were none of her attempts to give up chocolate really serious?)

Example [16] illustrates the fact that the constituent functioning as subject does not always begin the sentence. The question that corresponds to this example is:

[16]  As a matter of fact, has the man you paid to do it been arrested?

This question form identifies *the man you paid to do it* as the subject.

The phrase *as a matter of fact* has not moved in forming the question and is therefore not part of the subject. Since *as a matter of fact* belongs neither within subject nor within predicate, [16] is one sentence that cannot be exhaustively analysed into a two-part, subject-predicate structure. For the moment, however, I shall concentrate on those that can.

A temptation that the question movement test will help you avoid is that of taking the first string of words that could be the subject as actually being the subject of the sentence in which it appears. Look again at [13], [14], and [15]. [13] begins with the sequence *the clown*, [14] with *Elizabeth*, and [15] with *none of her attempts*. All these could be subjects (see [17]–[19] below), but not in the sentences we have considered.

[17]  The clown refuses to perform.
[18]  Elizabeth excels at Real Tennis.
[19]  None of her attempts were really serious.

The temptation to identify less than the whole of the relevant phrase crops up in all constituent analysis. In the case of subjects, the question movement test helps. For example, if the subjects of [17]–[19] are taken to be the subjects of [13]–[15], it is not clear how to form the appropriate questions, and all attempts to do so will result in ungrammatical sentences. (Why not check this for yourself?)

In general, you will usually find that taking less than the whole of the phrase leaves you with a residue that is not easily accounted for in structural terms. For instance, in the above cases, if *the clown, Elizabeth* and *none of her attempts* are taken to be the subjects of [13]–[15] respectively, the following strings are left as residues:

[20]  in the make-up room doesn't want to perform
[21]  and Leicester are rowing on the river
[22]  to give up chocolate were really serious.

But none of these strings seems to hang together as a phrase, they do not form units of sense, and it is difficult to see what their function could be. They cannot be predicates; we couldn't say, for example, that *to give up chocolate were really serious* is predicated as being true of *none of her attempts*.

In applying the question movement test to the following examples, you will find that you have to modify it slightly.

[23] My new duck lays lightly boiled eggs.
[24] Elizabeth and Leicester excel at Real Tennis.
[25] The chiropodist who attended her fell in love with most of his patients.

Form the yes/no questions that correspond to these examples.

---

As you will have discovered, the appropriate questions are formed by introducing a form of the verb *do*. For the purposes of this test, it is convenient to assume that *do* is introduced as in [26]–[28]

[26] My new duck *does* lay lightly boiled eggs.
[27] Elizabeth and Leicester *do* excel at Real Tennis.
[28] The chiropodist who attended her *did* fall in love with most of his patients.

and that the questions are formed from [26]–[28] by the now familiar movement of the subject, giving

[29] Does [my new duck] lay lightly boiled eggs?
[30] Do [Elizabeth and Leicester] excel at Real Tennis?
[31] Did [the chiropodist who attended her] fall in love with most of his patients?

(This difference between [12]–[16] and [23]–[25] is explained in Chapter 6, pp. 128–130.)

## Noun Phrase and Verb Phrase

So much, then, for the functions (subject and predicate) of the immediate constituents of the sentence. I will return to the functions of constituents, in a more general way, later in the chapter. The question that now arises is: **What KINDS of phrases function as subjects and predicates?** We have seen that such phrases can vary widely in their form and complexity. Nevertheless, all the SUBJECTS we have looked at have one thing in common: they all contain, and are centred on, the same CATEGORY of word, a NOUN. They are all NOUN PHRASES (NP). The single words that can replace them are all NOUNS or PRONOUNS. The phrases functioning as PREDICATES, on the other hand, all contain a VERB. They are all VERB PHRASES (VP). Predictably, they are all replaceable by single-word VERBS.

**Any phrase that can function as a subject is a Noun Phrase.** You might ask why we need to distinguish between the CATEGORY and the FUNCTION of a constituent. We need to do this because most categories of phrase have a variety of different functions. Although subjects are always Noun Phrases, this does not mean that all Noun Phrases function as subject. For example, we saw that the Noun Phrase *the chiropodist who attended her* was functioning as subject in [25]. In [32], though, it is not:

[32] The pianist has rejected the chiropodist who attended her.

Notice that it does not change position in the yes/no question (*Has the pianist rejected the chiropodist who attended her?*). In this sentence it is *the pianist* that has moved. *the chiropodist who attended her* is here part of the predicate *rejected the chiropodist who attended her*. It is a constituent of the Verb Phrase and has another function (discussed in Chapter 4).

Here is a list of phrases. Some are Noun Phrases, some are Verb Phrases, and some are phrases belonging to categories not yet introduced. Identify the phrases (as Noun Phrase, Verb Phrase, or 'other') by combining them (just two at a time) and seeing which combinations make well-formed subject-predicate sentences.

(a)    remind me of you
(b)    as quickly as he could
(c)    soggy chips
(d)    pamphlets advertising new syntactic theories
(e)    at the latter end of the day
(f)    were raining from the sky
(g)    are in demand.

---

The only well-formed subject-predicate combinations are: (c) + (a), (c) + (f), (c) + (g), (d) + (a), (d) + (f), and (d) + (g). Since (c) and (d) function as subjects they are NPs. (a), (f), and (g), which function as predicates, are VPs. Since (b) and (e) don't combine, in any order, with any of the other phrases nor with each other, they belong to categories other than NP and VP.

Information about the categories of the immediate constituents of the sentence can now be included in a phrase-marker, by labelling the appropriate nodes, as in [33]:

[33]

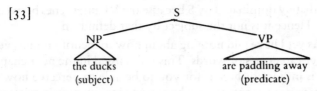

S

NP — the ducks (subject)

VP — are paddling away (predicate)

The diagram has the obvious interpretation: the sequence *the + ducks* is (or forms) a constituent belonging to the category Noun Phrase; the sequence *are paddling away* is (or forms) a constituent belonging to the category Verb Phrase; the NP and the VP together form a sentence (S).

Since I have been concerned only with the general structure of the sentence (that is, just the immediate constituents of the sentence itself) I have used the triangle notation for NP and VP to avoid having to give further details about their internal structure. And because I have not entered into any detail beyond identifying the subject and the predicate, the phrase-marker in [33] serves as a partial analysis of all the sentences considered in this chapter – with the exception of [16], which, for reasons already given, is a special case.

A point to note about [33] – and phrase-markers in general – is that a specification of the functions of the constituents (given in brackets in [33]) is not strictly part of the phrase-marker, and is not normally included. This is because it is possible to determine the functions of constituents from other information already contained in the phrase-marker – information about category and position.

For example, **the SUBJECT of a sentence can be defined as that NP which is immediately dominated by S. A PREDICATE is a VP immediately dominated by S.**

This definition of subject in terms of the phrase-marker will confirm that *the chiropodist who attended her* is not the subject of [32]. Draw the phrase-marker for that sentence.

[34]

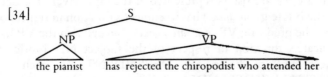

S

NP — the pianist

VP — has rejected the chiropodist who attended her

In [34] there are two NPs, *the pianist* and *the chiropodist who attended her*, but only one of those NPs is immediately dominated by S (*the pianist*). So *the pianist* is subject. *the chiropodist who attended her* is not immediately dominated by S because the VP intervenes between it and S. Hence it is not the subject by that definition.

As yet I have said nothing about how to identify nouns, verbs or other categories of words. This is discussed in the next chapter. What is important here is for you to be able to perceive how the various parts of a sentence can be expected to function in relation to each other. Without the idea of subject function and predicate function, it would be difficult to know where to begin the analysis of a sentence. In giving an analysis of a sentence, you should always satisfy yourself that any constituent you wish to say is contained in the sentence has a well-defined function and meaning. This goes not only for the immediate constituents of S but for all constituents. So I will generalise the discussion a little.

## Dependency and function

Since I am discussing the functions of constituents, it will help if I introduce some terminology to describe relationships between them. When two constituent nodes are immediately dominated by the same single node, as is the case with B and C in [35],

[35]

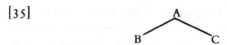

they are said to be SISTERS. As you might guess, since B and C are sisters in [35], they are also the DAUGHTERS of A, the node that immediately dominates them; and A is the MOTHER of B and C. Fanciful perhaps – but easily remembered!

It is the relationship of sister that concerns us here. SISTER constituents are usually represented at the same level of structure in phrase-markers. In general, **constituents have their functions in respect of their SISTER constituents.** Thus, in each of the sentences that we have considered so far, the subject NP and the predicate VP are sisters represented at the same level of structure, and the NP (e.g. *the ducks*) has its subject's function in respect of its sister, the predicate VP (e.g. *are paddling away*); and the VP has its predicate's function in respect of the subject NP. Notice that subject and predicate are DEPENDENT on each other (MUTUALLY DEPENDENT) in the sense that an NP only functions as a subject in the presence of a sister VP, and a VP only functions as predicate in the presence of a sister NP. The two of them together are required to form a complete sentence; neither can be omitted in a well-formed sentence.

Anticipating later chapters, let us now look at some other functional relations to see how an understanding of such functions can help in identifying constituents.

## Modifier and head

Consider the structure I assigned to *their rather dubious jokes* in Exercise 3 of Chapter 1. (Since I am concentrating on the relationship between constituency and function, I have omitted the CATEGORY labels which would be required for a complete analysis of the phrase.)

[36]

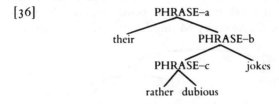

Make a list of all the sister relationships in that phrase.

There are three sister relationships:   (1) *their* and PHRASE–b (*rather dubious jokes*),  (2) PHRASE–c (*rather dubious*) and *jokes*,   (3) *rather* and *dubious*. The relation that holds between these sister constituents is of the same general kind, that of MODIFICATION.

To begin at the lowest level of structure, *rather* has its function in respect of its sister *dubious*. It specifies the extent of the dubiousness, telling us how dubious the jokes are. *rather* is DEPENDENT on *dubious*, in the sense that it is only present because *dubious* is. If we were to omit *dubious*, *rather* would have no function, and the omission would result in an ill-formed string (*\*their rather jokes*). Notice, however, that *dubious* is in no way dependent on *rather*. We can omit *rather* and still be left with a perfectly good phrase (*their dubious jokes*). This, then, is a ONE-WAY FUNCTION/DEPENDENCY. *rather* depends on *dubious* but not vice-versa. This function is called MODIFICATION. The function of *rather* is to MODIFY *dubious*.

What about *dubious* itself? **In a phrase containing a modifier, the element that is modified forms the essential centre of the phrase and is said to be the HEAD of the phrase.**

In this case, then, *dubious* is the head. I shall say more about heads of phrases in the next chapter.

A MODIFIER-HEAD relationship also holds, at the next (higher) level of structure, between the whole phrase *rather dubious* and the word *jokes*. *rather dubious* specifies the character of the jokes. Again, *rather dubious* as a whole is a DEPENDENT MODIFIER of *jokes* but not vice-versa. *rather dubious* could be omitted (giving *their jokes*), but *jokes* (the head of the phrase) could not (*\*their rather dubious*).

*rather dubious jokes*, then, forms a phrase but it does not tell us which rather dubious jokes are being referred to. It is the function of *their* to specify this. At this highest level of structure in the phrase, *their* is a dependent modifier of the head *rather dubious jokes*.

You might find it useful to picture the functional relations as in [37], where the direction of the dependencies is indicated by an arrow, and the functions by M (modifier) and H (head):

[37]

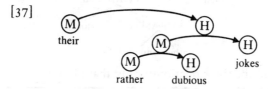

Now that the functions of these constituents have been specified, [36] should appear as a natural and obvious analysis. Compare it with some alternative analyses, [38] and [39]:

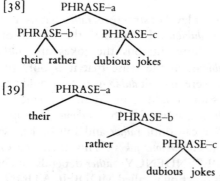

Both these analyses should now strike you as odd. *their* and *rather* both belong to categories that can only have modifying functions; they cannot themselves function as the head of a phrase. So they cannot have their functions in respect of each other. But in [38]

they are represented as sisters, forming a phrase ( − b). The fact that this supposed phrase does not seem to have a well-defined meaning is thus quite predictable. Notice that, since constituents function in respect of their sister constituents, *rather* is completely 'cut off' from the element (*dubious*) that it wants to modify.

[39] is marginally better, but still wrong. Before reading further, you might like to decide for yourself in the light of the preceding discussion exactly how it is better than [38], and exactly how it is still not so good as the analysis given in [36].

---

[39] is better than [38] in that *their* is correctly represented as a (modifying) sister of PHRASE–b (*rather dubious jokes*). It is still wrong, though, because it represents *rather* and *dubious jokes* as sisters, so that *rather* is now modifying, not just *dubious*, but the phrase *dubious jokes*. But we saw earlier that *rather* is dependent on (and belongs with) just *dubious*. It has to do with the dubiousness of the jokes, not the jokes themselves. The original analysis of PHRASE–b (given in [36]) rightly predicts that the string *rather dubious jokes* corresponds in meaning with the phrase given as [40]:

[40] *jokes* which are *rather dubious.*

By contrast, the oddity of the analysis of PHRASE–b given in [39] is brought out by the fact that it predicts that PHRASE–b corresponds in meaning with the ungrammatical [41]:

[41] *\*dubious jokes* which are *rather.*

*dubious* and *jokes* is another example of a sequence of words that forms a phrasal constituent in some contexts but not in others. We have seen that, in the context of *rather*, we need to relate *rather* and *dubious* before relating the whole phrase *rather dubious* to *jokes*. So *dubious* and *jokes* do not form a constituent in the context of *rather*. In the absence of *rather* (or any other modifier of *dubious*), on the other hand, there is no reason why *dubious* and *jokes* should not form a constituent, as in the phrase *their dubious jokes*:

[42]                                     PHRASE–a

                  their                        PHRASE–b

                            dubious            jokes

## Governor and complement

We have now looked at **the two-way (mutual) function/**

**dependency of subject and predicate** and several examples of
**the one-way function/dependency of modifier and head.** To
conclude this chapter, let us look again at the phrase *beside a stream*
(from the sentence *Old Sam sunbathed beside a stream*) in the light of
the discussion in this chapter. Do you recall the structure of the
phrase? Draw the phrase-marker.

How many sister relationships are there in the phrase?

[43]

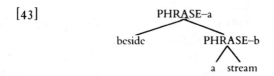

There are two sister relationships: (1) at the lowest level of
structure, that between *a* and *stream* and (2) at the next level up, that
between *beside* and PHRASE–b (*a stream*). The relationship
between *a* and *stream* is the same kind of modifier-head relationship
as that between *their* and *rather dubious jokes*. In the last chapter I
showed that *a* is dependent on *stream* and has its function only in
respect of *stream*. *Beside* and *a* do not relate to each other either
SYNTACTICALLY (that is to say, in terms of constituency or
function) or SEMANTICALLY (they do not form a unit of sense).
But what kind of relationship holds between *beside* and
PHRASE–b (*a stream*)? Try to determine whether the relationship
is a MUTUAL DEPENDENCY or whether it is an example of the
ONE-WAY DEPENDENCY OF MODIFIER AND HEAD.
(You will need to consider the phrase in the context of its sentence.)

The way to do this is to see if either of the constituents of the phrase
can be omitted individually in the context of the sentence. Can
they?

Both [44] (with *beside* omitted) and [45] (with *a stream*
omitted) are ungrammatical:

[44] *Old Sam sunbathed a stream
[45] *Old Sam sunbathed beside

Although the whole phrase could be omitted, neither of its
constituents can be omitted individually. It appears that *beside*
depends on the presence of *a stream* and that *a stream* depends on the

presence of *beside*. It is therefore a mutual dependency. As with the subject–predicate relation, neither element seems more central than the other, so we cannot speak here of the MODIFICATION of one element (the central head) by another (optional) element. Instead the relationship is described as being one of COMPLEMENTATION. In this case, **beside requires the presence of a phrase like *a stream* to complete its meaning; *a stream* is said to COMPLEMENT *beside*, which itself is described as the GOVERNOR of *a stream*.**

In a relationship of complementation, the first constituent is always the governor. If we were to give a graphic representation of the functional relations of the phrase, the mutual dependency could be represented by a double arrow as in [46]:

[46]

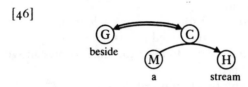

Notice that the mutual dependency of the two immediate constituents of the phrase can be predicted from its meaning. In the context of its sentence, *Old Sam sunbathed beside a stream, beside a stream* has the well-defined function of telling us where the sunbathing took place – that is, it specifies a LOCATION. The location of a thing (or an activity, like sunbathing) is usually expressed by orientating it in space in relation to some other thing (or activity). In this case, *a stream* specifies that other thing and *beside* specifies the spatial orientation. Neither *beside* or *a stream* alone could express the location, both are needed – hence their mutual dependence.[1]

With this example, and throughout the chapter, I have aimed to show how constituency, function, and meaning are interrelated. Giving appropriate analyses of sentences in terms of their constituents depends on how you actually understand those sentences. Constructing the phrase-marker of a sentence involves giving an explicit graphic representation of what you, as a speaker of the language, know about that sentence. The meaning of a sentence depends not just on the meaning of its words, but on how those

---

1. The mutual dependence of subject and predicate is usually treated as being in a class of its own, not as an example of complementation such as that which holds between *beside* and *a stream* and the other mutual dependencies we shall encounter in later chapters.

words are structured into phrases, and on the functions of those words and phrases. If you insist that each sequence of words you want to say forms a constituent has a well-defined meaning and function, you will find that an appropriate analysis will suggest itself naturally.

## Exercises

1.   Identify the subjects and predicates of the following sentences.
(a)   Her memory for names and dates was a constant source of amazement to him.
(b)   The prune fritters left something to be desired.
(c)   There are too many uninvited guests here.
(d)   Only six of the thirty domino-toppling contestants came properly equipped.
(e)   It was Lydia who finally trapped the pig.
(f)   The fact that you received no birthday greetings from Mars doesn't mean that it is uninhabited.
(g)   In the machine, the gremlin could be heard juggling with ball-bearings.

2.   Identify the category of the following phrases (as Noun Phrase, Verb Phrase, or 'other').
(a)   installed for only £199.95
(b)   were being given away
(c)   too far to drive in a day
(d)   obsolescent washing machines
(e)   ten long holidays at the Hotel Mortification
(f)   which I had bought only the day before
(g)   have made me realise that 'cheap' does indeed mean 'nasty'.

3. (a) The phrase *more exciting ideas* is ambiguous and needs a different structural analysis for each of its two interpretations. Draw the phrase-markers, giving an indication of which interpretation goes with which analysis.
(b)   Draw the phrase-markers for the following phrases:
      (i) young car salesmen    (ii) second-hand car salesmen.

4.   The phrase *the old Rumanian history teacher* has several different interpretations. Here are three structural analyses.

(a)

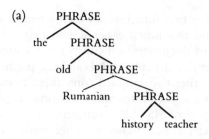

(b)

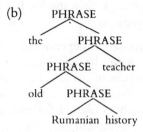

(c)

(i) Which analysis corresponds with the interpretation 'the old teacher of Rumanian history'?

(ii) Give the interpretations that correspond with the other analyses.

(iii) 'the history teacher from Old Rumania' is perhaps a less likely interpretation. Nevertheless it is possible to construct a phrase-marker that would impose that interpretation on the phrase. Draw the phrase-marker.

5. Decide on the functions of the italicised constituents in the following sentences.

(a) Old Sam sunbathed *beside a stream*.

(b) The *well-built* gentleman offered me a cigar.

(c) People *in running kit* are popping up from under the table.

(d) People in *running kit* are popping up from under the table.

(e) Max spotted *those wildcats*.

To answer this properly, you should not only state the function of the constituent but also indicate in respect of what other constituent it has that function. As mentioned in this chapter, you will find this much easier if you first satisfy yourself that you know the general structure of each sentence (i.e. that you can identify the subject NP and the predicate VP). First decide whether the italicised constituent belongs within the subject or the predicate. Since constituents have their functions in respect of SISTER constituents, a constituent within the subject can only relate to other constituents within the subject, and a constituent within the predicate to other constituents within that predicate.

6.(a) We have now looked at all the functions/dependencies in *old Sam sunbathed beside a stream*, with the exception of the function of *old*. Decide the function of *old* and then, using single and double arrows, give a complete representation of all the dependencies in that sentence. Use M for modifier, H for head, G for governor, C for complement, S for subject, and P for predicate.

(b)    The discussion of this chapter and the previous exercise have given you just enough information for you to work out a complete representation of the two-way and one-way dependencies in *Max spotted those wildcats*. Try it.

## Discussion of exercises

1.(a) [Her memory for names and dates] [was a constant source of amazement to him].

(b)    [The prune fritters] [left something to be desired]. A form of the verb *do* would have been required in applying the question test here.

(c)    [There] [are too many uninvited guests here]. This subject-predicate division is probably not very obvious, since *there* (like *it* in *it is raining*) does not mention anything. Nevertheless, the question movement test gives a clear result: cf. *Are there too many uninvited guests here?*.

(d)    [Only six of the thirty domino-toppling contestants] [came properly equipped].

(e)    [It] [was Lydia who finally trapped the pig]. Again, *it* is an empty subject, but it undergoes movement in the question (cf. *Was it Lydia who finally trapped the pig?*).

(f)    [The fact that you received no birthday greetings from Mars] [doesn't mean that it is uninhabited].

(g)  This is an example where the subject does not begin the sentence; *in the machine* is not part of the subject. *the gremlin* is subject and *could be heard juggling with ball-bearings* is the predicate.

2.  The following are the only well-formed subject-predicate combinations:  (d) + (b);  (d) + (g);  (e) + (b);  (e) + (g). Since they can function as subjects, (d) and (e) are the NPs; (b) and (g), functioning as predicates, are the VPs. (a), (c), and (f) belong to other categories.

3.(a)  One interpretation (i) is equivalent to that of 'more ideas that are exciting'. The other (ii) corresponds with 'ideas that are more exciting'. On both interpretations, the syntactic function of *more* is that of a modifier (notice that it can be omitted). The difference in interpretation is a matter of whether *more* modifies just *exciting*, as in (ii) or *exciting ideas* (that is, *ideas*, which happens to be modified by *exciting*), as in (i). The two phrase-markers are:

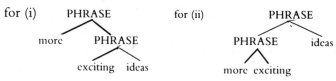

for (i)   PHRASE       for (ii)   PHRASE

    more   PHRASE       PHRASE   ideas

       exciting  ideas     more  exciting

(b)  (i)  Since people (salesmen, for example), but not things (cars, for example) can be described as 'young', *young* must modify a constituent of which *salesmen* is the head. It cannot modify *car* and hence cannot form a constituent with *car*. The natural phrase-marker, then, is:

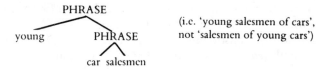

        PHRASE        (i.e. 'young salesmen of cars',

  young     PHRASE    not 'salesmen of young cars')

        car  salesmen

(ii)  Things, but not people, can be second-hand, so *second-hand* must modify (and hence form a constituent with) *car*, rather than any constituent having *salesmen* as its head.

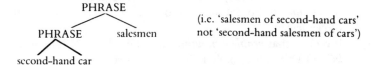

        PHRASE        (i.e. 'salesmen of second-hand cars'

  PHRASE    salesmen    not 'second-hand salesmen of cars')

second-hand  car

**4.**(i) Phrase-marker (c). This should be clearer after the following discussion.

(ii) In diagram (a) *Rumanian* modifies a phrase (*history teacher*) which has *teacher* (modified by *history*) as its head, so it is the (history) teacher that is Rumanian, not the history. The same goes for *old*: it modifies a phrase (*Rumanian history teacher*) which has *teacher* as its head. So, again, it is the teacher who is old. The interpretation can be expressed as 'the old teacher of history who comes from Rumania'. In diagram (b), *Rumanian* is the sister, and hence the modifier of, *history*. Here it is the history that is Rumanian rather than the teacher. And *old* modifies a phrase that has *history* as head, so again it is the (Rumanian) history that is old, not the teacher. So the interpretation is 'the teacher of old Rumanian history'.

(iii)

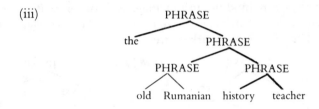

**5.**(a) You know that the sentence is divided into subject and predicate as follows: [Old Sam] [sunbathed beside a stream], so *beside a stream* must have its function in respect of its sister within the predicate, *sunbathed*. We have already noted that it is optional and that it specifies something about the sunbathing, namely its location. Therefore the function of *beside a stream* is that of modifier of *sunbathed*. This is our first example in which the modifier follows the head.

(b) *well-built* is a constituent in the structure of the subject NP *the well-built gentleman*, so it must have its function in respect of either *the* or *gentleman*. *well-built gentleman* seems to form a unit of sense, in contrast to *the well-built*. In fact, the structure of this phrase is almost identical to that of *their rather dubious jokes* (which, incidentally, is also a noun phrase – as you may have already noticed). *well-built* corresponds structurally with *rather dubious*. So the function of *well-built* is that of modifier of *gentleman*.

(c) It is clear that *people in running kit* is the subject NP. *in running kit* must therefore have its function in respect of *people*. It is also optional. It seems natural then that *people* is the head of that NP, and that *in running kit* is the modifier of that head. Another example of the modifier following the head of the phrase.

(d)   Notice that neither *in* nor *running kit* can be omitted individually: **people running kit are popping up from under the table*; **people in are popping up from under the table*. This indicates that *running kit* is required to complete the meaning of *in* and that *running kit* is only present because *in* is. We have here the mutual dependency of complementation, and – as usual in complementations – the second constituent (*running kit*) is said to complement the first (*in*), which is described as the governor. This is the same category of phrase as *beside a stream*.

(e)   The immediate constituents of the sentence are [*Max*] (subject NP) and [*spotted those wildcats*] (predicate VP). *those wildcats* must therefore relate to its sister constituent within the predicate, namely, *spotted*. Now notice that *those wildcats* cannot be omitted. This suggests that it is not modifying *spotted*. Is *spotted* modifying *those wildcats*? If it were, we should expect to be able to omit it. But we can't (cf. **Max those wildcats*). It appears that *spotted* depends on *those wildcats* to complete its meaning, (you can't just spot, you have to spot something) but also that *those wildcats* is present only because *spotted* is. In other words, we have here another example of the mutual dependency of complementation. *those wildcats* complements *spotted* (the governor).

**6.**(a) It has already been shown that *old Sam* is the subject NP in this sentence and that *old* is omissible. Furthermore, *old* gives us further information about Sam. The function of *old* is as a modifier of *Sam*, the head of the NP. In addition, as you discovered in Exercise 5, the function of *beside a stream* is to modify *sunbathed*. Integrating these, and the other dependencies into a single representation yields:

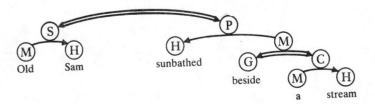

(b)   *Those* has the same function with respect to *wildcats* as *their* has to *rather dubious jokes*, and *a* has to *stream*. In addition, in Exercise 5 you discovered that there is mutual dependency between *spotted* and *those wildcats*. The only remaining relation is that between *Max* and *spotted those wildcats* – which is the familiar subject-predicate relation. Integrating these dependencies into a single representation yields:

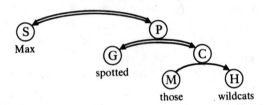

# CHAPTER 3

# Sentence Structure: Categories

I have explained the oddity of *their rather jokes* as being due to the fact that *rather* had a function only in respect of *dubious* and that, if you omit *dubious*, *rather* is left without a function. But why is *rather* left without a function? In the absence of *dubious*, why can't *rather* modify *jokes* instead? Or couldn't we say that *rather* modifies (or is modified by) *their*?

In a sense, you already know the answers to these questions. You already know that *rather* just isn't the KIND of word that can modify (and thereby form a constituent with) *jokes* – or, put the other way round, that *jokes* isn't the kind of word that can be modified by *rather*. You already know that *dubious* differs from *rather* in being the kind of word that can modify *jokes*, and differs from *jokes* in being the kind of word that can be modified by *rather*. *Their* is the kind of word that can modify (and hence form a constituent with) *jokes* (cf. *their jokes*), or any constituent that has *jokes* as its head (cf. [*their* [*dubious jokes*]]). But it is not the kind of word that can modify the kinds of word that *rather* and *dubious* are.

It is a brute fact about the way speakers understand their language that they recognise several different kinds of word – or, put another way, that they assign the words of their language to several distinct CATEGORIES. In doing so, they recognise that each word has a restricted range of possible functions and that there are restrictions on how the words can combine to form phrases. In illustration of the fact that you yourself do this, try the following exercise. Decide which of the following words belongs to the same category as *rather*, which to the same category as *dubious*, and which to the same category as *joke*. One of the words is of a category distinct from all three.

*tactics, extremely, could, subtle*

Consider the following strings:

[1a]  their tactics
[1b]  their dubious tactics
[1c]  *their rather tactics
[1d]  *their tactics dubious jokes
[1e]  *their rather tactics jokes

[2a]  *their extremely
[2b]  *their dubious extremely
[2c]  *their extremely jokes
[2d]  their extremely dubious jokes
[2e]  *their rather extremely jokes

The strings in [1] show that **tactics** has the same DISTRIBUTION as *jokes*. **By this I mean that *tactics* has the same range of functions, can combine with the same other elements, and can occupy the same positions as *jokes*.** Like *jokes*, it can be modified by *their* [1a] and by *dubious* [1b]. Like *jokes*, it cannot be modified by *rather* [1c]. [1d] and [1e] show that it cannot occupy the positions or assume the functions of either *rather* [1d] or *dubious* [1e]. **In short, *tactics* and *jokes* belong to the same category**, which is probably the decision you came to by intuition.

Now check list [2], making a note of what each string tells you about *extremely*.

---

In contrast to *jokes* and *tactics*, *extremely* cannot be modified by either *their* [2a] or *dubious* [2b]. And in contrast to *dubious*, it can neither modify jokes [2c], nor be modified by *rather* [2e]. *extremely* has all this in common with *rather*. More positively, in common with *rather*, when it appears in a position in which it can be interpreted as modifying *dubious* [2d], it is acceptable. *extremely* and *rather*, then, have the same distribution and so belong to the same category. They both specify the degree of the dubiousness of the jokes.

The same considerations would lead you to assign *subtle* to the same category as *dubious*. They both specify some characteristic of the jokes. The odd one out is *could*. Every attempt to incorporate *could* into the structure of the phrase results in ill-formed strings, so it must belong to yet another category.

I have mentioned only the category of WORDS (these are called LEXICAL CATEGORIES). But you know from Chapter 2 that PHRASES have their different categories too (i.e. that there are different PHRASAL CATEGORIES). Notice that, since *their rather dubious jokes* is a well-formed phrase, and since *rather* and *extremely*, *dubious* and *subtle*, and *jokes* and *tactics* belong to the same categories, it is predictable that *their extremely subtle tactics* should be a well-formed phrase as well. It is also predictable that the two phrases should belong to the same PHRASAL CATEGORY, and that they should have the same internal structure. As at the word level, this allows us to predict that, as whole phrases, they have the same DISTRIBUTION — they will be able to occupy the same positions in sentence structure and have the same range of functions.

It is clear that, instead of talking about individual words and phrases, we need to make more general statements about what does and what does not constitute a well-formed expression in the language in terms of the CATEGORIES involved. But first of all, we need to name these categories. In the rest of this chapter, then, I shall introduce some lexical categories by name and give hints on how to identify their members. I shall also discuss the category of phrases and how this relates to the category of the words that they contain.

## Nouns

For the purposes of identification, it is perhaps best to start with a very traditional definition of what a noun is: **A noun is the name of a person, place, or thing.** There are problems with this definition. For example, 'thing' has to be interpreted very broadly, to include substances like butter and foam (since *butter* and *foam* are nouns), abstract concepts like honesty and multiplication (since *honesty* and *multiplication* are nouns), collections of things like federations, crowds, and cutlery, and phenomena like gravity and time (for the same reason). Suspicions, accidents, refusals, and facts are not obviously things, yet *suspicion*, *accident*, *refusal*, and *fact* are all nouns. On the other hand, while *behind* and *ahead* might be said to stand for places, they are not normally taken to be nouns. Nevertheless the definition is useful as a starting point. Here are some further examples of nouns:

*January, Frankenstein, Bugsy, Jessica, Java, Portsmouth, gorilla, university, jam, theory, inspector, nationalisation, gremlin, joke, tactic, gallon, furniture, year, couple.*

You might well ask why I so confidently insist that *suspicion*, *honesty* and *January* are nouns when suspicions, honesty, and January are not strictly either people, places or things. In answer to this, you need to recall what the point of categorising words was in the first place. **By assigning a word to a particular category, we make a general statement about its DISTRIBUTION** – i.e. about its possible syntactic positions and functions. *honesty*, *suspicions*, and *January* are nouns because they occupy the same range of positions and have the same range of functions as other words that obviously are nouns by that traditional definition. In the final analysis, then, it is the syntactic criterion of distribution that decides the matter. So I shall supplement the traditional account of nouns with some distributional clues to their identification.

In addition, every category of words has its own range of possible WORD FORMS (its MORPHOLOGICAL possibilities). Nouns are no exception. As we shall see, this too can be useful in identifying them.

A MORPHOLOGICAL identifying feature of all nouns is that they have a GENITIVE (or POSSESSIVE) form. For example, *Bill's* (as in *Bill's pancakes* or *those are Bill's*), *mud's* (as in *the mud's consistency*).

Other features are shared by some nouns and not by others (in other words, there are several SUB-CATEGORIES of the noun category).

To begin with PROPER NOUNS – these are NAMES (with an initial capital letter). Examples from the above list are: *January*, *Frankenstein*, *Bugsy*, *Jessica*, *Java*, *Portsmouth*.

All other nouns are COMMON NOUNS. Most of what follows normally applies only to common nouns.

All COMMON NOUNS can be preceded by *the* (THE DEFINITE ARTICLE) to form a Noun Phrase (e.g. *the accident*, *the mud*, *the cutlery*).

Common nouns that refer to 'things' that can be COUNTED (COUNT NOUNS)

(a)   can be preceded by the definite article or *a*/*an* (THE INDEFINITE ARTICLE) (e.g. *a stream*, *an accident*) to form a Noun Phrase.

(b)   can be preceded by NUMERALS (*one*, *two*, *three* . . .) to form a Noun Phrase, and by expressions like *several*, *many* etc.

(c)   regularly appear in a PLURAL FORM in addition to a SINGULAR form:

| SINGULAR | PLURAL |
|----------|--------|
| *accident, man,* | *accidents, men,* |
| *foot, analysis.* | *feet, analyses.* |

This MORPHOLOGICAL possibility readily identifies a word as a noun.

Nouns that refer to 'things' that cannot be counted (NON-COUNT NOUNS, sometimes called MASS NOUNS – e.g. *butter, foam, cutlery, furniture, honesty, grace*) do not normally display any of these possibilities. They cannot normally be preceded by *a/an* (\**a foam*, \**a butter*, \**a furniture*) nor by numerals or similar expressions (\**two foams*, \**nine furnitures*, \**several muds*). Nor can they normally appear in a PLURAL form (\**foams*, \**butters*, \**honesties*). But they can be preceded by *some* (*some foam, some furniture, some honesty*).

The above remarks have been qualified by 'normally' because it is in fact often possible to turn a NON-COUNT NOUN into a COUNT NOUN precisely by modifying it by *a/an*, or a numeral, and/or giving it a plural form. This usually involves a change of meaning: *a mud, two butters* (a kind of mud, two kinds of butter); *a beer, three beers* a kind of beer, or a drink of beer). (See also *with an honesty that surprised me*).

Many nouns are both count and non-count. For example, *theory* can stand alone or with *some* (cf. *some theory*) as a non-count noun, but it can also be preceded by *a* and by numerals and have a plural form as a count noun (*a theory, theories, three theories*). Other examples that are both count and non-count are *suspicion, egg, cake*, and *charity*.

PROPER NOUNS, because they anyway stand for single, identifiable individuals, do not normally have any modifiers at all or appear in a plural form. However, in special circumstances, they can be modified by *the* or *a* and appear in a plural form: *the Ewings* (= the Ewing family), *the Borg of Wimbledon fame, the Einsteins of this world, a pensive Holmes.*

There is more one could say about these various SUB-CATEGORIES of nouns, but the above should suffice for the purposes of identification.

Now identify all the nouns in the following passage:

As Max and Adrian were talking, the daylight was fading from the West. Clouds were gathering and there was a chill in the air. They decided to end their conversation. Lights were shining from a passing steamer. Pessimistic thoughts filled the minds of both men,

but Adrian pushed them aside as being merely the result of his
tiredness. Besides, he had sand in his shoes.

---

The nouns in the passage are: *Max, Adrian, daylight, West, clouds,
chill, air, conversation, lights, steamer, thoughts, minds, men, Adrian,
result, tiredness, sand, shoes.*

   If you included *they, them* and *he* on the grounds that they
stood for persons and things, this is perfectly reasonable. They are
PRONOUNS. **PRONOUNS are used to stand in place of
complete Noun Phrases (NPs).** In the above passage, *they* stands
for *Max and Adrian, them* stands for *pessimistic thoughts,* and *he*
stands for *Adrian.* As you saw in Chapter 1, substituting single
words like these is an important test for whether a sequence of
words constitutes a phrase or not. In substituting a pronoun, we
test more specifically whether the phrase is a Noun Phrase or not.

   Here are some further examples of PRONOUNS:
DEFINITE PRONOUNS: *she/her, it, I/me, we/us, you, they/them*
INDEFINITE PRONOUNS: *some, something, someone, anything,
anyone*
DEMONSTRATIVE PRONOUNS: *this, that, these, those*
INTERROGATIVE (QUESTION) PRONOUNS: *who, which,
what, whose*
POSSESSIVE PRONOUNS: *my/mine, your/yours, his, her/hers,
its, our/ours, your/yours, their/theirs*

## Lexical and phrasal categories (Noun and Noun Phrase)

Before introducing further lexical categories, I shall look at the
relation between lexical and phrasal categories, using nouns and
Noun Phrases as an example. In Chapter 2 (p. 33) I said that a Noun
Phrase is a phrase that contains, and is centred on, a noun. *Their
rather dubious jokes* is a Noun Phrase and it contains the noun *jokes.*
But it contains words of other categories as well. Why does the
phrase as a whole have to be of the same category as *jokes*? Why
can't it be of the same category as *their* or *rather* or *dubious*? The
answer crucially involves the notion of HEAD introduced in
Chapter 2.

   In Chapter 2 I showed how *rather* modified *dubious, rather
dubious* modified *jokes,* and *their* modified *rather dubious jokes.* At
every level of structure in the phrase, it is *jokes* that functions as

HEAD. **In a modifier-head relation it is the category of the HEAD word that determines the category of the phrase a whole.** The other words are present only because of the function they (directly or indirectly) have in respect of the head noun. In a sense, then, *their rather dubious jokes* and *their extremely subtle tactics* can be seen as expansions of *jokes* and *tactics* respectively.

**It is the HEAD noun that determines the NUMBER (SINGULAR or PLURAL) and the GENDER (MASCULINE, FEMININE, or NEUTRAL) of the Noun Phrase as a whole.** This can be seen by considering what pronoun could be used to replace the Noun Phrase in a sentence:

[3] their extremely subtle tactics – they, them
[4] their extremely subtle tactic – it
[5] the extremely subtle manageress – she, her
[6] the extremely subtle manager – he, him.

*tactics*, to take just the first example, is the plural head noun. The NP as a whole is plural, as indicated by the fact that it could only be replaced by the plural pronouns *they* or *them*.

Before I make any further comments on the relation between NP (Noun Phrase) and N (Noun), here is a phrase-marker of *their extremely subtle tactics*, in which I have filled in all the information about categories that have been introduced:

[7]

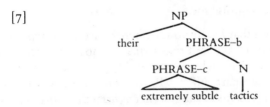

For the topmost node, all I have done is categorise PHRASE–a as a Noun Phrase (NP). In order to say that *tactics* is a noun, I have introduced an extra node, immediately dominating *tactics*, which I have labelled N.

Noun Phrases, of course, may contain more than one noun. But (with one exception to be discussed in a moment) **only one noun in a Noun Phrase can function as its head.** In each of the following sentences, first identify the subject NP, and then all the nouns contained in those subject NPs, indicating which is the HEAD noun.

[8] The man devouring the plums is grinning broadly.

[9] The comedy actress John met in the foyer seemed happy.

---

In [8] the subject NP is *the man devouring the plums*. It contains two nouns, *man* and *plums*, and it is clear that *man* is the head noun. The appropriate pronoun to replace the whole Noun Phrase would be *he* – a singular masculine pronoun – which is consistent with the number and gender of *man* but not with the number and gender of *plums*. In [9] the subject NP is *the comedy actress that John met in the foyer*. It contains the nouns *comedy, actress, John, foyer*. The appropriate pronoun is *she*, a feminine pronoun that is consistent only with the gender of *actress*. *Actress* is therefore the head noun.

As the discussion of these examples implies, **it is the HEAD NOUN that determines what sort of thing or person the whole NOUN PHRASE refers to.** The subject NP of [8] refers to a man – it is a man (not plums!) that is doing the grinning. In [9] the NP refers to an actress – it is an actress who seemed happy (not John, or comedy – and certainly not the foyer!).

I have mentioned that, in a Noun Phrase, constituents that modify the head noun are typically optional – they can be omitted without affecting the well-formedness of either the NP itself or the sentence in which it appears:

[10] Their extremely subtle tactics confuse me.
[11] Their tactics confuse me.
[12] Tactics confuse me.

The question that I want to raise here concerns sentence [12]. On the one hand, I have said that *tactics* is a noun. On the other hand I have said that, wherever possible, sentences should be analysed into a two-part, NP + VP, structure. Clearly, the VP is *confuse me*. But this seems to suggest that *tactics* is therefore NP – i.e. a full Noun Phrase. In [12] then, is *tactics* just a noun, or is it a full Noun Phrase? There seems to be a conflict here. The same apparent conflict crops up with proper nouns, which generally don't appear with modifiers, as in [13]:

[13] Max confuses me.

In [13], is *Max* just a noun or is it a full Noun Phrase? Think about this question before reading further. Can you think of any way of resolving the conflict?

---

As suggested, the conflict is only apparent. We do not have to choose between these alternatives. *Max* in [13] (and *tactics* in [12]) is both a noun and a full Noun Phrase. In saying this, I am allowing that **a Noun Phrase can consist simply of a head noun.** If you think about it, we must allow for this possibility: if we say that a Noun Phrase consists of a (head) noun plus its modifiers, and if modifiers are typically optional, it follows automatically that Noun Phrases can consist just of a head noun.

In terms of a phrase-marker representation, then, we must allow for Noun Phrase configurations like that shown in [14]:

[14]

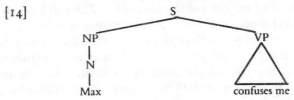

Some further remarks may help to clarify this point. Earlier I mentioned that pronouns stand in place of full NPs. Just as we can replace the subject NPs of [10] and [11] by *they*, so we can replace the subject NPs of [12] and [13] by pronouns (*they* and *he* respectively). On the other hand, if you try replacing a simple noun (as opposed to a full NP) with a pronoun, you will get very odd results. Consider again

[15] The ducks are paddling away.

*The ducks* is a Noun Phrase and it contains the noun *ducks*. Only the whole NP can be replaced by a pronoun (as in [16]), not the simple noun *ducks* (see [17]):

[16] They are paddling away.
[17] *The they are paddling away.

This clearly shows that simple nouns as such cannot be replaced by a pronoun. Since *tactics* in [12] and *Max* in [13] can be replaced by pronouns, they must be analysed as being full NPs as well as simple nouns.

In [16] we see that the pronoun *they* has assumed the position and function of a full NP. So *they* is itself an example of a one-word NP. In terms of a phrase-marker it would be represented as in [18], with PRONOUN abbreviated to PRO.

[18]

Now decide whether *tactics* in [10] (*their extremely subtle tactics confuse me*) is a full NP or not.

---

By the pronoun test, it is not a full NP; cf. *\*Their extremely subtle they confused me*. An NP consists of a simple noun and its optional modifiers. *their* and *extremely subtle* are the modifiers and *tactics* is the (simple) noun.

The discussion illustrates the close relation between the FUNCTION of subject and the phrasal CATEGORY of NP. In [12] and [13] *tactics* and *Max* are functioning as subjects. They therefore count as full NPs in those sentences. But in *their tactics confuse me*, it is the whole phrase, *their tactics*, that is functioning as the subject, not the simple noun *tactics* itself, which is just a constituent (albeit the central constituent) of the phrase that is functioning as subject.

So, more generally, when single words have the functions that full phrases have, it is standard practice to treat them as full phrases of the appropriate category. This means that we allow for **one-word phrases** in certain circumstances; not only one-word Noun Phrases, but one-word phrases of other categories as well. In fact, I opened Chapter 2 by discussing a sentence that consisted of two one-word phrases, namely *Ducks paddle*, where *Ducks* is a simple noun that counts also as the subject Noun Phrase, and *paddle* is a verb that counts as a Verb Phrase. The latter counts as a full Verb Phrase because it functions, by itself, as a complete predicate.

The idea of one-word phrases sometimes causes difficulty because WORDS are traditionally contrasted with PHRASES. After all, words are just words, but PHRASES are sequences, or strings, of words. However, in this context at least, it is necessary to understand 'word-sequence/string' as meaning 'a sequence/string of ONE OR MORE WORDS'.

## Adjectives and adverbs

*Dubious* and *subtle* are adjectives. Any word that has the same DISTRIBUTION as those words is an adjective. Many adjectives have characteristic endings, such as *-able, -al, -ate, -ful, -ic, -ing, -ive, -less, -ous, -y*. Examples are:

*capable, economical, Italianate, beautiful, microscopic, surprising, priggish, inventive, hopeless, callous, fluffy.*

There are other adjectival endings, and the endings given are only typical of adjectives, not an infallible guide. The more common adjectives tend not to have characteristic endings (e.g. *old, hot, short, tight, full, long*) and this goes for the colour adjectives (*blue, yellow* etc.).

Many adjectives have the morphological possibility of taking a COMPARATIVE (*-er*) and a SUPERLATIVE (*-est*) inflection, as in *newer*, and *newest*, *subtler* and *subtlest*. Others do not (cf. *\*beautifuller/\*beautifullest, \*dubiouser/\*dubiousest*) but instead may be modified by the COMPARATIVE and SUPERLATIVE DEGREE ADVERBS *more* and *most*, *less* and *least*. Yet others have irregular comparative and superlative forms (*good, better, best*).

I have mentioned the comparative and superlative DEGREE ADVERBS *more* and *most*, *less* and *least*. Since the main function of degree adverbs is to modify adjectives (specifying the degree of the attribute expressed by the adjective), this seems the appropriate place to mention DEGREE ADVERBS as a category. They are words having the same distribution as *rather* and *extremely*, for example:

*very, quite, so, too, slightly, hardly, highly, moderately, completely, increasingly, incredibly* etc.

Adjectives that accept the *-er/-est* inflection or modification by degree adverbs are called GRADABLE ADJECTIVES. Unfortunately for the purposes of identifying adjectives, not all adjectives are gradable. NON-GRADABLE ADJECTIVES do not accept the *-er/-est* inflection, or modification by degree adverb. Here are some examples of non-gradable adjectives:

*atomic, dead, potential, right, main, consummate, medical, fatal, final, second, third, supreme.*

Note the oddity of the following: *\*supremer, \*supremest, \*more supreme, \*very supreme, \*rather supreme, \*too supreme*.

As I introduce further categories in later chapters, we will encounter words which are adjectives but less obviously so. With these introductory remarks I have restricted myself to the clear cases.

Now, bearing in mind that adjectives have a variety of functions (not only the illustrated function of modifying nouns), identify the adjectives in the following passage. There are a few degree adverbs too. Make a note of them.

The great architectural interest of the royal palace did not strike William at that precise moment, grotesque and flamboyant though it was. He had eyes only for Goneril's gorgeous purple hair. Could it be artificial? He found it difficult to believe she was so self-conscious as to have dyed it such a fantastic hue. She seemed too modest for that. In silent admiration, he concluded that it had to be completely natural.

---

The adjectives are: *great, architectural, royal, precise, grotesque, flamboyant, gorgeous, purple, artificial, difficult, self-conscious, fantastic, modest, silent, natural.* The degree adverbs are: *so, too, completely.*

## Adjective Phrases and Adverb Phrases

*rather dubious, extremely subtle,* and *too modest* are Adjective Phrases. As with the NP, the phrase is of the same category as its head word, i.e. Adjective Phrase (AP) is centred on Adjective (A). And, again like NPs, an AP can consist of an unmodified head, a simple adjective.

For example, in *Aldo's very colourful pizzas* the Adjective Phrase, *very colourful,* functions as the modifier of *pizzas* and *colourful* is a simple adjective functioning as the head of the AP. On the other hand, in *Luigi's colourless pizzas,* the simple adjective functions both as the head and, in itself, as the complete modifier of *pizzas,* so it counts as a full Adjective Phrase as well.

By contrast with adjectives and nouns, **DEGREE ADVERBS cannot themselves be modified.** So there is no distinction between a degree adverb and a degree Adverb Phrase. In phrase-markers, then, I shall simply employ the label 'DEGREE' (shortened to 'DEG').

You should now be able to draw the phrase-marker for *very energetic,* using all the appropriate category labels. It is given as phrase-marker (a) at the end of this chapter.

---

Other constituents can appear in adjective phrases. I shall mention here only the GENERAL ADVERBS. Examples are:

*frankly, potentially, oddly, enthusiastically, immediately, suspiciously, awkwardly.*

As these examples illustrate, the vast majority of general adverbs (and, you will have noted, some of the degree adverbs) are formed from adjectives by the addition of -ly, and so are easily identified.

Like degree adverbs, general adverbs can modify adjectives within Adjective Phrases (though general adverbs typically have other functions as well): cf. *theoretically untenable, oddly inconclusive, diabolically tinted, immediately recognisable.*

General adverbs differ from degree adverbs in specifying a wider range of concepts than just degree. But this, in itself, is not the reason for distinguishing between general adverbs and degree adverbs in terms of syntactic category. The reason for the categorial distinction is that general adverbs can themselves be modified by degree adverbs, to form ADVERB PHRASES (AdvPs) – for example, *very oddly, quite frankly.* As already mentioned, degree adverbs cannot be modified. Since modification of a general adverb by a degree adverb is optional, an Adverb Phrase, (like an NP and an AP) can consist of just a simple (general) adverb.

By way of a summary, I will give an analysis of *more obviously artificial.* It is an ADJECTIVE PHRASE (AP), whose immediate constituents are the (head) ADJECTIVE (A) *artificial* and the (modifying) ADVERB PHRASE (AdvP) *more obviously.* This in turn consists of the (head) ADVERB (Adv) *obviously* and the (modifying) DEGREE ADVERB (DEG) *more.* Now incorporate this information about constituency and category into a phrase-marker of *more obviously artificial* (omitting the information about function). The phrase-marker is given as (b) at the end of the chapter.

## Prepositions and Prepositional Phrases

The last category to be introduced in this chapter is PREPOS-ITION (P), and its associated phrasal category, PREPOSITION-AL PHRASE (PP). *Beside* is a preposition (cf. *Old Sam sunbathed beside a stream*). Other examples are: *of, at, in, from, to, towards, with, from, by, for.*

I discussed the phrase *beside a stream* in Chapter 2. This is an example of the basic PREPOSITIONAL PHRASE, consisting of a preposition (as governor), complemented by a Noun Phrase. You will recall from Chapter 2 that the relation between *beside* and *a stream* is a MUTUAL DEPENDENCY – in contrast to the one-way modifier–head dependency exhibited in Noun Phrases, Adjective Phrases, and Adverb Phrases. **Phrases consisting of mutually dependent constituents are by convention named after the governing constituent,** in this case, the preposition. This may give the misleading impression that the preposition bears the same relation to the whole Prepositional Phrase as a noun does to a Noun Phrase, as an adjective to an Adjective Phrase, and as an adverb to an Adverb Phrase. While the NP, for example, is centred on a noun, the Prepositional Phrase is not really centred on the preposition. Because the dependency that holds in a PP is mutual, the preposition is not the head of the Prepositional Phrase. In other words, PPs cannot be regarded as expansions of Ps in the way that NPs can be regarded as expansions of Ns.

Now draw the phrase-marker of *to Max*, including all the categorical information. (Phrase-marker (c) at the end of the chapter.)

---

Prepositional Phrases, if they contain very long and complex NPs can appear to be long and complex themselves (e.g. *through the trampoline he'd just bought off Jim*). Nevertheless, with one exception to be discussed immediately, such PPs can always be analysed as consisting simply of a P and an NP.

## Co-ordinate Phrases

I have now introduced four main lexical categories, NOUNS, ADJECTIVES, ADVERBS (GENERAL and DEGREE), and PREPOSITIONS, and taken a brief look at the phrasal categories associated with them. I will conclude this chapter with a very general point about categories and constituency.

Discussing nouns and Noun Phrases, I mentioned that, in a Noun Phrase, only one noun can be head of the phrase. I pointed out that there was an important exception to this. The exception is illustrated in the following examples.

[19]  Max and Adrian are being melodramatic.
[20]  The clowns and the acrobats declined to co-operate.

Identify the subject NPs of these sentences.

---

Now identify the nouns in those NPs.

---

Of the nouns in each NP, can you, in fact, decide which is the head noun?

---

The subject NPs are [19] *Max and Adrian* and [20] *The clowns and the acrobats*. The first contains the two nouns *Max* and *Adrian* and the second *clowns* and *acrobats*. In each subject NP it is in fact impossible to identify any single noun as being the head. Of *Max* and *Adrian* neither seems more central than the other. It is not just Max, nor just Adrian, who is being melodramatic, both are. The same goes for the clowns and the acrobats.

In such cases, if any noun is head of the NP, then both nouns must be. In phrases such as these, we must allow that NPs can have more than one head. Both *Max* and *Adrian* are the noun heads of the NP *Max and Adrian*. Such phrases are called CO-ORDINATE PHRASES. *Max and Adrian* is a CO-ORDINATE NOUN PHRASE, with *Max* and *Adrian* CO-ORDINATED by *and*. **Co-ordinate NPs have as many heads as there are nouns co-ordinated in them.** Other CO-ORDINATORS are *but* and *or*.

In view of all that has been said so far, you might feel inclined to say that *Max and Adrian* does not constitute a single phrasal constituent but is a sequence of two separate constituents. The weight of evidence is against this view. Can you think of any arguments against it?

---

In the first place, you have already identified *Max and Adrian* as a single constituent in saying that the sequence functions as the subject of its sentence. You can check for yourself that it is that complete phrase (rather than any sub-part of it) that changes position in the question. Also, we can use an interrogative pronoun to replace the complete phrase, and answer the resulting question with it:

[21] Who is being melodramatic? – Max and Adrian.
[22] Who declined to co-operate? – The clowns and the acrobats.

Likewise, the co-ordinate NP can be replaced by *they*:

[23] They are being melodramatic.
[24] They declined to co-operate.

As you may have noted, with co-ordinate NPs it is usual to find that the NP as a whole is PLURAL regardless of whether the heads are singular or plural. Hence, although *Max* and *Adrian* are individually singular, the NP as a whole needs to be replaced by the plural pronoun *they*.

What, then, is the structure of these phrases? Ask yourself first whether the subject NP of [20], consists directly of the nouns it contains (plus *and*), or whether you can identify any intermediate constituents. If you can, what are their categories?

---

It should have been a simple matter to identify both *the clowns* and *the acrobats* as constituent phrases. They are, of course, Noun Phrases themselves. This can be demonstrated by showing that, even within the co-ordinate NP, they can themselves be replaced by pronouns, as in [25] and [26]:

[25] They and the acrobats declined to co-operate.
[26] The clowns and they declined to co-operate.

What about *Max* and *Adrian* in [*Max and Adrian*]? Are they just nouns or full NPs as well?

---

[27] and [28] are both well-formed

[27] He and Adrian are being melodramatic.
[28] Max and he are being melodramatic.

indicating that both *Max* and *Adrian*, in addition to being simple nouns, are full NPs in their own right.

In short, the subject NPs of [19] and [20] are co-ordinations of NPs. The whole co-ordinate phrase and the elements that are co-ordinated in them have the same distribution and so are of the same category. They can be represented as in [29] and [30]:

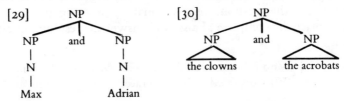

There is a general point here which I will approach by first asking you to judge which of the following strings are well-formed phrases and which not.

[31] Max and quickly
[32] the acrobats and wellnigh incomprehensible
[33] the actress that John met in the foyer and the acrobats

[34] in the foundations and under the rafters
[35] obviously intelligent and to Porlock
[36] moderately cheap and extremely nasty
[37] rather and inconsistent

---

For the purposes of this exercise, let's assume that we agree in our judgements: [33], [34], and [36] are well-formed phrases; [31], [32], [35], and [37] are ill-formed. Can you suggest a general explanation for the ungrammaticality of the latter set of examples?

---

Let us approach this by considering first of all the well-formed phrases. Consider [33]. What category of phrase is it, and how do you know?

---

[33] passes all the tests for NP. In the light of the above discussion, one could reliably guess that it is an NP since it is a co-ordination of phrases that have already been identified as NPs. Now identify the category of phrases that are co-ordinated in [34] and [36] and make a (reliable!) guess as to the category of the phrases as a whole.

---

*In the foundations* and *under the rafters* are both Prepositional Phrases. You will probably not be surprised to hear that [34] is itself a PP. *In the foundations* has the same distribution as *in the foundations and under the rafters* (wherever the one could appear so could the other) – so they must belong to the same category. In [36] *moderately cheap* and *extremely nasty* are both Adjective Phrases. Not surprisingly, [36] is an Adjective Phrase.

Now identify the phrases that have been co-ordinated in the ill-formed examples. On the basis of that, try to decide the category of the whole string. The difficulty you will experience in attempting to do this provides the explanation for their oddity. Try to formulate in your mind what the problem is.

---

[31] is a co-ordination of a Noun Phrase and an Adverb Phrase. How do we decide what category the whole co-ordination should belong to? We cannot decide. Both the co-ordinated phrases are heads of the co-ordinate phrase, but their categories conflict. In [32] a Noun Phrase and an Adjective Phrase have been co-ordinated and we have the same problem. In [35] it is a Prepositional Phrase and an Adjective Phrase, in [37] a Degree Adverb and an Adjective Phrase. And again, there is no way of deciding what the category of the whole string is.

To sum up, **any constituent, of any category, can consist of a co-ordination of constituents of the same category.** It follows from this that only constituents of the same category can be co-ordinated.

This very general principle has provided an often-used test in language study. It has been used as a test of two things, (a) constituency and (b) category. As regards (a), notice that the general principle allows only CONSTITUENTS to be co-ordinated. So if you can co-ordinate a string of words with another string of words, this indicates that each of those strings can be a constituent. As regards (b), if you know the category of one of those strings of words, you know that the other string of words must be of the same category, since only identical categories can be co-ordinated.

I have illustrated this general principle with co-ordinations of phrasal categories only. But the principle holds for all categories, including lexical categories and sentences themselves. Compare [38] and [39]:

[38]  Stuffy and too hot.
[39]  Too hot and stuffy.

Both are APs. [38] is a co-ordination of APs (the first consisting of a simple A). The most likely interpretation of [39], on the other hand, is that it means the same as *too hot and too stuffy*. In this case, the modifier of *hot* is shared by *stuffy*, so that *too* modifies not just *hot* but the whole phrase *hot and stuffy*. *hot* and *stuffy*, therefore, are each simple adjectives, and *too* must be analysed as modifying a CO-ORDINATE ADJECTIVE. So, as with many other APs discussed, this AP consists of a degree adverb and a (co-ordinate) adjective, as shown in [40]:

[40]

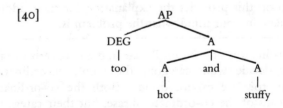

*Up and down the staircase* exemplifies the co-ordination of another lexical category. Draw the phrase-marker.

The whole string is a prepositional phrase, but it does not consist of co-ordinated prepositional phrases, since the co-ordination is of just prepositions. Here *the staircase* complements both *up* and *down*. The way to represent this is to analyse *up and down* as a co-ordinate preposition, as in [41]:

[41]

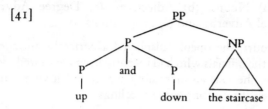

In these first three chapters, I have discussed constituency, function, and category, and how these concepts relate to each other. It is appropriate to conclude the chapter by showing how the points made about constituency and category in connection with co-ordination can be looked at in terms of function.

Co-ordinations of different categories are ill-formed because they could have no coherent function. Consider again [31] – *Max and quickly* – the co-ordination of an NP and an AdvP. Both the NP and the AdvP, remember, are heads. Attempting to make the whole co-ordinate phrase function in the way that an NP does, while alright as far as *Max* is concerned, involves making the AdvP function like an NP. But if it could function like an NP, it would be an NP, not an AdvP. And if we attempt to make the whole phrase function like an AdvP, the same problem arises in respect of the NP. So the phrase as a whole is without any possible function. In fact, it may well be that this lack of any possible FUNCTION will turn out to be more important than the mixing of CATEGORIES: for when the different categories can function in the same way it is sometimes possible to co-ordinate them. An example of this is *in a pickle and very worried*, which is a co-ordination of PP and AP. Compare it with [35] above.

## Diagrams for in-text exercises

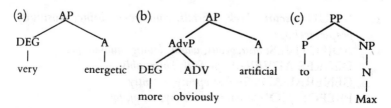

## Exercises

1.  Identify the following LEXICAL categories in the passage
    below: (a) Nouns, (b) Adjectives, (c) Degree Adverbs,
    (d) General Adverbs, and (e) Prepositions.

    On the court, she openly displayed a perfectly outrageous
    cheek towards the officials who had recently been appointed by the
    club. At home, she was an incredibly warm and loving human
    being, full of sensitivity for people's feelings.

2.  We have now identified two functions of NPs: subject, and
    complement to a preposition. There are other functions.
    Bearing this in mind, identify the NPs in the first sentence of
    the above passage. Remember to identify first the largest NPs
    and only then any NPs that may be contained within them.
    Then identify the head noun of each NP. Which NPs are
    functioning as subject? Which NPs are functioning as the
    complement to a preposition? Is there an NP functioning in
    some other way?

3.  Draw the phrase-markers for the following expressions. In
    some cases, you will find that you do not have all the
    information necessary to give a complete analysis. Where this
    is so (and only where this is so!), follow the example of the
    preceding chapters – avoid giving lexical category nodes, or
    just label phrase nodes as 'PHRASE', or use the triangle
    notation, as appropriate.

(a)  for you and Pete
(b)  rather nervous but very excited
(c)  her happy and glorious reign
(d)  a perfectly outrageous cheek
(e)  Herbert struck the board and I had to mend it

## Discussion of exercises

1.  NOUNS: *court, cheek, officials, club, home, being, sensitivity,*
    *people, feelings*
    ADJECTIVES: *outrageous, warm, loving, human, full*
    DEGREE ADVERBS: *perfectly, incredibly*
    GENERAL ADVERBS: *openly, recently*
    PREPOSITIONS: *on, towards, by, at, of, for*

**2.** NPs: (a) *The court* (b) *she* (c) *a perfectly outrageous cheek* (d) *the officials who had recently been appointed by the club* (e) *the club.* You may have missed *she*: it is a pronoun having one of the functions of full NPs. It is, I think, just about possible to analyse *a perfectly . . . the club* as an NP. *The officials* has not been analysed as an NP for reasons to be outlined in Chapter 7, alluded to in Chapter 2 (cf. the discussion of *a stream that had dried up*).

HEADS: (a) *court*    (b) *she*    (c) *cheek*    (d) *officials*    (e) *club.*

FUNCTIONS: *The court* is functioning as the complement of the preposition *on*. *she* is functioning as subject. *a perfectly outrageous cheek* has a function other than subject or complement to a preposition. *the officials appointed by the club* is complement to the preposition *towards*. *the club* is complement to the preposition *by*.

**3.** (a)

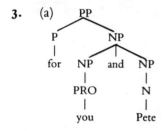

(b)

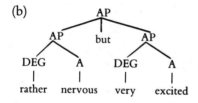

(c)

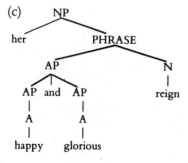

(d)

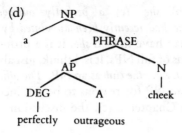

(e) This is a co-ordination of sentences.

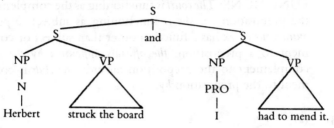

# CHAPTER 4

# The Verb Phrase

You know that the basic sentence consists of a Noun Phrase (as subject) and a Verb Phrase (as predicate), and you have encountered several examples of Verb Phrases though very little has been said about them. This chapter is concerned with the general structure (the immediate constituents) of the Verb Phrase half of the basic sentence. *Paddle, sunbathed beside a stream, love fish, hate chips, spotted those wildcats*, and *seemed happy* are all Verb Phrases. As these VPs illustrate, categories introduced in previous chapters may appear in the Verb Phrase, including Noun Phrases themselves. In the Verb Phrase, however, they have different functions. It is with these different functions that I am primarily concerned here.

## A first look at verbs and the Verb Group

**The one constituent that a Verb Phrase (VP) must contain is the VERB GROUP (Vgp). The Verb Group consists of a (LEXICAL) VERB which is optionally preceded and modified by other (AUXILIARY) verbs.**

Lexical verbs are very easily identified by their morphological possibilities. **They are those words that can take some if not all of the following INFLECTIONS: -s, -ing, -ed, -en.** For example:

*play*:  *plays, playing, played*
*write*:  *writes, writing, written.*

Examples of COMPLEX Verb Groups (that is, Verb Groups in which the head verb [in italics] has auxiliary modification) are:

[1]  is *writing*

[2] may have *written*
[3] could have been *writing*.

A general point to note in identifying categories, one that applies particularly to verbs, is that **words can belong to more than one category**. For example, *interest* is certainly a verb: cf. *interests, interesting, interested*. It is functioning as a verb in [4].

[4] Her hair interested him.

But both *interest* and *interests* can also be nouns (singular and plural respectively) as in [5].

[5] Its great architectural interest did not strike him.

And *interesting* and *interested* can be adjectives, as in [6] and [7].

[6] A very interesting manoeuvre was executed.
[7] He wasn't very interested in the bean-production.

When you find such words functioning in the context of a sentence, no confusion should arise. Notice in passing that the adjectives *interesting* and *interested* are gradable and so can be modified by *very*. By contrast, no verb can be modified by *very*:

[8] *Her hair very interested him.

Decide on the category (or categories) of the following words. Most of them belong to more than one category. You may find it helpful to construct sentences in which they can function.

*open, impossible, up, content, between, export, edit*. The exercise is discussed at the end of the chapter (Discussion 1, p. 84).

---

The Verb Group itself, together with the morphology of the verb and the lexical/auxiliary distinction, is treated in Chapter 6. For the moment, all that is required is that you be able to identify verbs, and the above should suffice for that purpose. Since I am not concerned with the structure of the Verb Group here, I shall use the triangle notation to represent it in phrase-markers and say no more about it in this chapter.

## The complements of the Verb Group

This chapter is concerned with the functional relations between the Verb Group (Vgp) and the other constituents that appear in the basic Verb Phrase. In Exercise 5(e) of Chapter 2 you were asked to determine the function of *those wildcats* in the sentence

[9]  Max spotted those wildcats.

The Verb Phrase is *spotted those wildcats*, and *spotted* is the single-word verb of the Vgp. Discussion of the exercise suggested that the relation between the Vgp and the Noun Phrase is one of complementation: there is a mutual dependency between the Vgp (as governor) and the Noun Phrase (as complement). The use of *spotted* without a following NP is ungrammatical, and so is the use of the NP without *spotted*:

[10]  *Max spotted
[11]  *Max those wildcats.

Not all Vgps do require a following NP. In fact, if we change the verb from *spot* to *sunbathe*, for example, we get a pattern of grammaticality exactly the opposite of the pattern of [9] and [10]:

[12]  *Max sunbathed those wildcats
[13]  Max sunbathed.

*spot*, it seems, must take an NP, while *sunbathe* cannot take an NP. So, the NP depends not just on there being a Vgp present, but also on what kind of verb is the head of that Vgp. *spot* and *sunbathe* are examples of two very general SUB-CATEGORIES of the verb category (and of the Verb Groups of which they are head). **Verbs are SUB-CATEGORISED according to what other elements must appear with them in the VP. In other words, they are sub-categorised in terms of their complementation types.**

Just because an NP cannot follow the Vgp *sunbathe* does not of course mean that nothing can follow it. You know that it can: for example, the PP *beside a stream* can. But this PP is not part of the COMPLEMENTATION of *sunbathe*, in the sense that it is not required to complete the meaning of the Vgp. It just gives extra information. If we omit it, we are not left with an incomplete predicate. It is an optional MODIFIER. (Compare the discussion of Exercise 5(a) and that of 5(e) in Chapter 2.) The fact that a PP can follow *sunbathe* cannot therefore be used to sub-categorise the verb. Another reason why it cannot be used to sub-categorise the verb is that **all Verb Phrases optionally include modification by a PP.** Notice, for example, that a PP can be added after *spotted those wildcats*:

[14]  Max spotted those wildcats *in the Spring*.

In short, *spot* and *sunbathe* can be distinguished by the obligatory presence or absence of a following NP, but not by the (optional) presence or absence of a following PP.

For the moment I shall concentrate on the complementation of the verb. More is said about the distinction between complementation and modification in the Verb Phrase in Chapter 5.

To see how general these sub-categories are, decide which of the following verbs belong to the same sub-category as *spot* (requiring an NP) and which to the same sub-category as *sunbathe* (requiring no NP). One of them belongs to both sub-categories.

*disappear, treat, inspect, die, vegetate, play, decamp, throw.*

---

Taking just the first two examples, note the following patterns of grammaticality:

[15a] Max disappeared        [16a] *Max treated
[15b] *Max disappeared Bill   [16b] Max treated Bill

*disappear* clearly belongs to the same sub-category as *sunbathe*, as do *die*, *vegetate*, and *decamp*: none of these verbs allows a following NP. But *treat* clearly belongs with *spot*, as do *inspect* and *throw*: these demand a following NP. *play*, on the other hand, belongs to both sub-categories, since both [17] and [18] are well-formed:

[17] The children played (beside a stream).
[18] Max plays the tuba (beside a stream).

*paddle*, *reflect*, and *break* are further examples of verbs that belong to both sub-categories. Check this for yourself. Sentences containing them in their different uses are given at the end of the chapter (Discussion 2, p. 84).

---

The two sub-categories discussed above are not the only ones. I shall deal here with **six main sub-categories of Vgp: (1) TRANSITIVE (sometimes called MONOTRANSITIVE), (2) INTRANSITIVE, (3) DITRANSITIVE, (4) INTENSIVE, (5) COMPLEX TRANSITIVE, (6) PREPOSITIONAL.**

## Monotransitive Verb Groups

**A MONOTRANSITIVE Vgp is one which requires a single Noun Phrase to complement it.** Of the verbs considered above, then, *spot*, *treat*, and *inspect* are monotransitive verbs. **The Noun**

**Phrase that complements a transitive verb is said to function as its DIRECT OBJECT.** So, in *Max spotted those wildcats*, the NP within the VP (*those wildcats*) is complementing the transitive verb *spot* as its direct object.

I have described the Vgp in this verb–object complementation as the GOVERNOR. Notice that, where an NP functioning as the direct object of a verb is a pronoun, it has a special form. This form is called the OBJECTIVE CASE (or, more traditionally, the ACCUSATIVE CASE). Thus the direct object pronouns in the objective case are grammatical in [19], but the corresponding pronouns in the SUBJECTIVE (traditionally, the NOMINATIVE) CASE are ungrammatical, [20]:

[19]    Max spotted $\left\{ \begin{array}{l} \text{me} \\ \text{her} \\ \text{him} \\ \text{us} \\ \text{them} \end{array} \right.$     [20]    *Max spotted $\left\{ \begin{array}{l} \text{I} \\ \text{she} \\ \text{he} \\ \text{we} \\ \text{they} \end{array} \right.$

**When the form of an NP is determined by its complement relation with another constituent, it is said to be GOVERNED by that other constituent (in this case, the verb). Notice that this goes for NPs complementing prepositions in Prepositional Phrases.** The preposition governs the NP, demanding that it appear in the objective case: *for him* vs. *\*for he*, *against them* vs. *\*against they*. *You* and *it* are the only pronouns that do not have a special distinct form in the objective case.

Since the Vgp and the NP are in a functional relationship, the NP needs to be represented as a sister of the Verb Group (and therefore as a daughter of the VP) as in [21]:

[21]

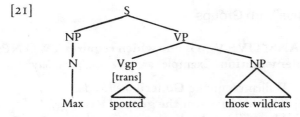

In [21] I have added to the Vgp node the extra label '[trans]'. This extra label is called a FEATURE, and it simply sub-categorises the Verb Group as being monotransitive. This sub-categorisation feature is partly needed in order to specify the function of the following NP in terms of the phrase-marker itself. Thus, **when an NP is the sister of a Verb Group bearing a [trans] feature, we**

**know that the function of the NP is that of direct object.** The
point of having this feature within the phrase-marker will become
more apparent when I deal with other sub-categories of Verb and
Verb Group.

## Intransitive Verb Groups

**An INTRANSITIVE Vgp is one that does not require any
further constituent as a sister in the VP.** So, *disappear*, *die*,
*vegetate* (and *play* on one interpretation) are intransitive verbs.

Since an intransitive Verb Group does not require any further
element to form a complete predicate, a single-word verb can
count not only as a complete Verb Group but also as a complete
Verb Phrase. (Remember the discussion of *Ducks paddle* in Chapter
3.) So, a very simple sentence like *Omar sighed* is represented as in
[22] – with an [intrans] feature on the Vgp.

[22]

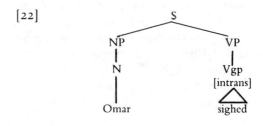

## Ditransitive Verb Groups

**A DITRANSITIVE Vgp is one which requires TWO NPs as
its complementation.** Examples are *give*, *send*, and *buy*:

[23a]  William is giving **Goneril** *the bleach*.
[24a]  The staff have sent **the general** *a message*.
[25a]  Max will buy **his butler** *a salami-slicer*.

In [23a]–[25a] the first complement NP (in bold) is said
to function as the INDIRECT OBJECT of the ditransitive
verb. The second complement NP (in italics) functions as
the DIRECT OBJECT (i.e. it has the same function as the NP
that complements a monotransitive Vgp). Here is a phrase-marker

of [23a] – with a [ditrans] feature on the Vgp:

[26]

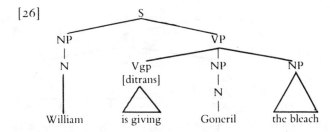

Both NPs are governed by the Verb Group *is giving* and would appear in the objective case if they were pronouns.

Now decide which of the following verbs are distransitive.

(a) *show* (b) *offer* (c) *see* (d) *tell* (e) *announce*

---

Consider the following sentences:

[27]  Max has already shown **Mathilda** *his collection of razors.*
[28]  Tarzan offered **Jane** *his hairy arm.*
[29]  Hazeltine told **the computer** *his news.*

(a), (b), and (d), since they accept two consecutive NPs, are ditransitive verbs. (c) and (e) do not:

[30]  *Max saw Mathilda his collection of razors.
[31]  *Hazeltine announced the computer his news.

An important characteristic of Verb Phrases consisting of a ditransitive verb complemented by two NPs is that they are systematically related to Verb Phrases in which **the indirect object NP (bold in [23a]–[25a]) corresponds to a Prepositional Phrase (PP) in a position following the direct object.** Thus [23a] corresponds with [23b]:

[23b]  William is giving *the bleach* **TO Goneril**.

The PPs that correspond in this way with indirect objects are always introduced by *to* or *for*.

What are the appropriate [b] forms for [24a] and [25a]?

---

[24b]  The staff have sent *a message* **to the general**.
[25b]  Max will buy *a salami-slicer* **for his butler**.

These [b] sentences can be represented as in [32]:

[32]

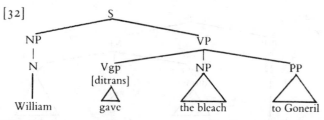

The PP corresponding to an indirect object NP has a rather special status. Usually, when a PP follows the direct object NP, it is not part of the complementation of the verb but is an optional modifier. However, in using a DITRANSITIVE verb such as *send*, we normally need to specify not only (a) a sender (usually subject), and (b) what is sent (usually the direct object), but also (c) **to whom it is sent (usually indirect object). (c) can be specified either by an NP or by a PP containing *to* or *for*.** So PPs that correspond to indirect objects are part of the complementation of ditransitive verbs. Whether they appear within PPs or not, I shall always refer to NPs like those in bold in [23a]–[25a] and [23b]–[25b] as indirect objects.

INDIRECT OBJECT, then, is either the first of two NP sisters of a Verb Group bearing a [ditrans] feature (as in [26]) or the NP daughter of a PP which is a sister of a Verb Group bearing a [ditrans] feature (as in [32]).

As for DIRECT OBJECT, as well as being the NP sister of a Verb Group bearing a [monotrans] feature, it can in addition be either the second of two NP sisters of a [ditrans] verb group, or the NP sister of a [ditrans] Verb Group which also has a PP sister.

## Intensive Verb Groups

**An INTENSIVE Vgp differs from a monotransitive and a ditransitive verb in that it can be complemented by a single Adjective Phrase, or Noun Phrase, or Prepositional Phrase.** The most common and obvious intensive verb is *be*:

[33]  Ed is being *rather extravagant*. (AP)
[34]  Sigmund was *an auctioneer*. (NP)
[35]  Oscar should be *in the engine-room*. (PP)

The intensive verbs include *become* and, in some of their uses, *seem, appear, turn, remain, look, taste, feel, smell*, and *sound*.

To bring out the character of the intensive verb and its complementation, compare [34] – repeated here – with [36]:

[34] Sigmund was an auctioneer.
[36] Sigmund spotted an auctioneer.

At first glance, these may not seem very different. In both, we have a verb complemented by an NP. In [36], as you know, the verb is monotransitive and the NP therefore functions as direct object. In [34], the verb is again complemented by an NP, but the meaning relation between that NP and the Verb Group, and between that NP and the subject NP, is different. In saying that Sigmund *spotted* an auctioneer, we mention two individuals – Sigmund on the one hand and the auctioneer on the other – and state that the former spotted the latter. This is nothing like what is happening in [34]. In using that sentence, we mention only one individual – Sigmund. The expression *an auctioneer* is not actually used to mention anyone in addition to the person mentioned by means of the subject NP. The rest of the sentence (*was an auctioneer*) is used to characterise the subject, Sigmund – to attribute to him a property, that of being an auctioneer. Much the same goes for [37] as compared with [36]:

[37] Sigmund became an auctioneer.

[37] expresses a change in Sigmund himself, rather than any kind of relation between Sigmund and another person.

The NPs complementing the intensive verbs in [34] and [37] have exactly the same function as the Adjective Phrase complementing the intensive verb in [33]. Here it is more obvious that the complement of the verb (which is an AP) cannot be used to mention somebody. It is simply used to attribute extravagance to the person mentioned by means of the subject NP, namely Ed.

**When an NP, AP, or PP complements an INTENSIVE verb, its function can be described as that of PREDICATIVE.** (This function is sometimes described as 'complement', in a sense that distinguishes it from 'object'. I have not adopted that terminology here since I have used 'complement' in a wider sense in this book.)

Now decide whether the (italicised) complement of the Verb Group in the following sentences is a predicative or a direct object.

[38] Max turned *a subtle shade of green*.
[39] Max turned *the card*.
[40] Tarzan felt *a tap on the shoulder*.

[41] Tarzan felt *a real idiot*.
[42] The leopard-skin pillbox hat didn't become *her*.
[43] The hat became *a very useful wastepaper basket*.

*A subtle shade of green* in [38], *a real idiot* in [41], and *a very useful wastepaper basket* in [43] characterise the subjects of their sentences and do not mention distinct individuals. They are therefore predicatives. More specifically, they are SUBJECT-PREDICATIVES – since they characterise the subjects. (In introducing complex transitive complementation below, I shall mention object-predicatives.) In those sentences, then, *turn, feel* and *become* are used in their intensive senses. *The card* in [39], *a tap on the shoulder* in [40], and *her* in [42], by contrast, mention things distinct from the subject. They function as direct objects, complementing *turn, feel* and *become* in their monotransitive senses.

Most of my illustrations have shown NPs complementing intensive Vgps (as predicatives). But the distinguishing mark of an intensive Vgp is that [intensive] is the only sub-category of Vgp that may be complemented just by an AP (as in [33]). Note the ungrammaticality of:

[44] *Max has spotted rather extravagant.
[45] *Stella has given very dubious a whole bunch.

So, if you are in doubt as to whether a VP consisting of Vgp + NP is an example of a monotransitive Verb Group + direct object or an example of an intensive Verb Group + subject-predicative, you can test it by replacing the NP with an AP. If the result is grammatical (and does not involve a change in the sense of the verb), this indicates that it is an intensive verb.

The phrase-marker representation of sentences with intensive Verb Group + NP as subject-predicative will be identical to that of sentences with a monotransitive Verb Group + NP as direct object except for the different sub-categorisation feature on the verb Group:

[46]

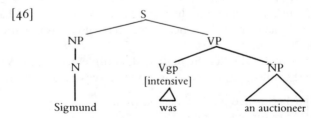

Since intensive verbs only take subject-predicatives and monotransitive verbs only take direct objects, we can rely on this difference in sub-categorisation to distinguish the direct object function from the subject-predicative function in terms of the phrase-marker configuration itself. Thus **an NP, an AP or a PP functions as subject-predicative if it is the sister of a Verb Group bearing an [intensive] sub-categorisation feature.** A word now about PPs functioning as subject-predicatives. I have already mentioned that all VPs can include optional modification by PPs. PPs should only be treated as part of the necessary complementation of an intensive verb (i.e. as subject-predicatives) if they cannot be omitted. So, *in the engine room* in [35] IS a predicative since [47] is not a complete sentence (even though the missing element might be understood in context – see Chapter 5):

[47] *Oscar should be.

I look again at PP complements below.

## Complex transitive Verb Groups

**COMPLEX TRANSITIVE** Vgps combine monotransitive complementation with intensive complementation. In other words, **(like monotransitives) complex transitives are complemented by an NP functioning as a DIRECT OBJECT (in italics below) and (like intensives) an NP, an AP, or a PP functioning as a PREDICATIVE (in bold).** Examples are:

[48] Melvin found *his own jokes* **extremely funny**.
[49] They are making *Stella* **their spokesperson**.
[50] Liza has been putting *the liquor* **under her bed**.

There is an important difference between the predicative in an intensive sentence and the predicative in a complex transitive sentence. As mentioned, the former characterises the subject (hence 'subject-predicative'). In complex transitive sentences, on the other hand, the predicative characterises the direct object, and so is called an OBJECT-PREDICATIVE. The relation between the DIRECT OBJECT and OBJECT-PREDICATIVE in a COMPLEX TRANSITIVE sentence parallels that between the SUBJECT and the SUBJECT-PREDICATIVE in an INTENSIVE sentence. For example, if [48] is true, then, at least as far as Melvin is concerned, his own jokes **are** extremely funny; if [49] is true, then Stella is going to **become** their spokesperson; and if [50] is true, then the liquor **is** under Liza's bed.

Here is a phrase-marker representation of [48]:

[51]

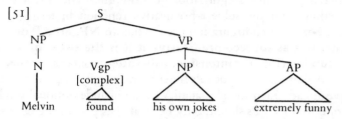

A further phrase-marker definition of direct object is required which allows that it can be that NP which is a sister of a [complex] Verb Group and which precedes either an NP, AP, or a PP sister. The phrase-marker definition of object-predicative is that NP, AP, or PP which is preceded by and is a sister of both an NP and a [complex] Verb Group.

## Prepositional Verb Groups

*glance*, *reply*, *refer*, and *look* are examples of **PREPOSITIONAL** verbs – they must be complemented by a Prepositional Phrase. Take *glance*, for example:

[52] *Max glanced
[53] *Max glanced the falling acrobat
[54] Max glanced at the falling acrobat.

[55]

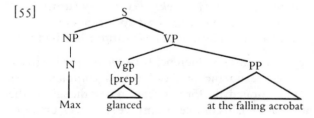

As we shall see in the next chapter, these need to be distinguished from [intransitive] verbs with optional modification by PP. I shall call the PP that complements a [prepositional] Vgp, a **PREPOSITIONAL COMPLEMENT**. In the sub-categorisation offered in this chapter such Vgps also need to be distinguished from [intensive] Vgps when these are complemented by a PP, as in *Oscar should be in the engine room* – [34] above. The Vgp in [34] has been sub-categorised as [intensive] rather than [prepositional] because it can alternatively be complemented by an AP or an NP functioning as subject-predicative. Prepositional verbs can only be complemented by Prepositional Phrases.

We have now looked at a six-way distinction among Verb Groups and their associated sentence patterns. Not all verbs (and not all uses of all verbs) fit neatly into this classification or do so only with a certain amount of ingenuity on the part of the analyst. The distinctions given nevertheless provide an introduction to the topic of sub-categorisation and in discussing them, I have mentioned all the major constituent functions.

In terms of these major functions, the sub-categorisation can be summarised as follows:

MONOTRANSITIVE – '[trans]':
    subject – verb – direct object
    (S)      (V)      (dO)

INTRANSITIVE – '[intrans]':
    subject – verb
    (S)      (V)

DITRANSITIVE – '[ditrans]':
    subject – verb – indirect object – direct object
    (S)      (V)      (iO)        (dO)

or:
    subject – verb – direct object – *to/for* indirect object
    (S)      (V)      (dO)        (iO)

INTENSIVE – '[intens]':
    Subject – verb – subject-predicative
    (S)      (V)      (sP)

COMPLEX TRANSITIVE – '[complex]':
    subject – verb – direct object – object-predicative
    (S)      (V)      (dO)        (oP)

PREPOSITIONAL – '[prep]':
    subject – verb – prepositional complement
    (S)      (V)      (PC)

As mentioned, other elements may optionally appear. These, though, are not part of the necessary complementation of the verb, but are modifiers. Chapter 5 is concerned with these and with some of the factors that need to be taken into account in distinguishing between complements and modifiers in the VP.

## Discussion of in-text exercises

### Discussion 1

The following sentences illustrate the different uses of the words given. The category of the word in each sentence is given below. You may find it useful to treat the sentences as an exercise: identify the category of the italicised word in each sentence.

1. Morgan *opened* his mouth.
2. Morgan's *open* mouth admitted the fly.
3. That was clearly *impossible*.
4. Mary *appealed* to John to take the rubbish out.
5. Her repeated *appeals* were unsuccessful.
6. He booted his drunken colleague *up* the gangway.
7. They *up* the rent every other month.
8. Georgette is perfectly *content*.
9. Jenny criticised the *content* of the paragraph.
10. Watching you work so hard *contents* me.
11. The recalcitrant mango slipped *between* Grace's fingers.
12. Toffee-wrappers are the main *export*.
13. Boggis and Stone *export* toffee-wrappers to Mesopotamia.
14. Max has *edited* a grand total of 253 books.

---

*open*: 1. Verb. 2. Adjective.    *impossible*: 3. Adjective.    *appeal*: 4. Verb. 5. Noun.    *up*: 6. Preposition. 7. Verb.    *content*: 8. Adjective. 9. Noun. 10. Verb.    *between*: 11. Preposition.    *export*: 12. Noun. 13. Verb.    *edit*: 14. Verb.

### Discussion 2

1. The ducks are paddling (across the lake). – [intransitive]
2. He paddled the raft (across the lake). – [monotransitive]
3. Morgan is reflecting (quietly). – [intransitive]
4. The glass reflected Max's ugly mug. – [monotransitive]
5. The samovar broke. – [intransitive]
6. Anna broke the samovar. – [monotransitive].

### Exercises

1. Identify the major functions in the following sentences (subject, direct object, indirect object, subject-predicative,

object-predicative and prepositional complement). Identify
the Verb Groups and sub-categorise them. Example:

Otto        is devouring    the cous-cous
(subject)   (Verb Group)    (direct object)
            [trans]

(1) The girl in the palace had dyed her hair deep purple.
(2) The balloons are ascending.
(3) Richard has promised me his spaghetti machine.
(4) This sedan-chair should prove useful.
(5) Someone has stolen my contact-lenses.
(6) It doesn't sound much fun.
(7) The candidate's antics did not amuse the board of examiners.
(8) The committee nominated her Acrobat of the Year.
(9) Egbert has been feeding the cat smoked salmon.
(10) I would like my curry as hot as you can make it.
(11) We don't allude to his third ear.
(12) The main witness for the prosecution has disappeared.
(13) He has applied for a gun licence.

2.   Decide whether the PP in the following sentences is part of
     the complementation of a DITRANSITIVE Verb Group or
     not.

(1)  Holden is writing letters to Africa.
(2)  Holden is writing letters to The White House.
(3)  Max took the hyena to the station.
(4)  Max lent his hyena to the Dramatics Society.
(5)  William baked a cake for Goneril.
(6)  William baked a cake for Christmas.
(7)  She is saving the money for a Bechstein Grande.
(8)  She is saving a place for Sophie.

3.   Using any of the following phrases, construct (a) a sentence in
     which *smelt* is used as an intransitive Verb Group; (b) a
     sentence in which it is used as a monotransitive Verb Group;
     (c) a sentence in which it is used as an intensive Verb Group.

     (i) *smelt*   (ii) *the apprehensive butler*   (iii) *Jim's attempt at a
     stew*   (iv) *loathsome*.

4.   Joachim found Bill an amusing companion.

     This sentence is ambiguous. Explain the ambiguity in terms
     of the functions of its constituents. Draw a phrase-marker for

each interpretation (making clear which phrase-marker corresponds with which interpretation).

5.    The functions of the major constituents in

(a)    Widmerpool will make Pamela a disastrous husband.

are difficult to accommodate within the six-way sub-categorisation introduced in this chapter. Explain why. You may find this easier if you compare it with (b) and (c)

(b)    Widmerpool will make Pamela a good wife.
(c)    Widmerpool will make Pamela lots of money.

which are much more easily handled (though in different ways).

6.    Using the triangle notation for all major constituents (as used in this chapter) draw phrase-markers for the following sentences.

(a)    Nicholas was feeling strangely euphoric.
(b)    The gallery wouldn't lend them the triptych.
(c)    The condition of the cakes left out overnight had deteriorated.
(d)    They voted the Grand Master out of office.
(e)    A bucket of cold water will revive this particular patient.
(f)    The Venetians have submitted to Napoleon's demands.

## Discussion of exercises

1.(1) The girl in the palace    had dyed    her hair    deep purple.
               S    V    dO    oP
                          [complex]

(2)    The balloons    are ascending.
         S    V
              [intrans]

(3)    Richard    has promised    me    his spaghetti machine.
       S    V    iO    dO
            [ditrans]

(4)    This sedan chair    should prove    useful.
         S    V    sP
            [intens]

(5)  Someone  has stolen  my contact lenses.
      S       V              dO
         [trans]

(6)  It  doesn't sound  much fun.
    S      V        sP
      [intens]

(7)  The candidate's antics  didn't amuse  the board of examiners.
           S           V           dO
             [trans]

(8)  The committee  nominated  her  Acrobat Of The Year.
        S       V     dO      oP
        [complex]

(9)  Egbert  has been feeding  the cat  smoked salmon.
     S      V        iO       dO
      [ditrans]

(10)  I  would like  my curry  as hot as you can make it.
     S    V     dO         oP
    [complex]

(11)  We  don't allude  to his third ear.
     S     V       PC
      [prep]

(12)  The main witness for the prosecution  has disappeared.
                S              V
          [intrans]

(13)  He  has applied  for a gun licence.
    S    V      PC
    [prep]

**2.**  As mentioned in this chapter, a PP is counted as part of the complementation of a distransitive verb only if it corresponds to an NP functioning as an indirect object. Take examples (1) and (2). (1a) (below) is not a reasonable paraphrase of (1), but (2a) (below) is a reasonable paraphrase of (2):

(1a)  Holden is writing Africa letters.
(2a)  Holden is writing The White House letters.

So the PP in (2) is part of the complementation of the verb, and *write* in that sentence must be sub-categorised as [ditrans]. In (1), on the other hand, *write* is a monotransitive verb, complemented by the direct object *letters* or perhaps *letters to Africa*. Note that, if *to Africa* is not part of the direct object NP in 1, then it must be analysed as an optional modifier within the VP. I discuss why there should be this difference between

(1) and (2) after dealing with the remaining examples.

(3) No. cf. *Max took the station his hyena.* The PP is a modifier.

(4) Yes. cf. *Max lent the Dramatic Society his hyena.* Lend is a [ditrans] verb.

(5) Yes. cf. *William baked Goneril a cake.*

(6) No. cf. *William baked Christmas a cake.*

(7) No. cf. *She is saving a Bechstein Grande the money.*

(8) Yes. cf. *She is saving Sophie a place.*

Notice that it is only NPs denoting ANIMATE things (or things that could be interpreted as being animate) that can be indirect objects. For example, the moment you interpret *Christmas* as a person rather than a festival, *William baked Christmas a cake* sounds perfectly grammatical. Even in (1b) *The White House* can be an indirect object because, as well as being a building, it is an organisation of human beings, as is the Dramatic Society. On the other hand, since there is no single human institution that represents Africa as a whole, *Africa* remains an inanimate location, and cannot function as indirect object.

3.  INTRANSITIVE:   1. The apprehensive butler smelt.
     2. Jim's attempt at a stew smelt.

     MONOTRANSITIVE:  1. The apprehensive butler smelt Jim's attempt at a stew.

     INTENSIVE:   1. The apprehensive butler smelt loathsome.
      2. Jim's attempt at a stew smelt loathsome.

4.  On one interpretation *Joachim found Bill an amusing companion* corresponds in meaning with (a) 'Joachim found an amusing companion for Bill'. Here the verb *find* is ditransitive, *Bill* is indirect object, and *an amusing companion* is direct object. On the other interpretation, it corresponds with (b) 'Joachim found Bill to be an amusing companion', where *an amusing companion* characterises Bill (the direct object) and so is an object-predicative. On this interpretation, then, the sentence is complex transitive. The difference in interpretation and in the functions of the constituents can be represented in phrase-marker terms simply in the sub-categorisation of the Verb Group:

(a)

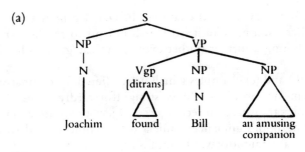

(b)

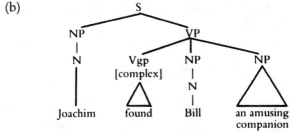

**5.** The sub-categorisation problem posed by the (a) sentence can be made clear by showing that it corresponds with

(d) Widmerpool will make a disastrous husband FOR Pamela.

Here the NP *Pamela* in (a) has moved and become a PP. This suggests that *make* in (a) is a [ditrans] verb, since *Pamela* seems to be functioning as INDIRECT OBJECT. But if *make* in (a) is [ditrans], we should expect *a disastrous husband* to be functioning as DIRECT OBJECT (since ditransitive complementation consists of indirect object + direct object). But it isn't. It does not mention an individual distinct from the subject *Widmerpool*. This suggests that it is a subject-predicative. So, it seems that in (a) we have:

subject – Verb Group – indirect object – subject-predicative.

If you look at the summary of the sub-categories given in this chapter, you will see that this particular combination of complements (indirect object + subject-predicative) is not allowed for. Indirect object only combines with direct object (in distransitive sentences) and subject-predicative only occurs by itself (in intensive sentences). We appear to have a combination of intensive complementation and one half of the distransitive complementation.

This is a very unusual example. In fact, I cannot think of another example like it, so I shall not go to the bother of establishing a further (rather exotic) sub-category to handle it.

The (b) and (c) examples which were offered for comparison present no problem. (b) is straightforwardly handled as complex transitive – direct object + object-predicative (under Widmerpool's guidance, Pamela will become a good wife). (c) is a straightforward ditransitive structure – indirect object + direct object (Widmerpool will make a lot of money FOR Pamela).

**6.**

(a)

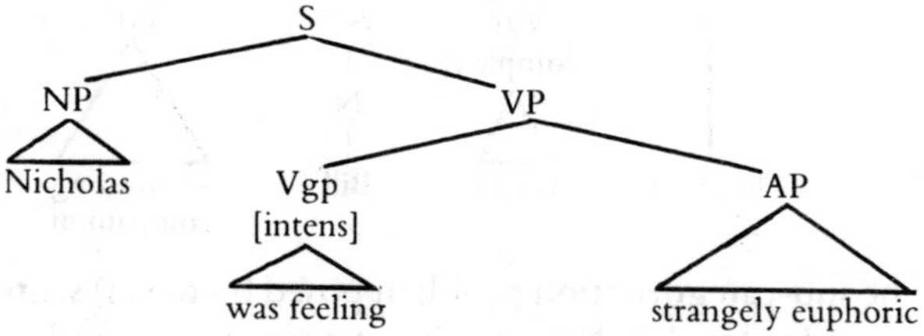

(b)

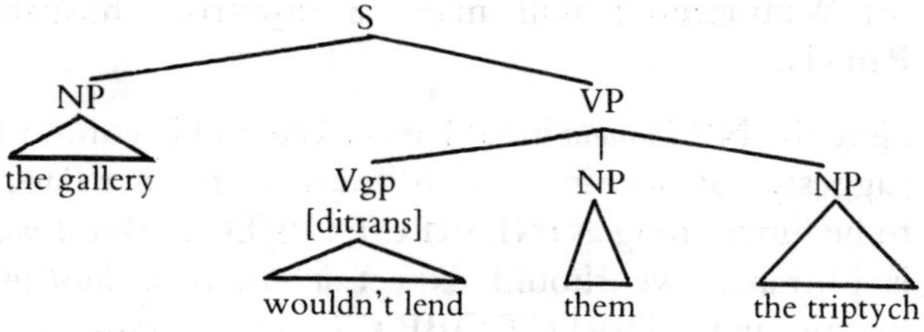

(c)

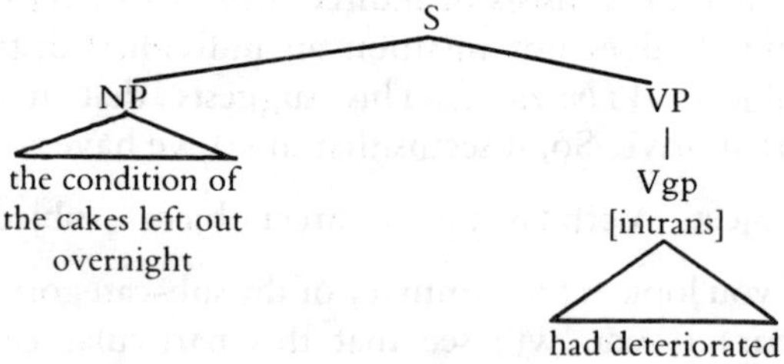

(d)

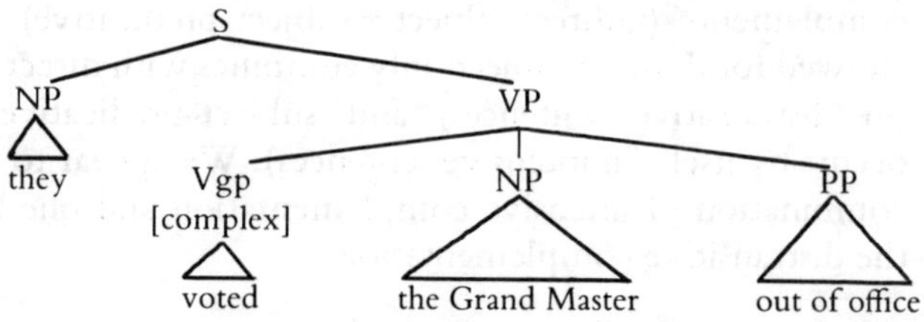

(e)

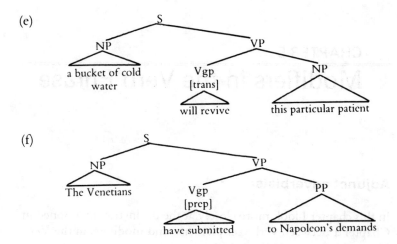

(f)

As you may have noticed, in these six phrase-markers, all six complementation types are represented, and hence all six types of basic sentence considered in this chapter.

# CHAPTER 5

# Modifiers in the Verb Phrase

## Adjunct adverbials

In this chapter I look more closely at the distinction mentioned in Chapter 4 between verb complements and modifiers in the Verb Phrase.

You have already encountered Prepositional Phrases functioning as modifiers in the VP:

[1] Old Sam sunbathed *beside a stream*
*like a maniac*

[2] Max spotted those wildcats *in the Spring*
*with his binoculars.*

As mentioned, since the (italicised) PPs are optional and can occur with almost any verb, they cannot be used to sub-categorise the verb. They give additional, though not essential, information.

When a constituent functions as the PPs in [1] and [2] are functioning, it is said to function as an ADJUNCT ADVERBIAL. At the end of this chapter, I shall say a word about CONJUNCT and DISJUNCT ADVERBIALS, but the chapter is primarily concerned with adjunct adverbials (ADJUNCTS for short).

[1] and [2] are examples of intransitive and monotransitive sentences with adjunct adverbials. Here are further examples of PPs functioning as adjuncts in intensive [3], [4], and [5], ditransitive [6], and complex transitive [7] structures:

[3] Ed was rather extravagant *in the bazaar.*
[4] Sigmund was an auctioneer *for three years.*
[5] Oscar was in the engine-room *in a flash.*
[6] William gave Goneril the bleach *on her birthday.*
[7] Liza put the liquor under the bed *for safekeeping.*

As the adjunct PPs in these examples illustrate, adjuncts

express a wide range of ideas, including manner, means, purpose, reason, place, and time (including duration and frequency). They tend to answer questions like *Where? Why? When? How? What for? How long? How often? How many times?*

Since adjunct is one type of ADVERBIAL function, you should not be surprised to learn that, **in addition to PPs, ADVERB PHRASES can also function as adjunct adverbials.** Nevertheless, take care not to confuse the label ADVERBIAL (which denotes a function) and the labels ADVERB/ADVERB PHRASE (which denote categories). We have seen that AdvPs can have functions other than that of adverbial. (They can modify adjectives, within APs). Conversely, you know that not all constituents functioning as adverbials are AdvPs: we have just seen that PPs can function as adverbials. Here are examples of AdvPs functioning, like the PPs above, as adverbials:

[8] Sam sunbathed *frequently*.
[9] He spotted the wildcats *quite accidentally*.
[10] She put it under the bed *surreptitiously*.

Many adverbs are not as easily identified as such by their *-ly* morphology, in particular the interrogative adverbs, *how, where, why, when*, and adverbs relating to time: *here, there, now, then, again, yet, still, already, seldom, often, ever, yesterday, tonight, tomorrow*.

In addition to AdvPs and PPs, **certain NPs can function as adverbials**: *home, last year, the day before yesterday, the day after tomorrow, this afternoon . . ..*

## Levels of Verb Phrase

How do adjunct adverbials fit into the structure of sentences? I have described adjuncts as modifiers within the VP but so far I have avoided saying exactly what they modify. Two possibilities seem to offer themselves. In [2], for example, does *in the Spring* modify just the Vgp *spotted*, or does it modify *spotted those wildcats* – that is, the Verb Group plus its direct object? Perhaps you have a view about this?

Answering this question involves making a decision about the constituent analysis of *spotted those wildcats in the Spring*. If the PP modifies just the Vgp *spotted*, then it should be a sister of the Vgp, along with *those wildcats*, as in [11]:

[11]

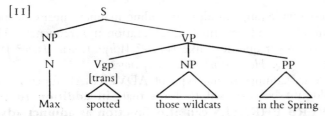

If, on the other hand, we want to say that *in the Spring* modifies *spotted those wildcats*, then it must be a **sister of a constituent consisting of the Vgp + direct object NP**. In other words, Vgp + NP must form a constituent. They don't form a constituent in [11], do they?

I shall choose this second alternative. Intuitively the adjunct PP does seem to modify a constituent consisting of Vgp + NP rather than just the Verb Group by itself. I have already noted that *those wildcats*, as a complement, completes the sense of the verb and, together with that verb, forms a unit of sense. It does this independently of the adjunct *in the Spring*.

We have seen that *Max spotted those wildcats in the Spring* can be analysed as a good subject-predicate sentence. So I shall analyse *spotted those wildcats in the Spring* as a VP. Furthermore we have already noted that *spotted those wildcats* forms a VP in its own right. Now, using the triangle notation for *spotted*, *those wildcats*, and *in the Spring*, draw the phrase-marker of the whole sentence.

[12]

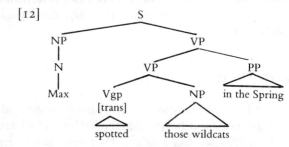

*spotted those wildcats* is a VP within the larger VP *spotted those wildcats in the Spring*. This analysis has the advantage of creating two levels of VP, distinguishing between COMPLEMENTS AS SISTERS OF THE VERB GROUP (within the 'lower' VP) and ADJUNCTS AS SISTERS OF A VERB PHRASE (within a 'higher' VP).

A piece of evidence that could be used to support this analysis was alluded to in the introduction. But first, draw the phrase-markers for [13] and [14] in the light of the discussion so far, bearing in mind that *mend* is a [monotransitive] verb and *put* is a [complex transitive] verb.

[13] Bevis mended the car in the garage.
[14] Bevis put the car in the garage.

Since *put* is [complex transitive], the PP in [14] is part of the complementation of the verb. By contrast, the PP in [13] is an (optional) adjunct adverbial. Thus, on the analysis adopted here, [15] and [16] are the appropriate phrase-markers (in which I have numbered the VPs for ease of reference).

[15]

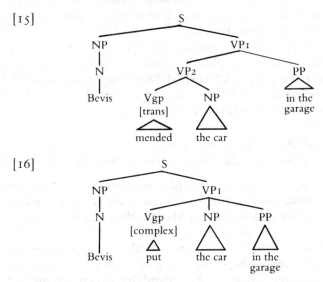

[16]

In the introduction, I noted that [17] was grammatical, but [18] ungrammatical:

[17] Bevis mended the car in the garage and Max did so in the lay-by.
[18] *Bevis put the car in the garage and Max did so in the lay-by.

The expression *do so* is used to avoid having to repeat material that has already appeared in the sentence. It stands for, or replaces, that material. Now, here are five questions for you:

(i)    What string of words does *do so* replace in [17]?
(ii)   What string of words does *do so* replace in [18]?

(iii)   What CATEGORY is the string of words that *do so* replaces in [17]?

(iv)   What CATEGORY is the string of words that *do so* replaces in [18]? You should find this difficult to answer.

(v)   On the basis of your answers to (i)–(iv) what can you say about the sequence of words that *do so* replaces?

---

(i)   *do so* replaces *mended the car.*

(ii)   *do so* replaces *put the car.*

(iii)   *do so* replaces a VP.

(iv)   *do so* does not replace any category. Only CONSTITUENTS can belong to categories, but in [18] *put the car* is not a constituent (there is no node that dominates all and only those elements).

(v)   Since [17] is grammatical and [18] ungrammatical, it appears that *do so* must replace a constituent. In [17] the constituent that it replaces is VP2 in [15]. Now check to see whether *do so* can replace *any* VP – that is, check whether it can also replace VP1 in [15] and VP1 in [16].

---

[19]   Bevis mended the car in the garage and Max did so (too).

[20]   Bevis put the car in the garage and Max did so (too).

From [19] we understand that Max mended the car in the garage. *Do so*, then, stands for *mended the car in the garage* (VP1 in [15]). From [20] we understand that Max put the car in the garage – *do so* stands for *put the car in the garage* (VP1 in [16]).

Both [19] and [20] are grammatical. So, it appears that we can use *do so* to replace either *mended the car in the garage* or just *mended the car* since both these strings of words have been analysed as VPs. But we can only use *do so* to replace *put the car in the garage*, not just *put the car*, since the former, but not the latter, has been analysed as a VP.

If we distinguish between [13] and [14] in the way suggested by [15] and [16], we are offering an explanation of why [17] but not [18] is grammatical.

In the light of this discussion, what do you suggest should be the phrase-marker of *Sam sunbathed beside a stream*? It is given as Discussion 1 at the end of the chapter.

---

Notice that, since the occurrence of adjuncts is not determined by the verb and its sub-category, there is no reason why we should not reiterate adjuncts to our hearts' delight, as in [21]:

[21] He guzzled creamcakes noisily under the blankets
    S     V        dO       aA         aA
in the outhouse   every night
    aA          aA

Now draw a phrase-marker of [22]:

[22] Humphrey drove his car on the left in France.

bearing in mind that [23], [24], and [25] are all grammatical:

[23] He drove his car on the left in France and Claude did so too.

[24] He drove his car on the left in France and he did so in Germany too.

[25] He drove his car on the left in France but did so on the right in the States.

(The phrase-marker is given at the end of the chapter – Discussion 2.)

## The mobility of adverbials

Well, this division of complements into a lower VP and adjunct adverbials into a higher VP looks very neat. Unfortunately, a very prominent characteristic of adverbials is that they can appear in all sorts of positions in the sentence, not just following the Vgp and its complements. Indeed, the very fact that you can move a PP around a sentence is a sure sign that it is functioning as an adverbial and not as the complement of the Vgp, see [26].

[26] Beside a stream, old Sam sunbathed.

Which positions can *surreptitiously* occupy in [27]?

[27] She put it under the bed.

[28] Surreptitiously, she put it under the bed.
[29] She surreptitiously put it under the bed.
[30] She put it surreptitiously under the bed.
[31] She put it under the bed surreptitiously.

Notice in passing that it cannot come between the Vgp and its direct object.

The position of the adjunct in [31], of course, poses no problem for the analysis of adjuncts as modifiers of VP within a higher VP. And neither does its position in [29]. What would you suggest as the most appropriate phrase-marker for [29]?

---

We can simply analyse *surreptitiously* as a PRECEDING sister of the VP within another VP (that is, as the PRE-MODIFYING sister of the VP) as in [32]:

[32]

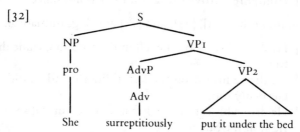

In [30], however, *surreptitiously* is going to have to appear within VP2 since it appears between the complements of the Vgp, between the direct object and the object-predicative. This is awkward for our analysis. If we want to say that the adjunct modifies the VP, it is odd to find it actually inside that VP.

And [28], of course, poses a problem because in it the adjunct is completely removed from the VP.

It is beyond the scope of this book to discuss this aspect of adverbials and its implications, important though it is. I shall not attempt to represent these 'displaced' adverbials in phrase-markers. Instead, I shall adopt a standard representation in which adjunct adverbials are always sisters of a VP within a higher VP. You should bear in mind, however, that this is a simplification of the facts. Of course, if we are simply enumerating the major functions in a sentence, ignoring constituency, no problems arise: [28] can be enumerated, using aA (for adjunct adverbial), as aA–S–V–dO–oP, [29] as S–aA–V–dO–oP and [30] as S–V–dO–aA–oP.

## Phrasal verbs

PPs functioning as adjuncts within VP must be distinguished from another apparently similar structure. Consider the difference between [33] and [34]:

[33] He called up the street.

[34] He called up the boss.

In [33] *up the street* is a PP functioning as an adjunct modifying a VP that consists of the intransitive Verb Group *called*. By contrast, you will have noticed that the string *up the boss* does not form a unit of sense in [34] – and in fact is not a constituent, and hence not a PP. Instead, *up* belongs more with *call*, to form the PHRASAL VERB *call up*. Now, if *called up* is the Vgp of [34], what do you suggest is the function of the NP *the boss*?

It is the single NP complement of the Verb Group, so it must be either subject-predicative or direct object. In fact, it is the direct object (if this is not clear, check in Chapter 4 on the difference between dO and sP). *Call up*, then, is a transitive phrasal verb. [34] can be represented as in [35]:

[35]

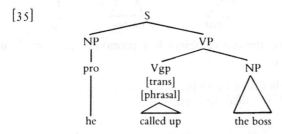

This representation of phrasal verbs can be refined when we consider the structure of the Verb Group in Chapter 6.

There are many such phrasal verbs in English – some more idiomatic than others, some transitive, some intransitive, e.g.

TRANS: *call off, look up, put down, hand down, hand over*
TRANS and INTRANS: *give up, give in, drink up.*

Although *up, off, down, over* look suspiciously like prepositions, they are traditionally distinguished from prepositions in this position and categorised as PARTICLES. So **a PHRASAL VERB consists of a VERB + a PARTICLE.**

Notice that sentence [36] is ambiguous.

[36] He looked up the street.

On one interpretation, the VP has an analysis like that of [33] – i.e. as Vgp + PP. This is the interpretation on which he would be looking up the street to see who was coming, for example. On the other interpretation, it is to be analysed as a phrasal verb with the

NP functioning as direct object (as in [34]). On this interpretation he would be trying to locate the street in a street atlas.

**A characteristic of particles is that they can appear in a position after the direct object.** Thus, [34] is acceptably paraphrased by [37].

[37] He called the boss up.

But [33] is not paraphrased by [38].

[38] *He called the street up.

The VP of [37] can be represented as in [39].

[39]

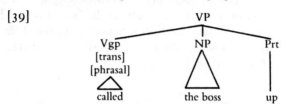

Indeed, when the direct object is a pronoun, the particle must appear after it:

[40a] He called him up.
[40b] *He called up him.

## Ellipsis

Now that I have introduced adjunct adverbials and distinguished them from the complements of the verb, we must look at a general issue that has a bearing not only on that distinction but on verb-sub-categorisation.

I have said that verb complements are a necessary part of sentence structure: they cannot be omitted without ungrammaticality. In this they contrast with adjunct adverbials. But look now at the following sentences:

[41] William gave the bleach *to Goneril*.
[42] William gave *Goneril* the bleach.
[43] William gave the bleach.

In Chapter 4 I sub-categorised *give* as a ditransitive verb. This is as good as saying that both the direct and the indirect object are necessary, non-omissible. But [43] does appear to be acceptable, even though it contains nothing that corresponds to an indirect object. Should we say, then, that the indirect object NP in [42] and the PP in [41] are optional? What effect would this have on the sub-category of the verb?

It would make *give* a monotransitive verb. If it is monotransitive, then the PP in [41] would be an adjunct rather than part of the complementation of the verb. Alternatively, we might want to assign *give* to both sub-categories, [ditrans] in [41] and [42], but [monotrans] in [43].

For various reasons, neither of these solutions is desirable. The most important reason is that neither solution does justice to the fact that, although [43] is acceptable, it nevertheless seems incomplete. Or, more to the point, it seems incomplete when considered OUT OF CONTEXT. Out of context, we would probably be prompted to ask who William gave the bleach to. However, in any context in which it could be understood who had been given the bleach, [43] is perfectly acceptable – for example, in the context of a conversation about Goneril's birthday presents. On the other hand, in the context of a discussion of what had happened to the bleach or of what William had done, its incompleteness would be unacceptable. Note the oddity of [44b] as an answer to [44a]:

[44a] Whatever happened to the bleach?
[44b] William gave it.

When a sentence is actually used by a speaker (i.e. when a speaker actually utters it), almost anything can be omitted, provided that the omitted elements can be understood from the context in which it is used. **The omission from sentences of REQUIRED elements capable of being understood in the context of their use is called ELLIPSIS.** Ellipsis creates acceptable, but nonetheless grammatically incomplete sentences.

Even subjects can be ELLIPTED, as in

[45] Visited Madame Sosostris this morning.

(Almost certainly the ellipted subject is *I*.) But we would not want to say, simply because the utterance of [45] is acceptable in certain contexts, that subject NPs are grammatically optional. To repeat, this would not do justice to our sense of the incompleteness of [45] as a sentence (or, put another way, our sense of [45] being an elliptical sentence).

In saying that certain constituents are necessary (obligatory), I have been relying implicitly on a distinction that is important in language description. This is **the distinction between THE GRAMMATICALITY OF A SENTENCE and THE ACCEPTABILITY OF AN UTTERANCE (that is, the acceptability of a sentence uttered by a speaker in a context)**. The study of syntax, in its purest form, is more concerned with the concept of GRAMMATICAL SENTENCE than with the concept of ACCEPTABLE UTTERANCE. In other words, **syntax is concerned with the form of sentences, without taking into account the effects of uttering sentences in a context**. Knowing what counts as a grammatical sentence plays an important part in a speaker's ability to interpret the utterances he actually hears (or reads), but it is only a part.

To sum up the discussion of ellipsis so far, in saying that a constituent is necessary and not optional, I am talking about SENTENCES, not UTTERANCES. The fact that a necessary constituent can be omitted, by ellipsis, in an utterance does not indicate that it is grammatically optional. Since this book is concerned above all with the form of sentences, I shall count elliptical sentences as grammatically incomplete (and hence as strictly ungrammatical).

You may, however, wish to apply the SENTENCE ANALYSIS offered here to UTTERANCES (that is, to actual USES of sentences by a speaker, whether in speech or in writing) rather than stick to made-up example sentences as I do in this book. If so, it will be useful to have a means of representing elliptical sentences. This is easily done. For example, we can capture the fact that, even though [43] has no indirect object, it still counts as a ditransitive sentence (albeit an elliptical one), as in [46]:

[46]

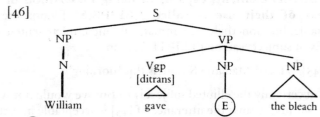

where (E) indicates an ellipted element, in this case an NP functioning as indirect object.

Before leaving ellipsis, it is worth spending a little time considering how ellipsis interacts with the analyst's decisions about sub-categorisation.

Compare [47] and [48]:

[47] Max played the tuba in the street.
[48] Max played in the street.

[47] is monotransitive with an adjunct PP (*in the street*). What about [48]? Well, in context, it could be an elliptical version of [47]. For example, if, as an utterance, it occurred in the context of a conversation about the players of the Chatanooga Stompers, and Max is known to be their tuba player, then [48] would reasonably be understood to mean exactly what [47] means. In such a context, it should be treated as an elliptical monotransitive sentence, with the dO ellipted. This analysis is only reasonable, however, because we can supply a particular direct object from the context, namely *the tuba*.

Out of context, (that is, as a sentence rather than an actual utterance), or in another context, [48] is interpreted differently. Here, *play* means the same as 'play about' or 'amuse oneself'. Notice that, out of context, we have no reason to suppose that *the tuba* or any other particular NP could be supplied. This is an intransitive sense of *play*.

As sentences out of context, then, [47] and [48] indicate that *play* belongs to two sub-categories [monotrans] and [intrans]. It has a distinct sense in each.

Compare now [49] and [50].

[49] Jean-Pierre ate the cous-cous rapidly.
[50] Jean-Pierre ate rapidly.

Should we assign *eat* to two sub-categories, [monotrans] in [49] and [intrans] in [50]? Or should we treat [50] as an elliptical [monotrans] with the direct object omitted?

*Eat* is different from *play* in that one always has to eat something. As we saw, one doesn't always have to play something; it depends on the sense of *play*. This might suggest that [50] should be treated as having an ellipted direct object. But notice that in that sentence it may be completely irrelevant what Jean-Pierre ate rapidly. It may be that it is just the activity of eating itself that is important. It may be that, whatever he ate, he did so rapidly. In this case, we cannot supply a particular phrase as being the ellipted direct object. So, even though the two uses of *eat* in [49] and [50] don't differ in sense, it seems reasonable not to treat [50] as an elliptical [monotransitive] sentence, but as a full [intransitive] sentence. So, *eat* belong to two sub-categories.

## Disjuncts and conjuncts

I will conclude this chapter by contrasting the adjunct adverbials we have looked at with DISJUNCT and CONJUNCT adverbials.

### Disjuncts

Many AdvPs and PPs can function either as adjuncts or disjuncts. Consider the following pairs:

[51a]  Buster admitted everything *frankly*.
[51b]  Buster admitted everything, *frankly*.
[52a]  Max can only do the tango *rather awkwardly*.
[52b]  Max can only do the tango, *rather awkwardly*.
[53a]  Mildred interfered continually *between you and me*.
[53b]  Mildred interfered continually, *between you and me*.

In the [a] examples the italicised constituent functions as an ADJUNCT. In the [b] examples, it functions as a DISJUNCT. In [51a], *frankly* tells us about the manner of Buster's admission (Buster was frank). As a disjunct, in [51b], *frankly* describes how the speaker of [51b] feels he himself is expressing what he has to say (the speaker is being frank in saying that Buster admitted everything). In [52b], with the disjunct, nothing is said about how Max dances the tango. The disjunct *rather awkwardly* expresses the speaker's assessment that Max's only being able to dance the tango is a rather awkward fact. Generally, disjuncts provide some comment by the speaker about the facts he is reporting or about how he feels he himself is expressing what he has to say.

Notice that, as a DISJUNCT, the adverbial does not modify anything within the sentence and is, in fact, felt to be only loosely associated with it. This feeling is borne out by the use of the comma in writing and by a distinct intonation in speech. Notice too that the disjuncts occur equally if not more naturally at the beginning of the sentence:

[51c]  Frankly, Buster admitted everything.
[52c]  Rather awkwardly, Max can only do the tango.
[53c]  Between you and me, Mildred interfered continually.

By contrast, it is rather difficult to interpret the adverbials as

ADJUNCTS in [51c] and [53c], and impossible to do so in [52c].

For some reason, over the last few years a certain amount of disgust has been expressed in the media about the use of *hopefully* in [54b] as against its use in [54a]:

[54a] He will look up hopefully.
[54b] He will look up, hopefully.
(Hopefully, he will look up.)

Why this should be is not clear. *hopefully* functions as an adjunct in [54a], but as a disjunct in [54b], just like *frankly, rather awkwardly, between you and me,* and innumerable other adverbials.

We need to distinguish adjuncts and disjuncts in terms of their phrase-marker representation. As mentioned, the disjunct seems separate from the rest of the sentence. Instead of modifying some element within the rest of the sentence, it appears to modify the rest of the sentence considered as a unit. Now the rest of the sentence considered as a unit is itself a perfectly good sentence. What, then, would you propose as the phrase-marker for [51b]?

[55]

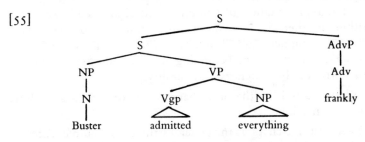

[55] shows a sentence that is not immediately analysible into NP and VP. The disjunct modifies a whole sentence and, together with that sentence, forms another sentence. (If the disjunct appears at the beginning, it should be represented as a preceding sister of S.)

Not all adverbials can function both as adjuncts and disjuncts. In [56] the adverbial must be interpreted as a disjunct, not as an adjunct:

[56] In short, you're fired.

Other adverbials that can only be disjuncts are: *unfortunately, admittedly, certainly, of course, perhaps.* Conversely, many other adverbials can only be interpreted as adjuncts:

[57a] He booted it sideways.
[57b] *He booted it, sideways. (*Sideways, he booted it.)

## Conjuncts

Conjunct adverbials, like disjuncts, are very loosely associated with the rest of the sentence, and I shall adopt the same phrase-marker representation for them as for disjuncts: as simultaneously the daughter of one S and the sister of another S. Examples of conjunct adverbials are: (adverbs) *nevertheless, therefore, furthermore, thus, however, incidentally*, (PPs) *on the contrary, for a start, in conclusion, on the other hand*.

[58]

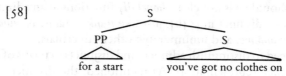

Notice that when conjuncts are present, the sentence sounds rather odd out of context. This is because conjuncts are used to indicate what kind of relation holds between the sentence and its linguistic context. They have no function in respect of any element within the sentence that they modify. They serve to link sentences into a coherent discourse.

The representation of conjuncts and disjuncts as sisters of S (within another S) is again a simplification, however. Like adjuncts, conjuncts and disjuncts can appear in a variety of positions, not only at the beginning and the end of sentences, but actually inside the sentences they modify:

[59] Rashid, on the other hand, came dressed as a washing machine.

In these first five chapters the general structure of simple sentences has been outlined. In the next two chapters, I go into more detail: Chapter 6 concerns the structure of the Verb Group itself, and Chapter 7 discusses in more detail the structure of Noun Phrases.

## Discussion of in-text exercises

### Discussion 1

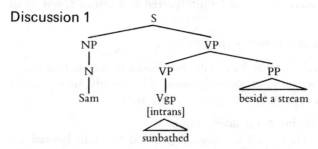

*beside a stream* is an adjunct and we are representing adjuncts as sisters of VPs. As an [intrans] Vgp, *sunbathed* forms a VP in its own right. Notice that we could continue with . . . *and Ferdinand did so behind the gas-house* meaning 'Ferdinand sunbathed behind the gas-house'.

## Discussion 2

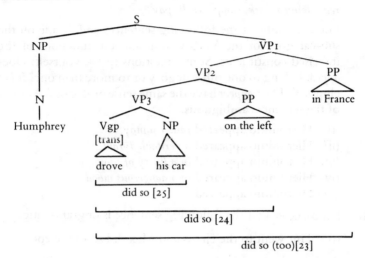

## Exercises

1.  Identify the sub-category of the Verb Group and the functions of the major elements in the following sentences (i.e. S, V, dO, iO, sP, oP, PC, and aA, dA, and cA for adjunct, disjunct and conjunct adverbials).

    (i) This so-called music will drive me mad very quickly.
    (ii) I will be with you in two shakes.
    (iii) We can celebrate this with an Indian take-away tonight.
    (iv) The academy has turned out some inspired confidence tricksters in its time.
    (v) Incidentally, I have sold your vests to the museum for a small fortune.
    (vi) Luckily enough, they gave in in seconds.
    (vii) Murdstone brought the child up too strictly, in my opinion.

2. Having checked the answers to exercise 1, draw phrase-markers for sentences (ii), (iii), (v), and (vi).

3. The following verbs are all monotransitive. Try and decide for each verb whether the absence of a direct object should be treated (a) as an instance of ellipsis or (b) as indicating that the verb also belongs to the intransitive sub-category. (cf. the discussion of *play* and *eat* in this chapter.)
   *read, launch, kick, jump, recall, pay.*

4. Look carefully at the following sentences and decide on the sub-category of the Verb Group and the functions of the italicised constituents. Some questions to ask yourself: Does *appear* belong to one sub-category or to more than one? Is (v) elliptical? Does *appear* have the same sense in all cases? Are any of the sentences ambiguous?

   (i)   Hieronimo appeared *rather jumpy*.
   (ii)  Hieronimo appeared *a veritable tyrant*.
   (iii) Hieronimo appeared *in a flurry of snow*.
   (iv)  Hieronimo appeared *in a dangerous mood*.
   (v)   Hieronimo appeared.

5. Let us agree that the following sentence is ungrammatical:

   (i) *Tim went to the circus and Max did so to the zoo.

   And let us assume that it is supposed to mean (or is an ungrammatical way of saying) (ii)

   (ii) Tim went to the circus and Max went to the zoo.

   Now tackle the following questions in order:

   (a) What string of words does *do so* replace in (i)?
   (b) What does the UNgrammaticality of (i) tell you about the CATEGORY of the string it replaces?
   (c) On the basis of your answers to (a) and (b), can you decide whether the PP *to the circus* is an adjunct or a complement of the verb?
   (d) On the basis of your answer to (c), how should we sub-categorise *go* in (i)?
   (e) Look at the following conversations:

       (iii) A: Where's Maria? B: She went.
       (iv)  A: Huge party, wasn't it! B: Even Maria went!

       How do you suggest we handle the sub-categorisation of *go* in each of these uses?

# Discussion of exercises

**1.**  (i)   This so-called music will drive me mad very quickly.
      S              Vgp    dO   oP        aA
                     [complex]

(ii)  I   will be   with you   in two shakes.
      S   Vgp        sP          aA
          [intens]

(iii)  We   can celebrate   this   with an Indian take-away
       S        Vgp          dO         aA
               [trans]

tonight.
aA

(iv)  The academy        has turned out
      S                  Vgp
                         [phrasal trans]

some inspired confidence-tricksters.        in its time.
dO                                            aA

(v)  Incidentally  I   have sold   your vests   to the museum
     cA            S   Vgp          dO            iO
                      [ditrans]

for a small fortune.
aA

(vi)  Luckily enough   they   gave in   in seconds.
      dA               S      Vgp        aA
                              [phrasal
                              intrans]

(vii)  Murdstone   brought   the child   up   too strictly
       S           Vgp        dO         Prt   aA
                   [phrasal
                   trans]

in my opinion.
dA

**2.**  (ii)

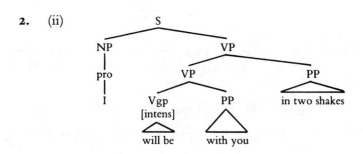

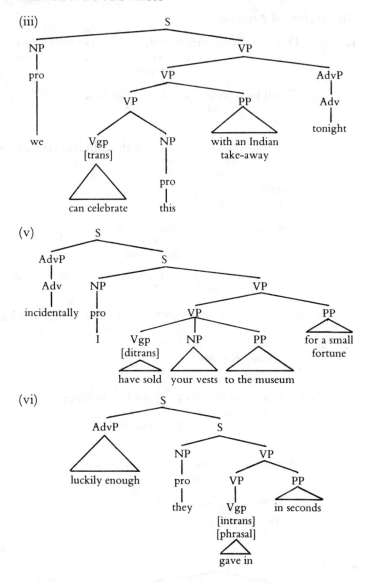

(iii)

(v)

(vi)

3. This exercise is a matter of judgement rather than getting the answer right or wrong. My judgements are as follows. The verbs seem to fall into four groups:

(i) *jump* and *kick* (ii) *read* (iii) *pay* (iv) *recall* and *launch*

(i) *jump* and *kick* are similar; you can jump a stack of books and kick an obstinate car but you can also jump without jumping something (as in jumping up and down) and you can just kick (babies do it all the time). So *jump* and *kick* clearly belong to both sub-categories [monotransitive] and [intransitive].

(ii) *read* is similar to *eat*. You do have to read something, but it is not always known or relevant what is being read when we report that someone is reading. Notice that we have no sense of incompleteness (which would indicate ellipsis) in *John is reading*. So *read*, like *eat*, belongs to both sub-categories.

(iii) When after a meal you inform your partner that he/she is paying, they will understand that it is the bill for the meal that is to be paid. In paying, you always pay the cost of something, in the form of a bill or an account. And while the object frequently is omitted with this verb, this is because it can be understood from the context of utterance. This indicates that *pay* is [monotransitive] only and that the absence of an object is elliptical. (There is, of course, another [ditransitive] use of *pay*, as in *I paid Buster his wages*.)

(iv) I have grouped *launch* and *recall* separately from *pay* since, while they are clearly [monotransitive] and require a direct object, they require it so strongly that it is almost unacceptable to omit the object by ellipsis. These too are [monotransitive] only.

4. In (i) *appear* is complemented by an Adjective Phrase. This indicates that the verb is [intensive], with the AP functioning as subject-predicative. The complement NP in (ii) has the same relation to the verb and the subject as the AP in (i), so again there is no reason not to take the verb in (ii) as [intensive], complemented by a subject-predicative. We usually find that [intensive] verbs can be complemented either by an AP, NP, or PP. So we might expect the verb in (iii) to be [intensive] again, with the PP functioning as subject-predicative. But notice that the sense of *appear* in (iii) is quite distinct from that in (i) and (ii). (i) and (ii) can be paraphrased by (vi) and (vii):

(vi)  Hieronimo appeared *to be* $\begin{cases} \text{rather jumpy} \\ \text{a veritable tyrant} \end{cases}$

(vii)  *It appeared that Hieronimo was* $\begin{cases} \text{rather jumpy} \\ \text{a veritable tyrant} \end{cases}$

where the verb has a sense similar to *seem*. (iii), on the other hand, cannot be paraphrased in these ways:

(viii)  Hieronimo appeared to be in a flurry of snow.

(ix)  It appeared that Hieroŋimo was in a flurry of snow.

In (iii) the verb has the sense of 'come into view' or 'turn up'. It can be paraphrased by (x).

(x)  Hieronimo appeared, and did so in a flurry of snow.

(Compare (i) and (ii).) In this sense the verb is to be treated as [intransitive] with the PP functioning as an (optional) adverbial.

Coming to (iv) now, notice that it is ambiguous: it can have either the sense it has in (i) and (ii) (*Hieronimo appeared to be in a dangerous mood*) or the sense it has in (iii) (*Hieronimo appeared and did so in a dangerous mood*). On the first interpretation, we have an [intensive] Verb Group complemented by a PP as subject-predicative; on the second, an [intransitive] Verb Group modified by an optional PP as adverbial.

As for (v) this must be taken as a non-elliptical [intransitive] sentence, not as an elliptical [intensive] sentence. Since *appear* also belongs to the [intransitive] sub-category, the subject-predicative cannot, in fact, be ellipted with the [intensive] sense of the verb. A speaker, in ellipting the subject-predicative, would risk having *appear* misunderstood and analysed by his hearers as [intransitive].

**5.**

(a)  *do so* replaces *went*.

(b)  Since *do so* only replaces VPs and since (ii) is UNgrammatical, we may conclude that *went* does not constitute, in itself, a VP (though it is, of course, a Vgp).

(c)  Yes, we can decide this. If *to the circus* was an adjunct it would be the sister of a VP (within a higher VP). In that case, *went* would have to be analysed as a VP. But *went* isn't a VP (as we showed in (b)). So the PP cannot be an adjunct. If, on the other hand, the PP is a complement, then it must a sister of the Vgp, and form a VP with that Vgp. And notice that *do so* can indeed replace the string *went to the circus* as in:

Max went to the circus and Hogarth did so (too).

So, it appears that we must analyse the PP as a complement. It is only by doing this that we can avoid analysing *went* as a full VP in its own right.

(d)  We must analyse *go* as a PREPOSITIONAL VERB.

(e)  Two quite different senses of *go* are involved. In (iii), the verb is used in the sense of 'leave' or 'depart' and is [intransitive]. *go*, therefore, is both an [intransitive] and a [prepositional] verb. In (iv), on the other hand, the verb is interpreted, in the given context, as *went to the party*. The prepositional complement is understood. This is an elliptical use of the [prepositional] verb.

# CHAPTER 6
# The Verb Group

This chapter is concerned with the internal structure of the Verb Group itself. The structure of verbal elements in English is a matter of some controversy: several different analyses have been proposed in recent years. What I aim to do here, then, is to offer an analysis that will be useful whether or not you intend to concern yourself later with the issues involved in deciding between competing analyses of English verbs.

From the last two chapters you will have gained an idea of what finite Verb Groups look like. **Every (non-elliptical) Verb Group contains a LEXICAL VERB as its HEAD. This lexical verb may or may not be modified by AUXILIARY verbs.** Lexical verbs are those that belong to the indefinitely large general vocabulary of the language (e.g. *run, eat, think, shatter, adjourn, depend, analyse . . .*). These lexical verbs always appear last in the Verb Group. Auxiliary verbs, by contrast, are a special and very restricted set of verbs. Their only function is to modify the lexical verb functioning as head of their Verb Group. Auxiliaries always appear in front of the head verb in the Verb Group. The auxiliary verbs are *be, have, do, can, may, must, will, shall, need, dare, ought, used to.*

A Vgp consisting of just a head verb (without auxiliary modification) I shall call a SIMPLE Verb Group. A Verb Group with modification by auxiliary verbs I shall call COMPLEX. A simple Vgp will have just a lexical verb (V) as its daughter, as in [1], while a complex Vgp will have two daughters, AUXILIARY (AUX for short) and V, as in (2). All the auxiliary verbs will fall under the AUX node.

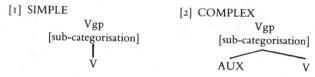

[1] SIMPLE

Vgp
[sub-categorisation]
|
V

[2] COMPLEX

Vgp
[sub-categorisation]
AUX        V

## The simple finite Verb Group

It is called SIMPLE because it contains just a single verb. But if you inspect the simple Verb Groups below, you will find that the single word can be further analysed:

| | |
|---|---|
| [3a] Max mows the lawn | [3b] Max mowed the lawn |
| [4a] It soon cracks | [4b] It soon cracked |
| [5a] He slots it in | [5b] He slotted it in |
| [6a] He gives her ten | [6b] He gave her ten |
| [7a] She goes nowhere | [7b] She went nowhere |
| [8a] Max meets the guests | [8b] Max met the guests |
| [9a] He puts it in his ear | [9b] He put it in his ear |

The [a] sentences are distinguished from the [b] sentences by a TENSE distinction in the verb. In the [a] examples, the verbs appear in a PRESENT TENSE form. In [b], they appear in their PAST TENSE form.

**A Verb Group that contains a TENSED verb (as in [3]–[9] above) is called a FINITE VERB GROUP.** Every sentence must contain one finite Vgp (whether simple or complex). But sentences can contain more than one Verb Group. In such cases, the further Verb Groups may or may not contain a tensed verb. **Verb Groups without a tensed verb are called NON-FINITE VERB GROUPS.** In this chapter, though, we shall be concerned just with sentences with one Verb Group and, therefore, just with FINITE (TENSED) Verb Groups.

In examples [3]–[5] – which all contain REGULAR verbs – the form the verb takes is readily separated into (i) the verb itself (called THE VERB STEM) and (ii) a PRESENT TENSE INFLECTION (e.g. *mow* + -*s*) or a PAST TENSE INFLECTION (e.g. *mow* + -*ed*). In the other examples, though, this separation is not so easily done. These all contain IRREGULAR verbs. In these, the verb form and the form of the marker of past tense are so bound up with each other that it is impossible to distinguish them. And sometimes there is no explicit marker of the tense at all – as in [9b].

You might ask: How do we know that *put* in [9b] IS the past tense form of the verb *put*? Well, consider [5a] and [5b]. The verbs in those sentences are very distinctly marked for present and past tense respectively. If I were to ask you to change just the verb in each of those sentences from *slot* to *put*, you would use *puts* instead of *slots*, and *put* instead of *slotted*. In short, you would use *put* as the past tense form of the verb *put*, just as you use *slotted* as the past tense form of the verb *slot*. (Other verbs that behave like *put* in not having a different past tense tense form from their STEM form are *bet* and *hit*.)

Although it is irregular for a verb not to change its form in the past tense, in the PRESENT TENSE it is quite regular for verbs not to change their form. In fact, verbs only change their form in the present tense when (as in all the [a] examples above) the subject NP is *he*, *she*, *it*, or any full Noun Phrase that could be replaced by one of those pronouns. Such NPs and pronouns are described as THIRD PERSON SINGULAR NPs. Otherwise, the present tense form of the verb is identical to the stem form. The only exception to this general rule is the verb *be*:

[10]

| NUMBER | PERSON | MOW PRES | BE PRES | BE PAST |
|---|---|---|---|---|
| | 1st (I) | *mow* | *am* | *was* |
| singular | 2nd (you) | *mow* | *are* | *were* |
| | 3rd (he, she, it) | *mows* | *is* | *was* |
| | 1st (we) | *mow* | *are* | *were* |
| plural | 2nd (you) | *mow* | *are* | *were* |
| | 3rd (they) | *mow* | *are* | *were* |

**This change of form in the finite verb according to the number and person of the subject NP is called SUBJECT-VERB AGREEMENT or SUBJECT-VERB CONCORD.**

**It is customary to recognise just PRESENT and PAST as the tenses of English.** Future TIME is expressible in a variety of ways (for example, by means of the auxiliary verb *will*, as in *He will go*), but there is no future TENSE as such. It is important to recognise that there is no simple correlation between the grammatical category TENSE and the notion of TIME. For example, in the right circumstances, both present tense and past tense are compatible with the expression of future time, as shown by [11] and [12]:

[11]  the boat leaves at ten this evening.
     (present tense – future time)
[12]  If he gave me the bleach tomorrow, I'd use it.
     (past tense – future time)

Furthermore, *will* is capable of expressing ideas other than future time, as in [13]:

[13]  He *will* keep burning the fritters!

How should we represent the tensed simple Vgp? In this book I am primarily concerned with whether a verb is finite (i.e. whether it is tensed) and, if so, whether the tense is present or past. These are matters of syntax. I am less concerned with the actual FORM a verb may take when it is tensed for present or past. This is more a matter of morphology, phonology, and spelling. So I shall not attempt to segment a tensed verb into a verb stem on the one hand and a tense inflection on the other in phrase-marker diagrams. Instead, I shall add the tenses as a FEATURE to the V node. The Verb Group *gives*, therefore, will have the representation in [14] and *gave* that in [15].

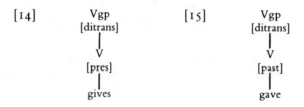

Now let us look at COMPLEX FINITE VERB GROUPS – Verb Groups containing auxiliary verbs.

## Auxiliary verbs in the complex Verb Group

There are two kinds of auxiliary verbs, modal auxiliaries and primary (non-modal) auxiliaries. **The PRIMARY AUXILIARY verbs are *do*, *have* and *be*.** As we shall see, in addition to being auxiliary verbs, these three verbs can function like lexical verbs in being the head of the Vgp. **The MODAL AUXILIARY verbs are: *can*, *may*, *must*, *shall*, *will*, *need*, *dare*, *used to*, *ought to*.**

Since some auxiliary verbs can also function as lexical verbs, it will be useful to mention some of the differences in behaviour between auxiliary verbs and lexical verbs. I shall mention just two:

1. In QUESTIONS an auxiliary verb can move in front of the subject NP. A lexical verb cannot.

2. In NEGATIVE SENTENCES, the NEGATIVE PARTICLE (*not* or *n't*) is attached to an auxiliary verb but never to a lexical verb.

Compare the auxiliary verbs in [16] and [17] with the lexical verbs in [18] and [19]:

[16]  [i] He can go      [ii] Can he go?   [iii] He cannot go
[17]  [i] He is going    [ii] Is he going?  [iii] He isn't going

[18]  [i] He spoke       [ii] *Spoke he?   [iii] *He spoke not
[19]  [i] He drinks      [ii] *Drinks he?  [iii] *He drinks not

The correct forms for [18] and [19], of course, are

[20]  [ii] Did he speak?    [iii] He didn't speak
[21]  [ii] Does he drink?   [iii] He doesn't drink

which involve the auxiliary verb *do*. This is explained further below.

Notice that, *need, dare, used to,* (and in some dialects, *ought to*) can behave either like auxiliary verbs or like lexical verbs. Take *need*, for example:

|  | As LEXICAL verb. | As AUXILIARY verb. |
|---|---|---|
| [22] | He doesn't need to go | He needn't go |
| [23] | Does he need to go? | Need he go? |

## The structure of AUX

AUX can contain up to four immediate constituents, each with its own auxiliary verb. The four possible constituents are:

1.  **MODAL** ('MOD' for short)
2.  **PERFECT ASPECT** ('PERF' for short)
3.  **PROGRESSIVE ASPECT** ('PROG' for short)
4.  **PASSIVE VOICE** ('PASS' for short).

All four are optional. Any combination of them is possible but, whatever the combination, they always appear in the order given. Each constituent can only appear once. This allows for exactly sixteen different combinations, as you may check for yourself.

A finite Vgp, remember, is one that contains a tensed verb. Only one verb can carry the tense and it is always the first verb in the Verb Group. If there are no auxiliary verbs, then (as we have seen) it is the lexical verb itself that carries the tense. Otherwise, the first auxiliary verb does so. The tense feature, therefore, will always be attached to the first verb.

I will take the four possible immediate constituents of AUX in the given order:

## 1. Modal

As the label suggests, MOD can be filled by any one modal verb. **Modal auxiliaries are distinguished from the primary auxiliaries and lexical verbs in always carrying tense.** They do not have untensed (non-finite) forms.

Some modals have both a present tense form and a past tense form:

| PRESENT: | can | will | shall | may |
|----------|-----|------|-------|-----|
| PAST: | could | would | should | might |

Compare [24] and [25]:

[24] (Present): He says he *will* come.
[25] (Past): He said he *would* come.

The other modals (for example, *must* and *need*) do not even have a past tense form but just the present tense form already given. Compare this situation with that which holds with a lexical verb like *give*. Besides its finite (present and past tense) forms, *give(s)* and *gave*, it has three non-finite forms: (i) *give* (the stem form, as in *to give*), (ii) *giving* and (iii) *given*.

**A further peculiarity of modals is that they do not exhibit subject-verb agreement.** That is, they do not change their form in the present tense even with a third person singular subject NP (so we have *He can go*, not \**He cans go*).

Finally, you should note that **the verb following the modal verb in the Verb Group appears in its basic stem form.** This applies whether the following verb is the lexical verb itself or another auxiliary verb.

You might like to review the foregoing sections before suggesting a phrase-marker analysis for the Verb Group *can give*.

[26]

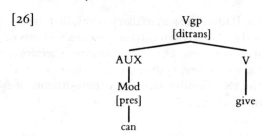

Now try *would meet*.

[27]

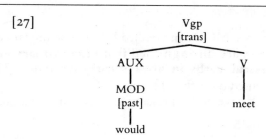

I shall describe [26] as a PRESENT MODAL VERB GROUP and [27] as a PAST MODAL VERB GROUP.

## 2. Perfect aspect

Here are some verb groups with the PERF option chosen:

[28]  will have given (a present modal perfect Vgp)
[29]  could have delayed (a past modal perfect Vgp)
[30]  has forbidden (a present perfect Vgp)
[31]  had gone (a past perfect Vgp)

These all contain a form of the **PERFECT AUXILIARY verb** ***have***. In [28] and [29] it appears in its untensed stem form because it follows a modal verb. In [30] and [31], however, perfect *have* is the first verb in the finite verb group so it appears in its tensed forms – present in [30], past in [31]. Remember, though, that a tensed verb does not always differ in its form from the basic stem. In [32], for example,

[32]  They have gone

*have* is the present tense of the perfect auxiliary. This can be confirmed by changing the subject NP to a third person singular NP (e.g. *she* or *Max*) and noting that *have* would then need to change to *has*.

You may be confused by the fact that, while [30] and [32] contain a present tense, they both refer to past time. Bear in mind the lack of correlation between time and tense, mentioned earlier. There are more ways of referring to the past than using the past tense. **The use of the perfect auxiliary *have* is one way of referring to past time independently of tense.** As [30] and [31] show, the perfect auxiliary itself can be tensed for present or past.

*Have* **can function both as the perfect auxiliary (modifying the head verb) or as the head verb itself.** [28]–[32] above illustrate its use as the perfect auxiliary. In [33] and [34], however, it functions as the head of the Vgp:

[33]  Tarzan *has* a bevy of apes at his disposal.

[34]  Tony *will have* mayonnaise with his chips.

You can tell that *have* is not functioning as the perfect auxiliary in these examples because the constituents that follow it are not verbs (they are NPs). As the perfect auxiliary, *have* must precede another verb within a Verb Group.

**The verb that follows *have* in the Verb Group always appears in its (non-finite) PERFECT PARTICIPLE form.** This applies whether this following verb is a lexical verb or another auxiliary. Look again at [28]–[31]. *given, delayed, forbidden,* and *gone* are the perfect participle forms of *give, delay, forbid, and go.*

As the perfect participle of *delay* illustrates, with many verbs (in fact, all regular and some irregular verbs) the perfect participle form is identical to the past tense form. However, no confusion should result from this since this form represents the (finite) past tense only if the verb is the first verb in the Verb Group. If a verb in that form is preceded by *have*, then that form represents the perfect participle. Here are some examples:

| [35] | STEM FORM | PAST TENSE | PERFECT |
|---|---|---|---|
| Regular: | delay | delayed | have delayed |
| Irregular: | give | gave | have given |
| ,, | show | showed | have shown |
| ,, | go | went | have gone |
| ,, | put | put | have put |
| ,, | be | was/were | have been |
| ,, | have | had | have had |

The last example (*have had*) shows the verb *have* functioning simultaneously as the perfect auxiliary AND as the head of the Verb Group. As you can see, *have* is one of the verbs whose perfect participle (*had*) is identical in form with the past tense. Here are example sentences in which *have* functions both as auxiliary and as head verb:

[36] Aldo *has had* a little chat with the doorman.
(present perfect Vgp)

[37] By two a.m., I *had had* enough. (past perfect Vgp)

Here is the phrase-marker analysis of the present perfect Vgp *has given*:

[38]

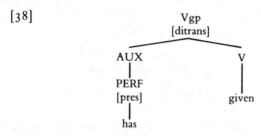

Now give the phrase-marker of the past modal perfect Vgp *would have given* (given as Discussion of in-text exercises, 1).

## 3. Progressive aspect

Try to identify what the progressive auxiliary is in the following Verb Groups:

[39a] was smoldering (past progressive Vgp)
[39b] is procrastinating (present progressive Vgp)
[39c] would be trampolining (past modal progressive Vgp)
[39d] have been cooking (present perfect progressive Vgp)

What these examples all have in common is a form of the verb *be* (*was*, *is*, *be*, and *been*). **Be is the progressive auxiliary.** They also have in common the *-ing* inflection on the verb following *be*. Just as the perfect auxiliary *have* determines the form of the following verb (requiring it to adopt the perfect participle form), so **the progressive auxiliary requires the following verb to adopt the V-ing form. This I shall call the PROGRESSIVE PARTICIPLE.**

Before reading further, name the four forms of *be* that appear in [39].

In [a] and [b] *be* is the first verb in the Verb Group and is, therefore, tensed. In [a] it appears in its past tense form, in [b] in its present tense form. In [c], it follows the past tense modal *would*, so it appears in its basic stem form *be*. In [d] it follows perfect *have* and so appears in its perfect participle form.

Like *have*, **be can function either as an auxiliary or as the head verb itself.** As a head verb, it is the intensive verb encountered in Chapter 4:

[40]   Kubla Khan *is* too extravagant.

In [41], *be* figures twice:

[41]   Nanny *is being* a nuisance again.

This is a present progressive Vgp. *is* is the present tense form of the progressive auxiliary *be*, and *being* is the progressive participle of the intensive verb *be*.

Now give the phrase-markers for [a] *was giving*, [b] *could be giving* and [c] *has been giving*. (These are given as Discussion 2 at the end of the chapter.)

___

Before considering the fourth auxiliary option, Passive Voice, it will be useful to review all the options made available by MOD, PERF, and PROG:

[42]   [i]    pres/past Vgp (simple)
      [ii]   pres/past modal Vgp
     [iii]  pres/past perfect Vgp
     [iv]  pres/past progressive Vgp
      [v]   pres/past modal perfect Vgp
     [vi]   pres/past modal progressive Vgp
    [vii]  pres/past perfect progressive Vgp
   [viii] pres/past modal perfect progressive Vgp

As an exercise, give an actual example of each type of Vgp listed in [42]. Use *forget* as the lexical verb and, where necessary, the modal *will*. Assume that all the Verb Groups have a third person singular subject.

___

| | PRESENT | PAST |
|---|---|---|
| [i] | forgets | forgot |
| [ii] | will forget | would forget |
| [iii] | has forgotten | had forgotten |
| [iv] | is forgetting | was forgetting |
| [v] | will have forgotten | would have forgotten |

[vi]   will be forgetting          would be forgetting
[vii]  has been forgetting         had been forgetting
[viii] will have been forgetting   would have been forgetting

## 4. Passive voice

**All the Verb Groups examined so far are said to be in THE ACTIVE VOICE, because they do not contain the passive auxiliary. Vgps containing the passive auxiliary verb are said to be in THE PASSIVE VOICE.** Compare the following active and passive Verb Groups.

|         |             | ACTIVE      | PASSIVE        |
|---------|-------------|-------------|----------------|
| [43a]   | simple past:| stole       | was stolen     |
| [43b]   | pres. prog: | is stealing | is being stolen|
| [43c]   | pres. perf: | has stolen  | has been stolen|
| [43d]   | pres. modal:| will steal  | will be stolen |

Identify the passive auxiliary verb.

All the passive Verb Groups contain a form of the verb *be: was* in [a], *being* in [b], *been* in [c], and *be* in [d]. **Be is the passive auxiliary verb.** Of course, *be* is also the progressive auxiliary. The difference between progressive *be* and passive *be* lies in the form taken by the following verb. Following progressive *be*, a verb adopts the progressive participle form (V–ing – e.g. *stealing*). **Following passive be, a verb adopts the PASSIVE PARTICIPLE form (e.g. stolen).** Notice that **the passive participle and the perfect participle of verbs always have the same form.** Since the two participles are the same with every verb in the language, it is traditional not to distinguish between them. This participle form is traditionally called THE PAST PARTICIPLE, though I have not adopted that term here since it misleadingly suggests that the form has something to do with past tense. But notice, in passing, that the passive option introduces no new form into the language; it just recombines forms which are anyway required for the formation of perfect and progressive Vgps:

PROGRESSIVE        PERFECT        PASSIVE
was  stealing      had stolen     was  stolen

Since the eight (active) Vgps enumerated in [42] can all be

passive, the passive option increases the total of possible Vgps by another eight, to sixteen. Here are the remaining Vgps (exactly the same as [i]–[viii] in [42] but with PASS in the AUX).

[42] (*continued*)
  [ix]  pres/past passive Vgp
  [x]  pres/past modal passive Vgp
  [xi]  pres/past perfect passive Vgp
  [xii]  pres/past progressive passive Vgp
  [xiii]  pres/past modal perfect passive Vgp
  [xiv]  pres/past modal progressive passive Vgp
  [xv]  pres/past perfect progressive passive Vgp
  [xvi]  pres/past modal perfect progressive passive Vgp

Again, using *forget* as the lexical verb and, where necessary, the modal *will*, give actual examples of the Vgps named in [42][ix] [xvi].

| | PRESENT | PAST |
|---|---|---|
| [ix] | is forgotten | was forgotten |
| [x] | will be forgotten | would be forgotten |
| [xi] | has been forgotten | had been forgotten |
| [xii] | is being forgotten | was being forgotten |
| [xiii] | will have been forgotten | would have been forgotten |
| [xiv] | will be being forgotten | would be being forgotten |
| [xv] | has been being forgotten | had been being forgotten |
| [xvi] | will have been being forgotten | would have been being forgotten |

Of course, the more complicated Vgps occur more rarely, with [xvi], the most complicated, hardly occurring at all. Nevertheless, it is a possible Vgp, available for use on the few occasions it is needed.

**A major difference between the passive auxiliary and all other auxiliaries is that the choice of passive affects not just the Vgp but the whole sentence.** If we want the progressive equivalent of [43]

[43] Everyone dreaded Jim's stew.

we simply change the simple past Vgp into a past progressive Vgp:

[44] Everyone was dreading Jim's stew.

This is not enough with PASS. The passive equivalent of [43] is not [45]

[45] *Everyone *was* dreaded Jim's stew

in which just the Vgp has been changed and which is anyway ungrammatical, but [46]

[46] Jim's stew was dreaded by everyone.

If you compare the active [43] with the passive [46], you will see that the object in [43] is the subject of [46] and the subject in [43] has become a Prepositional Phrase (functioning as an adverbial) introduced with *by* in [46]. What, then, is the passive counterpart of the following sentences?

[47a]  This earnest little wine will tantalise Fido.
[48a]  Mrs Golightly has threatened the lodger.
[49a]  Oddjob is ejecting the intruders.

If it is not immediately obvious to you what the passive counterpart of these sentences is, make the change in stages: first make the Vgp passive, then effect the changes in the rest of the sentence.

---

[47b]  Fido will *be* tantalised by this earnest little wine.
[48b]  The lodger has *been* threatened by Mrs Golightly.
[49b]  The intruders are *being* ejected by Oddjob.

In passive sentences the *by* Prepositional Phrase is by no means obligatory:

[47c]  Fido will be tantalised.
[48c]  The lodger has been threatened.
[49c]  The intruders are being ejected.

We have seen that **converting an active sentence into its passive counterpart involves making the object become subject.** Only verbs that can have objects, therefore, can appear in the passive voice.

Since INTRANSITIVE verbs do not take any complementation at all, sentences containing them do not have a passive counterpart.

In Chapter 4, MONOTRANSITIVE and INTENSIVE verbs were distinguished: while both sub-categories can be complemented by a NP, as in [50a] and [51a],

[50a] Everyone present saw a doctor. (transitive)
[51a] Everyone present was a doctor. (intensive)

the complement NP functions as object only in the transitive [50a]. In the intensive [51a] the complement NP functions as subject-predicative. So [50a] does have a passive counterpart, but [51a] does not:

[50b] A doctor was seen by everyone present.
[51b] *A doctor was been by everyone present.

Notice, with monotransitive verbs, that since the object becomes subject in the passive, monotransitive verbs don't have an object when the passive auxiliary is chosen. In the following phrase-marker (for [48b]) the PP is analysed as an adverbial:

[52]

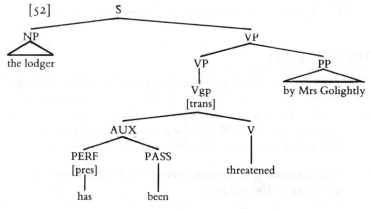

The same goes for COMPLEX TRANSITIVE Verb Groups in the passive voice: they lack an object in the passive voice. What is the passive counterpart of [53a]?

[53a] This so-called music is driving Otto mad. (S–V–dO–oP)

[53b] Otto is being driven mad by this so-called music.

Since the object of the complex transitive verb becomes subject in the passive, notice that the predicative no longer describes the object but the subject. For example, in [53b] *mad* still applies to *Otto* but *Otto* is now subject. So the object-predicative of a Vgp in the active voice becomes a subject-predicative when that Vgp appears in the passive voice.

Finally, let us consider the effects of PASS on DITRAN-

SITIVE verbs. Recall that ditransitive verbs can take two objects in the active voice (direct and indirect). It is always the first object that becomes subject in the passive. So what are the passive counterparts of [54a] and [55a]?

[54a]   The staff sent the general a pork-pie.
[55a]   The staff sent a pork-pie to the general.

In [54a] the indirect object (*the general*) precedes the direct object, so *the general* becomes subject, leaving *a pork-pie* in object position:

[54b]   The general was sent a pork-pie by the staff.

In [55a] *a pork-pie*, as direct object, precedes – so *a pork-pie* becomes subject, leaving the indirect object in the PP in its position:

[55b]   A pork-pie was sent to the general by the staff.[1]

## The auxiliary *do*

We have now reviewed all the options available under AUX with the exception of the auxiliary verb *do*. I now look again at how Verb Groups behave in YES/NO QUESTIONS and NEGATIVE sentences with *not* (or *-n't*) and the part played in this by *do*.

The rule for forming YES/NO QUESTIONS is this:

**The auxiliary verb that carries TENSE moves in front of the subject.**

Thus [56a] becomes [56b]:

[56a]   Byron could have escaped.
[56b]   Could Byron have escaped?

This is commonly called SUBJECT-AUXILIARY INVERSION.

How should we represent sentences exhibiting subject-auxiliary inversion like [56b]? I shall assume that the verb itself and the node that immediately dominates it (the node with which the TENSE feature is associated) are attached as a sister of the NP with which it is inverted. This means that it will be a daughter of the S. So, given that the representation of [56a] is [57a], the representation of [56b] will be [57b].

---

1. In saying that it is always the first object that becomes subject in the passive, I am assuming that the passive counterpart of [54a] in which *a pork-pie* becomes subject is ungrammatical:

*A pork-pie was sent the general by the staff.

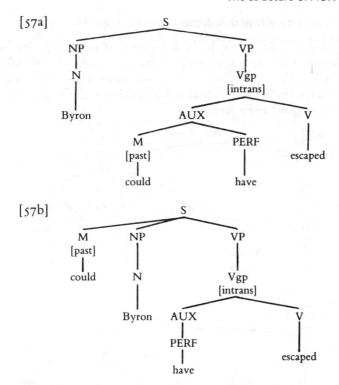

[57a]

[57b]

The question rule given above works fine just as long as there IS an auxiliary to move. But it does not cover those cases where there is no auxiliary: in simple Verb Groups the tense is not carried by an auxiliary but by the (non-auxiliary) head verb itself. And as we saw, head verbs do not normally invert with the subject in questions:

[58a]  Buster boiled the broccoli.
[58b]  *Boiled Buster the broccoli?

**If there is no auxiliary carrying tense, one has to be supplied in order to form the question. The auxiliary verb used for this is *do*.** So, corresponding to the simple past tense Verb Group *boiled* in [58a], we have a complex Vgp in which the past tense is carried by the auxiliary *do*, as in [59a]:

[59a]  Buster did boil the broccoli.

(Notice that *boil*, deprived of its tense, now appears in its stem form.) It is *did*, as the auxiliary carrying the tense, that inverts with the subject:

[59b]  Did Buster boil the broccoli?

**The auxiliary verb *do* is empty of meaning; its sole function is to carry the tense instead of the head verb when required.** In view of this, I shall represent *do* as immediately dominated by 'TENSE'. [60a] and [60b] are the representations of [59a] and [59b] respectively.

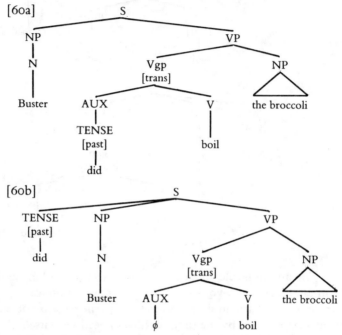

Notice that moving 'TENSE' from under the AUX node in [60a] leaves the AUX node empty. When a category node is left dominating nothing (in this case, AUX in [60b]), due to the movement of a constituent, I shall say that it dominates a GAP and symbolise this with 'ϕ' (the zero symbol).

The rule for forming NEGATIVE sentences with THE NEGATIVE PARTICLE *NOT* is similar to the question rule in making reference to the auxiliary that carries tense:

**The negative particle is placed immediately after the auxiliary that carries the tense.**

[61a]  Byron could have escaped
[61b]  Byron could not have escaped
[62a]  Byron has escaped

[62b]  Byron hasn't escaped

**Again, *do* is required to carry the tense in the absence of any other auxiliary.**

[63a]  Buster boiled the broccoli
[63b]  Buster didn't boil the broccoli
[64a]  Buster boils broccoli
[64b]  Buster doesn't boil broccoli

[62b] and [63b] can be represented as in [65] and [66] respectively, with the negative particle attached under the node bearing the tense feature.

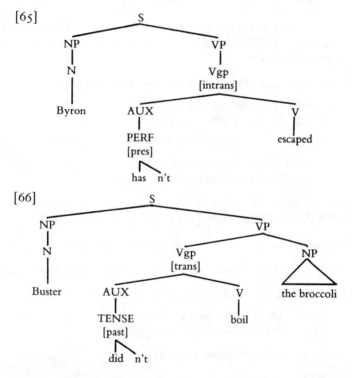

Like *have* and *be*, ***do* can function as an auxiliary verb and as a head verb.** Exercise 3 at the end of the chapter is concerned with this aspect of *do*.

## More on *have* and *be*

I have mentioned that *have* and *be* can function both as auxiliary verbs (modifying a head verb) and as head verbs themselves. As you might expect, when FUNCTIONING as auxiliaries, they must BEHAVE like auxiliaries, moving in front of the subject in questions and accepting the negative particle ([67] and [68]). *do*, which is normally required in the absence of an auxiliary, is ungrammatical with the auxiliary use of *have* and *be* ([69] and [70]).

[67a] **Are** they going?    [67b] They **aren't** going.

[68a] **Have** they gone?    [68b] They **haven't** gone.

[69a]*Do** they **be** going?   [69b] They **don't be** going.

[70a] *Do** they **have** gone? [70b]*They **don't have** gone.

What is more surprising, *have* can BEHAVE like an auxiliary when it is FUNCTIONING as a head verb. Both [71] and [72] are grammatical:

Functioning as a head verb, behaving like head verb:

[71a]  Do we have any garlic?

[71b]  We don't have any garlic.

Functioning as a head verb, behaving like an auxiliary:

[72a]  Have we any garlic?

[72b]  We haven't any garlic.

And *be* ALWAYS BEHAVES like an auxiliary whatever its FUNCTION. Thus, only [73] is grammatical, not [74]:

Functioning as a head verb, behaving like an auxiliary:

[73a]  Is Kubla extravagant? [73b]  Kubla isn't extravagant.

*Functioning as a head verb, behaving like a head verb:

[74a]  *Does Kubla be extravagant?

[74b]  *Kubla doesn't be extravagant.

[75]  is the representation of [73a].

[75]

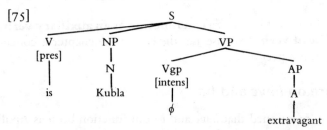

(The removal of *is* and its immediately dominating node leaves a gap in the Vgp, symbolised by $\phi$.)

This completes our review of the finite Verb Group.

## Discussion of in-text exercises

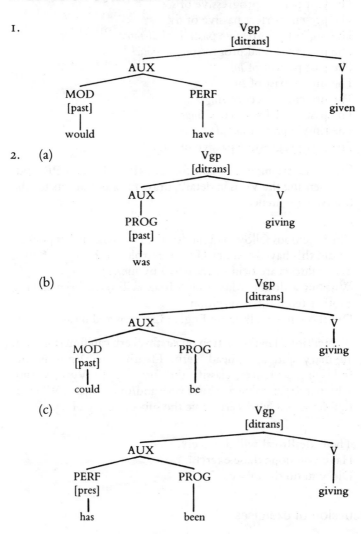

1.

2. (a)

   (b)

   (c)

## Exercises

1. Using the modal *can* where necessary (and assuming a third person singular subject), construct the following Verb Groups:
(a) The past modal passive of *see*
(b) The past perfect progressive of *see*
(c) The present perfect passive of *fly*
(d) The present progressive passive of *dictate*
(e) The present modal progressive of *slouch*
(f) The past perfect of *hit*
(g) The simple past of *sing*
(h) The present perfect of *sing*
(i) The past modal perfect of *have*
(j) The simple past of *forbid*
(k) The past progressive passive of *forbid*

2. Using the triangle notation for all NPs, APs, and PPs (but representing the Vgps in detail), draw phrase-markers for the following sentences:

(a) The ingenious fellow had hidden the moussaka in his pocket.
(b) Could this have been her famous purple wig?
(c) The wildcats are being persecuted by flies.
(d) Without a doubt, Max and Adrian will have been having another tedious conversation.
(e) Did those feet walk upon England's green and pleasant land?

3. As mentioned in the section on *do*, this verb can function as an auxiliary and as a head verb. Identify the Vgps in the following sentences, classify the form of the Vgps, stating whether *do* functions as a head verb and/or auxiliary. Where it functions as a head verb, give the sub-category of *do*.

(a) The Cafe Royal will do nicely.
(b) Have you done these exercises?
(c) Did you do the broccoli?

### Discussion of exercises

1. (a) could be seen (c) has been flown
   (b) had been seeing (d) is being dictated

(e) can be slouching       (i) could have had
(f) had hit                (j) forbade
(g) sang                   (k) was being forbidden
(h) has sung

2. (a)

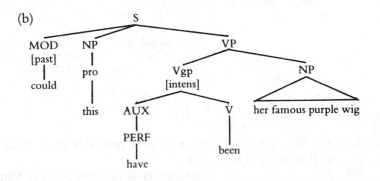

(b)

(c)

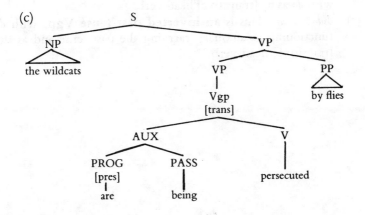

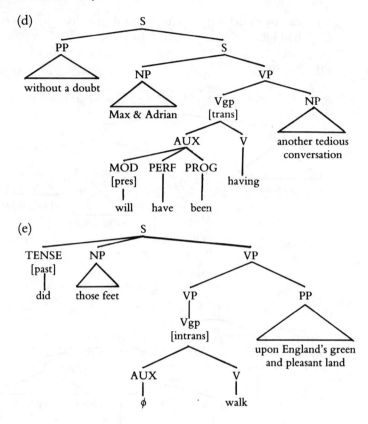

3. (a) The Vgp is *will do*. This is **a present modal Vgp**, with *do* as its [intransitive] head verb.

(b) *Have . . . done.* This is **an inverted present perfect Vgp**, with *do* as its [transitive] head verb.

(c) *did . . . do.* This is **an inverted past tense Vgp,** with *do* functioning as auxiliary carrying the past tense and as the [transitive] head verb.

# CHAPTER 7

# More on Noun Phrases

From the preceding chapters you will have gained a broad idea of how major phrases (NP, VP, Vgp, AP, PP, and AdvP) are structured into sentences. The basic VP itself was shown to consist of a Vgp complemented by NPs, APs, and PPs. Of these, only the internal structure of the Vgp has been examined in any detail. In this chapter, I look in more detail at the internal structure of NP and the elements to be found within NP.

The structure of NP is difficult to determine since the tests that are available do not always give clear results. As with verbs, several analyses have been proposed. I shall adopt an analysis in which **NP, in the basic case has just two immediate constituents. These are (1) DETERMINER (DET, for short) and (2) NOMINAL (NOM for short).** Here is a sample phrase-marker:

[1]

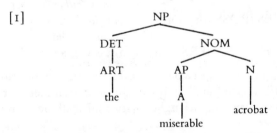

DET will always consist of just one constituent. NOM however can be complex, consisting of the head noun and any phrase that may be functioning as its modifier, its PRE-MODIFIERS (which precede the noun) and its POST-MODIFIERS (which follow it).

I will start with those elements that can come under the DET node.

## Determiners

These are a fixed set of 'grammatical' words which give information relating to DEFINITENESS and INDEFINITENESS (roughly, whether the thing referred to by the NP is familiar to both speaker and hearer or not) and information about QUANTITY and PROPORTION.

In some analyses, determiners have been described as modifying the NOM, though they are more commonly and more specifically described as DETERMINING it.

The basic determiners are *the* (THE DEFINITE ARTICLE) and *a* (THE INDEFINITE ARTICLE). The articles (ART for short) are basic in the sense that they provide a touchstone as to what counts as a determiner: **any expression that occupies the same position in NP structure as an article counts as a determiner.** If an expression can appear in sequence with (or CO-OCCUR with) an article in an NP, then that expression must be seen as occupying a different position and so cannot be a determiner.

There is a small set of words which seem to perform the same function as the articles and which cannot appear in sequence with them within an NP. These are therefore determiners themselves. They include:

DEMONSTRATIVES (DEM for short): *this, that, these, those*
Certain QUANTIFIERS (Q for short): *some, any, no, each,*
*every, either, neither*
POSSESSIVES (POSS for short) *my, your, its, her,*
*his, our, their, John's*
The 'WH' DETERMINERS: *whose* (possessive), *what, which*

In addition, there are two rather odd quantifier expressions, *a few*, and *a little*, which I shall analyse as simple determiners without further analysis (using the triangle notation). I shall mention these again later.

[2], [3], and [4] are the phrase-marker representations of *those trampolines, some mistake*, and *my address*.

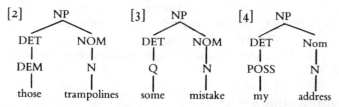

You should note that **the determiner position in an NP is not always filled by a real expression.** Many descriptions of the

English Noun Phrase propose that there is a **'ZERO ARTICLE'**, which has no form and is symbolised here by '$\phi$'. This is proposed on the grounds that the ABSENCE of a determiner in an NP gives information of a sort comparable to that given by *the*, *a*, and the other determiners. For example, the absence of a determiner indicates INDEFINITENESS. Compare the NP *mud* (as seen in the sentence *it's covered with mud*), which is indefinite and would be analysed as ø + *mud*, with *the mud*, which is definite. Compare also *tables* (an indefinite NP analysed as ø + *tables*) with *the tables*. The lack of a determiner is also capable of making the reference of an indefinite NP more GENERAL: compare *mud* with *some mud*, *tables* with *some tables*.

I shall adopt this 'zero article' analysis here. This means that the analysis of SINGLE-WORD NPs need not always be the same. Look at the phrase-marker representations of the three types of single-word NPs, *him* [5], *Maximilian* [6], and *mud* [7].

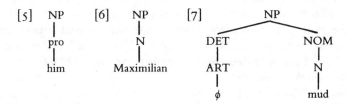

Only **MASS NOUNS** (like *mud*) and **COUNT NOUNS IN THE PLURAL** (like *tables*) are analysed as being determined by the 'zero article'. Proper nouns (names) like *Maximilian* in [6] are not, because they do not normally accept determiners anyway, and because the lack of a determiner does not indicate indefiniteness or generality, as it does with the common noun. As for pronouns such as *him* in [5], we saw in Chapter 3 that the function of pronouns is to replace NPs as a whole. It is predictable that pronouns should not accept determiners because determiners are just a constituent part of NPs.

In analysing *mud* as in [7] with a DET node and a NOM node, we predict that, although *mud* there appears without an overt determiner and without modification, it could accept an overt determiner and modification – as in *some glorious mud*. Proper nouns as such, and pronouns, do not admit of the structural possibilities made available by DET and NOM, and so are analysed without them. (I say proper nouns 'as such' because, as noted in

Chapter 3, it is possible to treat a proper noun like a common noun, giving it a determiner and modification, as in *the Borg of Wimbledon fame*.)

I have mentioned that no determiner can CO-OCCUR in sequence with any other determiner within an NP (i.e. within each NP, there can be only one determiner). Consider now the NP in [8]:

[8] The clown's pantaloons.

This NP might appear to be an exception to this in containing an article (*the*) followed by a possessive (*clown's*). Articles and possessives have both been categorised as determiners. It is not an exception, however. Can you see why it isn't and, if so, can you suggest an analysis for [8]?

---

You may have noticed that *John's* was listed among the possessive determiners. As you know, *John*, being a proper noun, counts not only as a noun but also as a full NP in its own right. So it appears that **a possessive determiner can consist either of a possessive pronoun (*my*, *your* etc.) or a full NP + -s e.g. *John's*. This is called the possessive, or GENITIVE, -s.** The sequence *the + clown + 's* in [8] is not a sequence of two determiners (article followed by possessive), since the article is actually contained inside a possessive determiner that consists of an NP (*the clown*) + GENITIVE-*s*. The correct analysis of [8], then, is [9]:

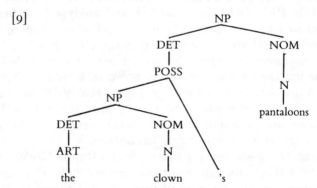

[9]

There is nothing to prevent the NP within such possessive determiners displaying all the structure that other NPs do – including the possibility of being determined by yet another possessive NP, as in [10] and [11]:

[10] Hieronimo's brother's pantaloons
[11] Hieronimo's brother's employer's pantaloons.

In principle, there is no limit to the number of times this can be done. Draw the phrase-marker for [10] (given as Discussion 1 at the end of the chapter).

---

## Pre-determiners

Consider now the words *all*, *both*, and *half*. These resemble the determiners we have looked at. However, because they co-occur in sequence with determiners, as in [12]–[14]:

[12] all the men
[13] both those trampolines
[14] half Jim's money

they cannot be categorised as determiners themselves. Instead, they are categorised as PRE-DETERMINERS (PRE-DET for short). Expressions like *double*, *treble* and so forth are also pre-determiners (cf. *double that amount*). In [15] and [16]

[15] all men
[16] both trampolines

*all* and *both* are still analysed as pre-determiners. In these the determiner position is regarded as being occupied by the zero article '$\phi$'. The proposal that there is a zero article present in [15], with *all*, is perhaps more plausible than in [16] with *both*. *all men* (*all $\phi$ men*) is both more indefinite and more general than *all the men*. However, *both the men* and *both men* (*both $\phi$ men*) differ neither in generality nor definiteness. Nevertheless, I shall continue to analyse *both* as a pre-determiner since, as [13] illustrates, it does co-occur with and precede determiners.

In deciding how pre-determiners fit into the structure of NPs, we must decide what constituent the pre-determiner determines. Give this a thought. This is a similar sort of exercise to the one we carried out in deciding how adjuncts fitted into the structure of VP. Notice the following: within the NP *all the men*, there is a sequence which looks very much like a constituent, namely *the men*. Furthermore, within *all the men*, the sequence *the men* can be replaced by a pronoun, as in *all them* or *all those*. What, then, would you suggest as a likely analysis of *all the men*?

---

The points made immediately above suggest that *all*, as a pre-determiner, determines a constituent consisting of *the* and *men* and that this constituent is itself a Noun Phrase. So **the pre-determiner should be represented as the sister of a NP within the NP as a whole:**

[17]

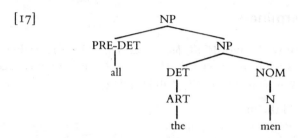

## Determiners and pre-determiners as pronouns

The majority of determiners and all the pre-determiners are capable of functioning rather like pronouns:

[18] I've always wanted *those*
[19] *Some* fell on stony ground
[20] *John's* are turning blue
[21] *All* is ruined.

I say 'rather like' pronouns because they differ from true pronouns in ways I discuss at the end of the chapter.

Among the determiners that cannot function as pronouns, there are some that correspond to forms that can. For example, the quantifier *no* cannot function as a pronoun (*\*I want no*), but corresponds to *none*, which can (*I want none*). And with the possessives, we find the following alternations:

DETERMINER:   my      your      her      our      their
PRONOUN:      mine    yours     hers     ours     theirs

*Its* cannot function as a pronoun; *his* can function as either determiner or pronoun.

It is predictable that pre-determiners, which pre-determine full NPs, should be able to co-occur with pronouns. Draw the phrase-marker of the subject NP in *All mine are at the cleaners* (given as Discussion 2 at the end of the chapter).

---

Now review these sections on determiners and pre-determiners before tackling the following exercise. The phrases in [23] and [24]

[23]  Both the man's eyes
[24]  Both the men's noses

look much the same when considered simply as strings of words, but a little thought shows that they must differ in hierarchical structure. Give the different phrase-markers. (Don't forget that possessive NPs have all the structural possibilities that other NPs do.)

---

We want the representation of the hierarchical structure to reflect the fact that the function of *both* in [23] extends over the whole of the rest of the phrase (i.e. *the man's eyes*); that it is pre-determining a constituent that has *eyes* as its head. [23], after all, means 'both eyes of the man', not '*the eyes of both the man'. The function of *both* in [24], on the other hand, extends only over *the men* (with *men* as its head); it has no function in respect of *noses* at all. [24] means 'the noses of both the men', not !'both noses of the men'. This distinction is reflected in the difference between [25] and [26]:

[25]

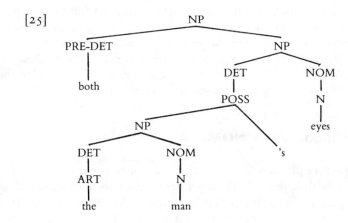

[26]

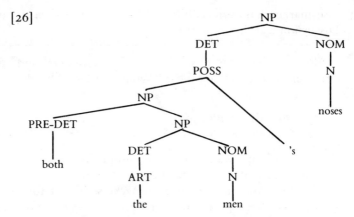

Notice that in [25] *both* has the NP *the man's eyes* as its sister constituent. In [26], it has *the men* as its sister constituent.

In distinguishing these examples, I introduced the idea of **the function of a constituent extending over a sequence of words. This phenomenon is more commonly referred to as SCOPE.** In these examples, we can say that the scope of *both* differs: in [23]/[25] the scope of *both* is *the man's eyes*; in [24]/[26] the scope of *both* is just *the men*. *eyes* is said to be included in the scope of *both* in [23]/[25], while *noses* is exluded from the scope of *both* in [24]/[26].

In this book, as you may have noticed, I have wherever possible assumed that the scope of a constituent (the extent of its function) is restricted to its sister constituents.

This concludes our brief survey of determiners and predeterminers. Several expressions which resemble determiners have not been dealt with yet, for example *much, many, few,* and *little.* For reasons to be explained immediately, I treat these as QUANTIFYING ADJECTIVES and include them under the NOM node along with pre-modifying adjectives.

## Pre-modifiers in NOM

**Adjective phrases (APs)** are the commonest pre-modifiers of the noun within the NOM constituent. These were introduced in Chapter 3. The position of premodifying APs in NP is illustrated in [1] at the beginning of the chapter. Here I shall mention other possible pre-modifiers before discussing the structure of NOMs in which there are several pre-modifiers.

## Quantifying adjectives

As mentioned, **I include among the pre-modifiers in NOM the Quantifying Adjectives (QA for short)** *much, many, few* **and** *little.* These items share important features with adjectives:

(i) Like adjectives, they co-occur with and follow determiners (*those many books, the little butter that I have, some few successes*) including the zero article *many books* ( = φ *many books*), *much garlic* ( = φ *much garlic*).

(ii) Like adjectives, they may occur in the VP, functioning as subject-predicatives:

[27] His mistakes were $\begin{cases} \text{many} \\ \text{few} \end{cases}$

[28] It wasn't much

[29] It was little enough.

(iii) Like adjectives they are gradable: *very many books, too much garlic, rather few ideas, very little tact.* The comparative and superlative forms of *many* and *much* are *more* and *most*; of *little, less* and *least*; of *few, fewer* and *fewest*. Notice that *more* in *more ferocious curries* is ambiguous. It could be either the comparative form of *many*, the quantifying adjective ('more curries that are ferocious') or it could be the comparative degree adverb mentioned in Chapter 3, modifying *ferocious*. This makes a difference to the constituent analysis (see Chapter 2, Exercise 3).

For convenience, I shall treat the following as quantifying adjectives: the CARDINAL NUMERALS (*one, two, three . . .*), the ORDINAL NUMERALS (*first, second, third . . .*) and the GENERAL ORDINALS (*next, last, other* etc.).

## Participle phrases

(PartP, for short). **The non-finite forms of verbs referred to in Chapter 6 as the progressive, perfect, and passive participles (V-PART, for short) may appear as pre-modifiers within NOM:**

|  PROGRESSIVE | PERFECT/PASSIVE |
|---|---|
| [30a] the leering manager | [31a] a faded dream |

[30b] the sleeping guard    [31b] the departed nymphs
[31c] sliced cake
[31d] a forgotten valley

In this position, the perfect and passive participles can only be distinguished by appealing to the meaning. [31a and b] are perfect, referring to a dream that has faded and nymphs who have departed; [c] and [d], on the other hand, are passive, referring to cake that has *been sliced* and a valley that has *been forgotten*.

Since these forms are verbal rather than adjectival, **they are not gradable:** *the very leering manager, *rather sliced cake, *the slightly sleeping guard*. They may, however, be modified by GENERAL adverbs, as in *the rapidly congealing gravy*. Draw the phrase-marker for this NP (given as Discussion 3 at the end of the chapter).

---

Certain true adjectives look very much like verb participles: *charming, pleasing, (un)interested, relieved, surprising, unexpected*. However, since they are gradable, they are easily distinguished from participles: *rather pleasing, very interested*. Some of these, for example *unexpected*, do not even correspond to any known English verb anyway (cf. *unexpect*.)

## Nouns

Nouns themselves may act as pre-modifiers of head nouns, as in *chess piece, roof maintenance*, and *computer game*. The relationship between a head noun and a pre-modifying noun is much closer than that between a head and any other pre-modifier. **Frequently the combination of modifier noun and head noun is referred to as a COMPOUND NOUN and is not treated as a PHRASAL constituent at all, but as a compound WORD.** Notice, for example, that in a sequence of modifiers that includes a noun modifier, it is the noun modifier that must appear last – it cannot be separated from the head noun.

[32] some expensive roof maintenance
[33] *some roof expensive maintenance

To reflect this closer (compound) relationship, I shall include modifiers under the N node rather than under the NOM node. [34], then, is the phrase-marker representation for [32]:

[34]

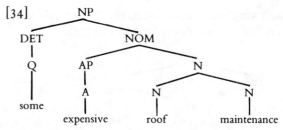

A small complication arises from the fact that noun modifiers can themselves be modified. Consider [35]:

[35] Some Japanese print collectors.

You will notice that it is ambiguous. On one interpretation it means 'Japanese collectors of prints'. Draw the phrase-marker for that interpretation (given as [40] below).

---

On the interpretation just given, *Japanese* modifies the compound noun *print collectors*. On the other interpretation, *Japanese* modifies just the modifying noun *prints*, meaning 'collectors of Japanese prints'. On this interpretation, we have a constituent *Japanese print* modifying the head noun and the question arises what category it should be assigned to.

Since it is centred on a noun and has modification, it might seem that it should be assigned to NP or NOM. However, it displays few of the structural possibilities displayed by either NPs or NOMs. It cannot be plural, nor can it take determiners or pre-determiners:

[36] *Some [Japanese prints] collectors.
[37] *Some [those Japanese print] collectors.

It is also restricted in the kind of pre-modifiers it accepts. While *Japanese* (or *rare*) is fine as a modifier, I find that [38]

[38] some beautiful print collectors

is better interpreted as 'beautiful collectors of prints' and not as 'collectors of beautiful prints'; that is, for me at least, *print*, when acting as a pre-modifier itself, does not accept *beautiful* as a modifier. Finally, the modifying noun does not itself accept post-modification:

[39] *Some [Japanese print after Kunisada] collectors.

In view of all this, I shall categorise modifying nouns as N even when they are themselves pre-modified. Here, then, are the phrase-markers for the two interpretations of [35].

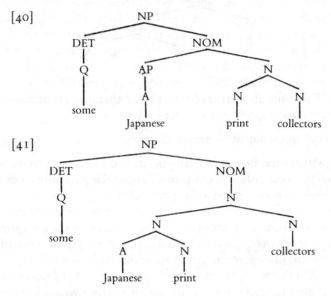

## More on the structure of NOM

Before considering the structure of pre-modifiers in NOM, draw the phrase-marker for the NP in [42].

[42] All those hairy ape men

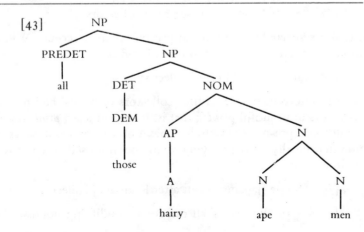

The claim made by this phrase-marker is that *all* pre-determines *those hairy ape men*, that *those* determines *hairy ape men*, that *hairy* modifies *ape men*, and that *ape* modifies *men*. This kind of configuration is called a NESTING STRUCTURE (as it were, *men* is nested in *ape men*, *ape men* is nested in *hairy ape men* and so on.) Given the distinction between pre-determiners, determiners, adjectival modifiers, and noun modifiers made in the preceding sections, the structure of [42] must be as represented in [43].

What about when we have a sequence of more than one adjectival modifier? Consider [44].

[44] A pessimistic structural engineer

How should this be represented? Well, in this case, it is fairly clear that *pessimistic* must be analysed as modifying *structural engineer* considered as a unit. *structural engineer*, after all, forms a unit of sense quite independently of *pessimistic*. Notice also that the order of the modifiers cannot be changed (*\*a structural pessimistic engineer*), indicating that the relationship between *structural* and *engineer* is much closer than that between *pessimistic* and *engineer*.

This suggests that [44] should be assigned the same (nesting) configuration as [43]; but we must decide what category *structural engineer* and *pessimistic structural engineer* belong to. I shall analyse *structural engineer* as a NOM, and *pessimistic structural engineer* as a NOM as well, as in [45].

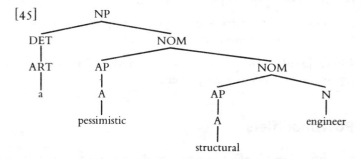

The same analysis is clearly appropriate for the interpretation of *more ferocious curries* in which *more* is the quantifying adjective.

In [45] the two modifiers have been analysed as functioning at different levels of structure (one nested inside the other). In addition, notice that they cannot be co-ordinated: a pessimistic structural engineer is not an engineer who is pessimistic and structural.

Now compare [44] with [46]

[46] A strong hairy ape

It is not so clear with this example that we should analyse *strong* as a modifier of *hairy ape* (that is, have the modifiers arranged hierarchically on different levels, in a nesting structure). By the co-ordination test *strong* and *hairy* do seem to function on the same level, each modifying *ape* independently of the other. A strong hairy ape, after all, is an ape that is both strong and hairy. Furthermore, *a hairy strong ape* (with the modifiers reversed) does not exhibit quite the same oddity as *a structural pessimistic engineer*.

Nevertheless, if only for the sake of consistency in the representation of adjectival premodifiers in NOM, I shall analyse [46] as having the same hierarchical, nesting structure as [44], taking *strong* as a sister of NOM (*hairy ape*) within another NOM. **One piece of evidence often cited in support of this nesting analysis involves the pronoun *one*.** (In fact, as we shall see, *one* is better described as a pro-Nom, since it replaces NOMs, not full NPs.) In answer to the question in [47a], one may reply with [47b].

[47a] Which structural engineer did you dismiss?
[47b] The pessimistic one.

[47b] means 'the pessimistic structural engineer', and *one* is understood as replacing *structural engineer* as a constituent. Similar-ly one could reply to [48a] with [48b]:

[48a] Which hairy ape did you attempt to feed?
[48b] The strong one

where [48b] means *strong hairy ape* and *one* is understood as replacing *hairy ape* as a constituent.

## Post-modifiers

In this section I look at just two of the categories that follow the head noun within NOM: Prepositional Phrases and certain types of Adjective Phrase. There are several other kinds of constituents that follow the head noun in NPs which I shall not mention here. These all involve structures that can be analysed as sentences themselves. Constituents that can be analysed as being sentences themselves are called CLAUSES, and these are the subject of the following three chapters.

## Prepositional Phrases as post-modifiers

In the basic case, PPs in NP are analysed as post-modifying sisters of the head noun, within NOM. Draw a complete phrase-marker for [49].

[49] An invitation to the ball.

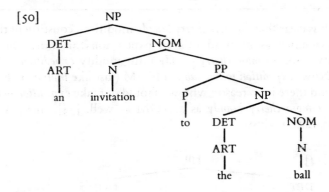

[50]

Notice that, within PP, the NP that complements the preposition may in turn contain a post-modifying PP, as in [51], where *in the village* post-modifies *pub*. Draw the phrase-marker.

[51] An expedition to the pub in the village

[52]

At first glance, [53] might appear to have the same structure.

[53] An expedition to the pub for more cherry brandy

However, unlike *the pub in the village* in [51]/[52], *the pub for more cherry brandy* does not form a constituent. Decide on the function of *for more cherry brandy*. Having done that, can you suggest an appropriate analysis for [53]? (Hint: look at [45] again.) Use the triangle notation for each of the PPs.

---

It is clear that *for more cherry brandy* modifies a constituent that has *expedition* as its head (it's an expedition for more cherry brandy). So, *for more cherry brandy* must modify *expedition to the pub*. Now, *expedition to the pub* is a NOM (just like *invitation to the ball*) and there is no reason why we should not take *expedition to the pub for more cherry brandy* as a NOM as well. [54], then, is an appropriate analysis.

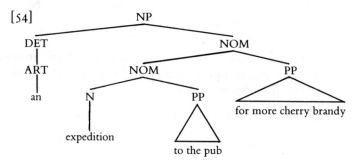

[54] illustrates a hierarchical (nesting) arrangement of post-modifying PPs that mirrors the arrangement of pre-modifying APs in [45].

As with the pre-modifiers, the pro-NOM *one* can be used in support of these analyses. In considering the following examples, you should note that *one*, as a pro-NOM, is determined by the zero article instead of the indefinite article *a*. (Notice that *one* contrasts in definiteness with *the one*, and that *\*a one* is ungrammatical.)

[55] Charles made an expedition to the pub for more cherry brandy and Diana made one for Ruddles Best.

From [55] we understand that Diana made an expedition to the pub for Ruddles Best. *one* is standing for *expedition to the pub*, which in [54] is indeed analysed as a constituent. Compare this with how the *one* test works in [51]/[52]. Since in [52] *the pub in the village* is analysed as a constituent, *expedition to the pub* cannot be a constituent. And, sure enough, replacing *expedition to the pub* in [56a] by *one* in this case yields very odd results – [56b].

[56a] Charles made an expedition to the pub in the village and Diana made an expedition to the pub at the crossroads.

[56b] *Charles made an expedition to the pub in the village and Diana made one at the crossroads.

The use of the pro-nom *one* in support of this nesting analysis of pre-modifiers and post-modifiers has yielded quite clear results. But all the examples considered have contained either just pre-modifiers or just post-modifiers. What happens when an NP contains both pre-modifiers and post-modifiers, as in [57]?

[57a] The *pessimistic* engineer *from Crumble & Rot*
[57b] An *expensive* bed *with built-in stereo*

The question is this: do the PPs post-modify a NOM constituent consisting of the AP and the head noun, or do the APs pre-modify a NOM constituent consisting of the head noun and a PP? In other words, is [58a] or [58b] the correct analysis of the NPs in [57]?

[58a]

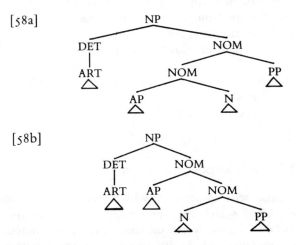

[58b]

Do you have any intuition about this? I don't. Both analyses seem fine to me. Interestingly, the *one* test does not oblige us to choose between them, but allows for both. We can replace either *pessimistic engineer* (as in [59]) or *engineer from Crumble & Rot* [60] with acceptable results.

> [59] Ludwig dismissed the pessimistic engineer from Crumble & Rot and hired the one from Jokers Anonymous.
>
> [60] Ludwig dismissed the pessimistic engineer from Crumble & Rot and hired the optimistic one.

Neither analysis is more correct, both are possible. This goes for the two cases considered in [57] and many others. In particular, as you may check for yourself, the *one* test allows for three different analyses of [61], which contains two pre-modifiers and a post-modifier.

> [61] This rather wet little wine from the Loire.

Although it is beyond the scope of this book to go further into the structure of the NOM constituent, brief mention should be made of examples in which one of the analyses must be chosen and the other definitely ruled out; that is, examples in which either the pre-modifier definitely is more closely associated with the head noun than the post-modifier or vice versa:

> [62] Pre-mod more closely associated with N than post-mod:
> The structural engineer from Jokers Anonymous
> cf. The one from Jokers Anonymous
> *The structural one
> [63] Post-mod more closely associated with N than pre-mod:
> The bearded exponent of the twelve tone scale
> cf. The bearded one
> *The one of the twelve tone scale

## Adjective Phrases as post-modifiers

There is a small set of adjectives (which includes *present*, *absent*, *responsible*, *visible*) which may pre-modify or post-modify the noun in NOM. To a greater or lesser extent, a difference in meaning is associated with the difference in position. Compare the [a] and [b] examples:

> [64a] the present members   [64b] the members present
> [65a] the responsible men    [65b] the men responsible
> [66a] the visible stars      [66b] the stars visible.

Post-modifying APs occupy the same position in the structure of NOM as post-modifying PPs.

Apart from such adjectives, there are just two circumstances under which the general run of adjectives must post-modify the noun.

1. The APs considered so far have either contained no modification or have been PRE-modified. But APs may contain material following the head adjective, for example:

[67a] Responsible *for the sauces*
[67b] Happy *in his job*
[68a] Too heavy *to lift single-handed*
[68b] Angry *that they have not been chosen.*

The precise relationship between the adjective and the constituent that follows it is unclear. The following constituent is often referred to as the COMPLEMENTATION OF THE ADJECTIVE. In [67] this complementation takes the form of a PP. In [68] it takes the form of a structure resembling that of a sentence, i.e. it is a CLAUSE. As mentioned, clauses are the topic of the following chapters, so I shall say no more about them here.

**When APs contain complementation of the adjective, they cannot pre-modify nouns but must post-modify them.**

[69a] The chef responsible for the sauces has absconded.
(*The responsible for the sauces chef)
[69b] A stuntman happy in his job is a Godsend.
(*A happy in his job stuntman)
[70] Any animals too heavy to lift single-handed should be referred to the ring-master.
(*Any too heavy to lift single-handed animals)

[71] is the phrase-marker analysis of the subject NP in [69a]:

[71]

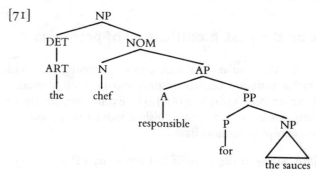

2. **When an AP modifies an indefinite pronoun, it always POST-MODIFIES it.**

[72] Something rather surprising
(*Rather surprising something)
[73] anyone very intelligent (*very intelligent anyone)

Such pronouns can also be modified by PPs, as in [74]:

[74] Someone in the crowd

NPs of the sort given in [72]–[74] pose something of a problem. I have said that expressions like *someone, something, anyone, anything, no-one, nothing* are pronouns. I also said that pronouns replace full NPs. This is why pronouns do not admit determiners, or pre- or post-modification. It is rather awkward, therefore, to find these pronouns taking post-modification, as in [72]–[74]. What has happened in the above examples is that, historically, a determiner (*some/any*) and a head noun (*thing/one*) have coalesced into a single word. This is particularly awkward since, in the context of post-modification, a determiner and a head noun do not even form a constituent in our analysis.

I am not aware of any solution to this descriptive problem so, for want of any better analysis, I shall adopt that given in [75]:

[75]

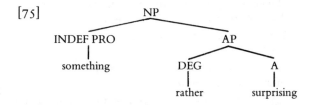

## More on the post-modification of pronouns

An apparently similar problem arises in connection with the pronominal function of determiners and pre-determiners, mentioned earlier (see examples [18]–[21]). Even when functioning as pronouns, these must be distinguished from true pronouns since they too accept post-modification:

[76] Some of the animals (postmod. by PP)

[77] both ⎫
     all  ⎬ of the sprouts (postmod. by PP)
     half ⎭

[78] those who have absconded (postmod. by clause)

The only determiners which function as true pronouns (in not allowing any nominal structure in the form of modification) are the possessives. (cf. *John's of the books)

The fact that these pronouns also function as determiners or pre-determiners provides one solution to the problem. The solution consists in continuing to analyse them as determiners or pre-determiners even when they appear to be functioning as pronouns, i.e. even when there is no overt head noun for them to (pre-)determine. This analysis involves allowing that the head noun position can be left unfilled with certain determiners and the pre-determiners. Under this proposal, [76] would have the following analysis:

[79]

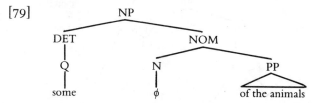

The idea is that the unfilled noun slot can be understood as being the same noun as appears in the Prepositional Phrase (in this case *animals*). This solution makes for a rather abstract analysis of *all of the sprouts* [77] as you may check for yourself (remember that *all* is a pre-determiner). The analysis is given as Discussion 4 at the end of the chapter.

A less abstract alternative would be to allow that certain pronouns can in fact be post-modified, treating these NPs as we treated NPs containing post-modified indefinite pronouns, as in [75] above:

[80]

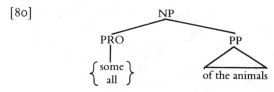

The first analysis (with the unfilled head noun) gives, I

believe, a more accurate picture of how we interpret such NPs, while allowing us to preserve the idea that a true pronoun replaces the whole of an NP. However, in cases like [72]–[74] I have anyway allowed that pronouns may co-occur with post-modifying phrases, so there is little reason to reject the second analysis, which at least has the advantage of being more concrete. Since it is beyond the scope of this chapter to discuss the matter more fully, I shall leave the choice between the two analyses to the reader.

## Discussion of in-text exercises

**I.**

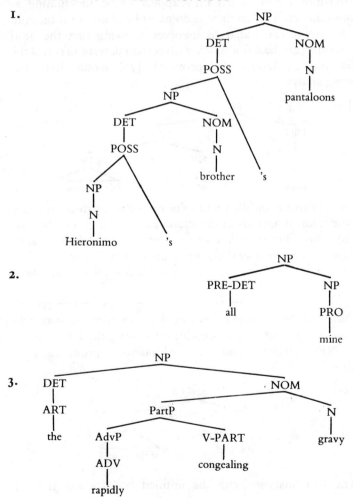

**2.**

**3.**

**4.**

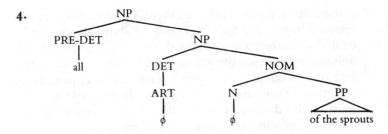

## Exercises

**1.** Draw complete phrase-markers for the following NPs. Note that several of them involve the zero article. (c) is ambiguous and should be assigned two phrase-markers. (f) and (g) contain co-ordinations; before attempting the phrase-marker, make sure of the category of the constituents that are co-ordinated (NP, NOM, or N).

(a) A book of quotations from Shakespeare.
(b) A book of quotations from Penguin.
(c) More ferocious curries.
(d) The dying king's final message.
(e) All Gulbenkian's contributions to charity.
(f) Some rather off-putting gestures and remarks.
(g) His partner in crime and lifelong cell mate.

**2.** In discussing determiners, I mentioned two expressions, *a few* and *a little*, proposing that they be treated as phrasal quantifiers functioning as DETERMINERS. Here are the phrase-markers.

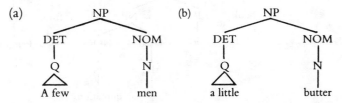

Later, in discussing pre-modifying adjectives, I mentioned the QUANTIFYING ADJECTIVES *few* and *little*. This exercise is about the difference between them. Can you think of any reason why *few* and *little* in (a) and (b) above should not be treated as quantifying adjectives? You might approach this question by drawing the phrase-markers that *a few men* and *a little butter* would have if *few/little* were treated as quantifying adjectives. Then comment on those phrase-markers in the light of the discussion of SCOPE in this chapter and the discussion of noun sub-categories in Chapter 3.

## Discussion of exercises

I.(a)

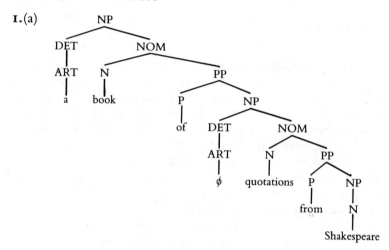

(c)

i.

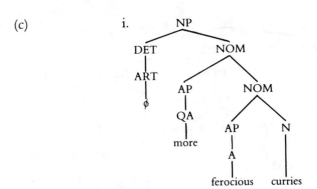

ii.

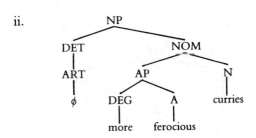

(d)

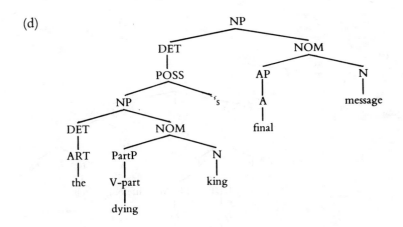

(e)

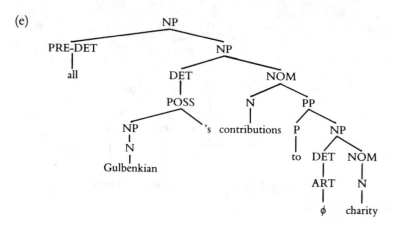

(f)

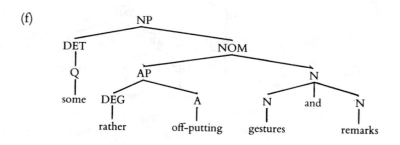

(g)

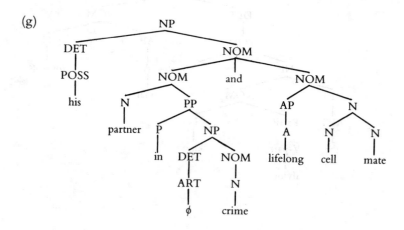

**2.** Look at phrase-markers (c) and (d), in which *few/little* in *a few men/a little butter* are treated as quantifying adjectives.

(c)

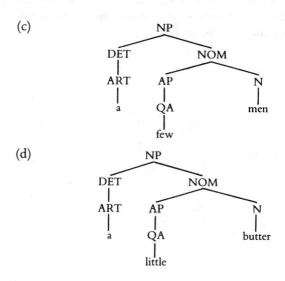

(d)

What is wrong with this analysis? Well, notice that the indefinite article is determining a NOM constituent that has *men* as its head in (c) and *butter* as its head in (d). That is, *men* and *butter* fall within the scope of *a* in each case. We want to avoid this. The indefinite article *a* can only determine constituents that have a singular count noun as head; it cannot determine plural count nouns (*★a men*) or mass nouns (*★a butter*). This is why *a few* and *a little* must be treated as constituents, as phrasal determiners. When they are so treated, as in (a) and (b), the head noun (*men/butter*) is analysed as falling outside the scope of the definite article (i.e. the head noun is neither a sister or the indefinite article nor contained within one).

In *few men* (*φ few men*) and *the few men, few* does function as the quantifying adjective, as does *little* in *what little butter I have* and *very little butter* (*φ very little butter*). Since *few* (as QA) only modifies plural nouns, it cannot appear in a NOM determined by *a*. Similarly, since *little* (as QA) only modifies mass nouns, it cannot appear in a NOM determined by *a*.

Finally, notice that in *a little window*, where *little* does modify a count noun within a NOM determined by *a*, *little* is not a quantifying adjective, nor is *a little* a phrasal determiner. This is a third use of *little* – as the ordinary general adjective (meaning the same as 'small').

# CHAPTER 8

# Sentences within Sentences

You will by now be familiar with the idea that a constituent may contain constituents of the same category as itself. You know, for example, that an NP may contain further NPs, that a NOM may contain further NOMs, a VP further VPs, and so on. This phenomenon is called RECURSION.

This and the next two chapters are mainly concerned with the description of sentences that appear within the structure of other sentences, i.e. with SENTENTIAL RECURSION. You should not have much difficulty in picking out, from within the structure of the following sentence, a sequence of words that can be analysed as a sentence in its own right.

[1] I said he wouldn't burn the fritters.

You might like to confirm for yourself that the sequence you have identified can indeed be analysed as a sentence, by drawing a complete phrase-marker of it. (Given as Discussion 1 at the end of the chapter.) The sequence is, of course,

[2] he wouldn't burn the fritters.

**When structures that can be analysed as well-formed sentences function as constituents in the structure of other sentences, they are called SUBORDINATE CLAUSES.** Subordinate clauses are often described as EMBEDDED SENTENCES (to be understood as 'sentences embedded in the structure of other sentences'). **The sentence that has a subordinate clause embedded in it is called the SUPERORDINATE CLAUSE.** Thus, the whole of sentence [1] is a SUPERORDINATE clause because it contains the SUBORDINATE clause *he wouldn't burn the fritters* as a constituent.

In [1] the superordinate clause is also the MAIN
CLAUSE. By this I mean that the clause is not itself
embedded in (or, subordinated to) any other clause. The
verb of the main clause is called THE MAIN VERB. A
superordinate clause is not always a main clause, though. Look at
[3].

[3] They believe I said he wouldn't burn the fritters.

[3] can be given an ABBREVIATED CLAUSAL ANALYSIS as
in [4]:

[4]

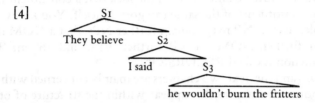

Here, as in [1], S2 (the *say* clause) is SUPERordinate to S3 (the *burn*
clause); but the *say* clause is not now the main clause because it is in
turn SUBordinate to the *believe* clause (S1). The *believe* clause is
SUPERordinate to both the *say* clause and the *burn* clause, but not
subordinate to any other clause. The *believe* clause (which includes
the *say* and the *burn* clauses) is therefore the main clause, and *believe*
is the main verb.

Now identify constituents that can be analysed as sentences in
the structure of [5] and [6]. Notice that [6] contains two such
constituents. Identify the main verb in [5] and [6].

[5] You should remind Private Brainwave that he is not the
captain at the earliest opportunity.
[6] The fact that you received no birthday greetings from
Mars doesn't mean that it is uninhabited.

---

Within the structure of [5], [7] can be identified as a sentence, and
within the structure of [6], [8] and [9] can.

[7] He is not the captain.
[8] You received no birthday greetings from Mars.
[9] It is uninhabited.

*(Should) remind* is the main verb of [5], and *(doesn't) mean* the main
verb of [6].

Note that, in [5], *at the earliest opportunity* belongs to the main clause (*You should remind Private Brainwave . . . at the earliest opportunity*); it cannot reasonably be considered as part of the subordinate clause since it is not clear what *he is not the captain at the earliest opportunity* might mean.

As already noted, the subordinate clauses examined above can be straightforwardly analysed as sentences, exactly as outlined in previous chapters. Not all clauses are quite so straightforward, however. Some kinds of subordinate clause have one or more elements missing from them. In particular, NON-FINITE SUBORDINATE CLAUSES lack at least a tensed verb. Other kinds are distorted from the familiar sentence patterns you encountered in previous chapters, in particular, WH-CLAUSES – clauses involving the 'wh' words *which, what, who* etc. These kinds are described in Chapters 9 and 10. This chapter concerns just clauses with a tensed verb, with all the normal elements present, and with no distortion from ordinary sentence structure – i.e. with FINITE NON-WH SUBORDINATE CLAUSES. Since the internal structure of these is straightforward, I shall concentrate on how they fit into the structure of their super-ordinate clauses and on their functions.

## The complementiser

You may have noticed that the subordinate clauses in [5] and [6] were preceded by the word *that*. **That serves to introduce finite non-wh subordinate clauses. When *that* functions in this way (rather than as a determiner or a pronoun) it is called a COMPLEMENTISER (COMP).**

You may have wondered whether to include *that* as part of the subordinate clause or whether to consider it as part of the main clause. How does this complementiser fit in? Well, I have already assigned the subordinate clause itself to a category (namely, 'S'), so the clause must be a constituent in its own right. Since the only function of this complementiser is to introduce this clausal constituent, it seems clear that the complementiser should form a constituent with the clause. So, to take the subordinate clause in [5] for example, *he is not the captain* and *THAT he is not the captain* are both constituents.

The category label generally used for constituents of the form [COMPlementiser + S] is 'S-BAR' – symbolised by an 'S' with a bar over it: 'S̄'. This symbol reflects the fact that *THAT he is not the captain* (S-bar) is, in some sense, clausal while at the same time distinguishing it from the clause itself (just S). The representation of the subordinate clause in [5], then, is as in [10], which can be further abbreviated as in [11].

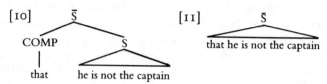

Now that you know how to handle the complementiser *that*, try an ABBREVIATED CLAUSAL ANALYSIS of [6], using the triangle notation shown in [11].

---

You may recall the subject-predicate analysis of this sentence from Chapter 2 Exercise 1: [*the fact that you received no birthday greetings from Mars*] [*doesn't mean that it is uninhabited*]. Notice that the first subordinate clause falls within the main clause subject, while the second falls within the main clause predicate. So that, although [6], like [3], contains two subordinate clauses, it differs in that its subordinate clauses are not nested one within the other; each subordinate clause is subordinated directly to the main clause, independently of the other.

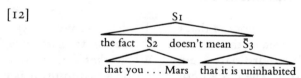

(Before reading further, you might like to gain more practice in identifying subordinate clauses by doing Exercise I at the end of the chapter.)

The complementiser of S̄2 in [12] is OBLIGATORY (see [13]), but that in S̄3 is OPTIONAL (see [14]):

[13] *The fact ⌃ you received no birthday greetings from Mars . . .

[14] . . . doesn't mean ⌃ it is uninhabited.

It is also optional in the subordinate clauses of [3]: although those clauses appear there without a complementiser, it is possible to have one:

[15] They believe *that* I said *that* he would burn the fritters.

For consistency, I shall follow the practice of always **using the S-bar analysis (with COMP) whenever the complementiser is possible, whether or not it is actually present.** Where there is no overt complementiser, the zero symbol should be used. This means that the subordinate clause *he would burn the fritters* in [2] and [3] is more strictly represented as in [16]:

[16]

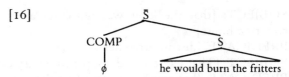

*That* is not the only element which is analysed as a complementiser, but it is the basic complementiser in the sense that, beyond having the basic complementiser's function of introducing the subordinate clause and indicating that it IS a subordinate clause, it has no meaning. **Clauses which can take *that* as their complementiser are called *that*-clauses.** In dealing with the adverbial function of finite clauses (i.e. **finite adverbial clauses**) at the end of the chapter, I shall mention SUBORDINATING CONJUNCTIONS (e.g. *because, if, so that, since, although*): these too function as complementisers, but they have 'conjunctive' meanings over and above their function of introducing the subordinate clause.

## The functions of *that*-clauses

I shall here consider four major functions:

1. Subject
2. Complement of a Vgp within VP
3. Complement of an A within AP
4. Complement of a N within NP

### Subject

Give a subject-predicate analysis of the following sentences:

[17a] That the King was not after all in his counting house disconcerted her.

[18a] That Goneril had a supernumerary eye has never been noted by the critics.
[19a] That Rashid's disguise was a success is undeniable.

Your analysis should show that **the subordinate *that*-clauses are functioning as the subject** in each case:

[17b] SUBJECT: [that the king was not after all in his counting house]
PREDICATE: [disconcerted her].
[18b] SUBJECT: [That Goneril had a supernumerary eye]
PREDICATE: [has never been noted by the critics].
[19b] SUBJECT: [That Rashid's disguise was a success]
PREDICATE: [is undeniable].

Recall from Chapter 2 that constituents functioning as subjects are always analysed as NPs. Can you think of any other reason why we should want to analyse these subordinate clauses as NPs?

Quite simply, they can be replaced by pronouns, as in [20] and [21]:

[20] *It* disconcerted her.
[21] *This* has never been noted by the critics.

So we need a representation that will allow that the subject of [18], for example, is both an NP and a clause. The way to do this is to make S̄ the sole constituent of NP, as in [22]:

[22]

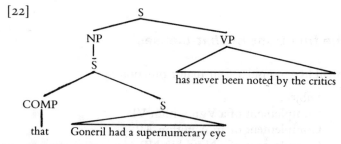

**A characteristic of clauses functioning as subject is that they can, as it were, be moved (or EXTRAPOSED) from under the NP node to the end of the sentence, leaving behind the pronoun *it*:**

[23] It disconcerted her [that the king was not after all in his counting house].

[24] It has never been noted by the critics [that Goneril had a supernumerary eye].

What sentence results if the subject of [19a] is extraposed?

[25] It is undeniable that Rashid's disguise was a success.

I shall represent these EXTRAPOSED SUBJECTS as daughters of the main clause S, as in [26].

[26]

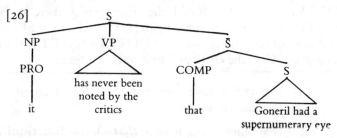

The *it* that takes the place of the subordinate clause is rather special because it is empty of meaning and does not refer to anything. It is called the EXPLETIVE (or ANTICIPATORY) *IT* to distinguish it from other pronouns that do refer to things.

There is a handful of verbs which can occur with a clause in this extraposed position but not in the normal subject position, for example *seem, appear, transpire, happen.*

[27a] It seems [that some rather dubious ingredients were involved].

[27b] *That some rather dubious ingredients were involved seems.

[28a] It just so happens [that dinosaurs are extinct].

[28b] *That dinosaurs are extinct just so happens.

Even though these clauses cannot appear in the normal subject position, they are still analysed as extraposed subjects. This is because, not only does the clause appear in the same position as an extraposed subject, but the expletive (empty) pronoun *it* occupies the subject NP position, just as in [23]–[25] above. Notice that, since the subordinate clause is regarded as a subject (as in [27b] and [28b]), this small groups of verbs must be sub-categorised, in this use at least, as [intransitive].

Now draw the phrase-markers for the following sentences, using the triangle notation for all NPs, APs, PPs, and Vgps.

[29] That the squid sauce had been a mistake soon became clear.

[30] It is not my fault Max trampled on your monocle.

(Given as Discussions 2 and 3 at the end of the chapter.)

## Complement of Vgp within VP

You may have noticed that the main clause of [18a] is in the PASSIVE voice. We should therefore expect there to be an ACTIVE sentence corresponding to [18a] in which the SUBJECT CLAUSE of [18a] functions as the DIRECT OBJECT of the main verb (*note*). Give the corresponding active sentence.

[31] The critics have never noted (that) Goneril had a supernumerary eye.

Here is another example of **a *that*-clause functioning as DIRECT OBJECT of a transitive verb:**

[32] Arnold claims (that) the sea was calm that night.

In addition to *note* and *claim*, transitive verbs that take clausal objects include: *mean* (as in [6] above), *say* and *believe* (as in [4] above), *mention, admit, expect, suggest, think, know, demand, hope* and *insist*.

*that*-clauses also function as DIRECT OBJECTS in the complementation of DITRANSITIVE verbs, as in:

[33] I advised him (that) his shirt was hanging out.
[34] She finally convinced him (that) he needed a shave.

Other ditransitive verbs that take clausal direct objects are: *remind* (as in [5] above), *persuade, teach, warn, tell, promise* and *inform*.

Subordinate clauses cannot function as INDIRECT OBJECTS of a ditransitive verb for the simple reason that indirect objects must be able to refer to ANIMATE entities, whereas clauses (sentences) refer to facts and ideas, which are abstract and hence INANIMATE.

Since *that* clauses may function as the complement of verbs which also take NPs and pronouns as direct objects, as in [35]

[35]

I have always { admitted  
denied  
known  
claimed } it

and since clauses functioning as objects in active main clauses become subject NPs in the passive, I shall analyse them as being dominated by an NP node, just like the clausal subjects considered in the last section e.g.

[36]

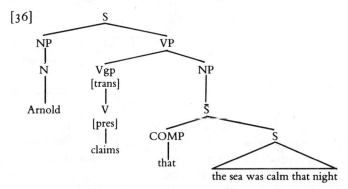

You should note, however, that not all verbs that take *that*-clauses in complementation can take NP/pronoun direct objects. *Hope, insist* and *pray*, for example, cannot.

[37]

*I { hope  
insist  
pray } it

Furthermore, not all object clauses can appear as subjects of passive main clauses. This is particularly so in cases where the clause complements a ditransitive verb, as in [39]:

[38] *That he should abandon the monocle was insisted by the whole company.

[39] *That his shirt was hanging out was advised him.

Nevertheless, for consistency, all such clauses will here be analysed as NP objects.

Now draw the phrase-marker for [33] above, using the triangle notation for NPs and Vgps.

[40]

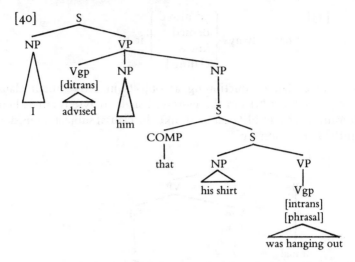

Since not all transitive verbs can take clausal objects (e.g. *kick*, *boil*, *engrave*, among many others) and not all transitive verbs that can take clausal objects can take simple (non-clausal) objects, there is a strong case for going beyond the sub-categorisation given in Chapter 4 and further sub-categorising verbs according to whether they can take clauses in complementation or not. Although this is, in fact, common practice, the basic sub-categorisation introduced in Chapter 4 and used here will suffice for present purposes.

In addition to functioning as direct objects in the complementation of the Verb Group, ***that*-clauses may function as SUBJECT-PREDICATIVES in complementation to the intensive verb *be*:**

[41] The consensus is that you should taste the stew first.

[42] The most relevant point is that you've burned the fritters again.

In this case, there is no motivation for analysing the subordinate clause as an NP: we have already allowed that a range of categories can function as subject-predicative (NP, AP, and PP) and there is no reason not to allow that S̄ itself can too. Draw the phrase-marker of [41], using the triangle notation for NPs and Vgps.

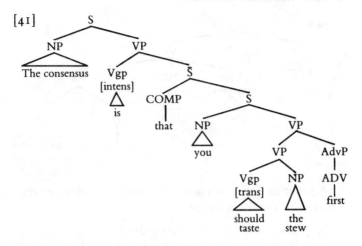

## Complement of A within AP

I mentioned in passing that **adjectives can be complemented by clauses within AP** in Chapter 7. Here are examples of APs in which the adjective is complemented by a *that* clause:

[43] Angry that they had not been chosen.
[44] Aware that he had overstepped the mark.

As noted, such Adjective Phrases may post-modify Ns within NP. In addition, they can function as subject-predicatives (as in [45]) and as object-predicatives (as in [46]).

[45] They seemed angry that they had not been chosen.
[46] She made him aware that he had overstepped the mark.

Like PPs, clauses complementing an adjective are represented as sisters of the adjective. Using the triangle notation for NPs, Vgps and Ss, draw phrase-markers for [45] and [46].

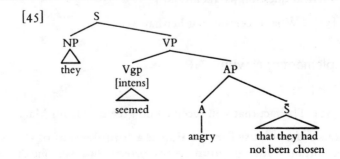

[46]

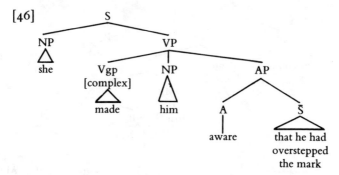

A point to notice in connection with complement clauses in AP is the distinction between:

[47] It is certain that her hair is dyed.
[48] William is certain that her hair is dyed.

Can you explain this difference? (Look again at pages 170–1)

---

Only one of them contains an AP with complementation of the adjective by a *that* clause. The other contains an extraposed (clausal) subject. In [48] [*certain that her hair is dyed*] is an AP functioning in the complementation of the verb *be* as subject-predicative: the clause complements the A. The same sequence in [47] is not a constituent: *certain* is the subject-predicative AP and *that her hair is dyed* is the extraposed subject; cf. [49]:

[49] That her hair is dyed is certain.

Notice that [48], with its full NP subject, could be the answer to the question

[50] Who is certain that her hair is dyed?

But for [47], with the empty expletive *it* as subject, there is no grammatical question parallel to [50]:

[51] *What is certain that her hair is dyed?

## Complement of N within NP

The NP [52]

[52] The fact that you received no greetings from Mars

contains **a *that*-clause functioning as a complement of the N.** An important feature of **noun complement clauses** – one that is useful in distinguishing them from other clauses that can appear in NP – is that they can complement only ABSTRACT nouns like the following: *fact, rumour, idea, contention, law, statement, message, indication, announcement.* Thus we have [53] but not [54]:

[53]    The {
news
contention
idea
suggestion
rumour
} that Bjorn is a machine

[54]    *The {
book
newspaper article
programme
bucket
} that Bjorn is a machine

The structure of such NPs – and the function of the clause – is not entirely clear. The clause is not in general taken to be a post-modifier of the N. It is called the COMPLEMENT of the noun because it has the same relation to the noun in NP as clauses that complement the Verb Group in VP and the Adjective in AP:

[55a] His absence *INDICATES that he disapproves* (VP)
[55b] His absence is *INDICATIVE that he disapproves* (AP)
[55c] His absence is an *INDICATION that he disapproves* (NP)

I shall represent clausal complements of N as in [56]:

[56]

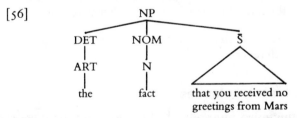

Other analyses are possible. I adopt this particular analysis purely for convenience: to distinguish these complement clauses from other clauses that clearly do post-modify the N within NOM. The full character of noun complement clauses will become more apparent when I compare them with post-modifying clauses in NP in Chapters 9 and 10.

Needless to say, NPs containing noun complement clauses have the full range of functions that other NPs have. When they function as subject-predicatives, however, a possible confusion with extraposed subject clauses arises again. Only two of the following sentences contain NPs with a complement clause. Identify them.

[57] It's a disappointment that the monocle wasn't stolen.
[58] One small difficulty is the fact that dinosaurs are extinct.
[59] It was a message that the party was off.
[60] It's a well-known fact that beavers build dams.
[61] It's our contention that you can dispense with the monocle.

---

In [57], [60], and [61] the subordinate clauses are not noun complement clauses but extraposed subject clauses. They do not form a constituent with the NP that precedes them. Check that the clauses can function as subjects replacing the empty pronoun *it*. Only in [58] and [59] is the subordinate clause functioning as complement of the preceding noun within a larger NP: [*the fact that dinosaurs are extinct*], [*A message that the party was off*]. Notice that [59], perhaps the most easily confused with the extraposed subject, is not paraphrased by [62]:

[62] *That the party was off was a message.

The subject pronoun in [59] actually refers to something (a piece of paper or a 'phone call perhaps). In connection with [60], it is worth noting that a clause can complement the noun *fact* only when the NP as a whole is singular and determined by the definite article not the indefinite article or any other determiner:

[63] *A fact that dinosaurs are extinct makes all the difference.

## Finite adverbial clauses

What distinguishes finite adverbial clauses from the finite clauses considered so far is that they take SUBORDINATING CONJUNCTIONS as complementiser, rather than *that*. Here are some examples of subordinating conjunctions: *after, before, until, since* (these four are also prepositions), *(al)though, unless, if, because, once*. There are also word-sequences which I shall take as phrasal complementisers without further analysis (using the triangle notation): *now (that), so (that), in that, except that, as if, in case, in order that, as soon as*.

It is the subordinating conjunction – and the extra meaning that it carries with it – that allows the clause to function as an adverbial. [64], for example, functions as a TIME adverbial (as in [65]) because the subordinating conjunction *after* carries a TEMPORAL meaning in addition to having the basic complementiser's function of introducing the clause.

[64]

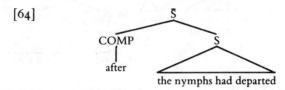

[65a] Things were rather dull *after the nymphs had departed*.
[65b] *After the nymphs had departed* things were rather dull.

As indicated in [65], clauses functioning as adverbials have the same freedom of position as the simple (non-clausal) adverbials considered in Chapter 5, though they tend to occur less frequently in the position following the subject because of their length.

As in Chapter 5, I shall analyse clauses functioning as **adjunct adverbials** (as in [66]–[68]) as **modifying sisters of VP within VP.**

[66] I'm pleased *because I prefer burnt fritters*.
[67] I'll have Lobster Thermidor, *since you're paying*.
[68] The sedan-chair was moving *as if it was propelled by rockets*.

**As disjuncts** (see [69]–[70] below) **they will be analysed as sentence modiers**, as in Chapter 5.

[69] *Unless I am gravely mistaken*, you are King Kong.
[70] *Since you ask*, my name is Ozymandias.

Using the triangle notation for NPs, PPs, Vgps, and subordinate Ss, draw phrase-markers for [68] and [69].

[68]

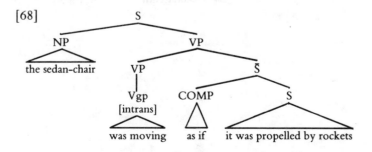

[69]

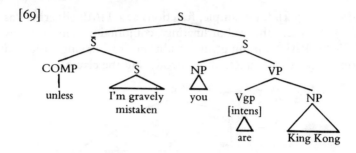

This completes the survey of the functions of finite non-WH clauses. The fact that sentences contain constituents that can themselves be analysed as sentences, and that these embedded sentences may have yet further sentences embedded in them, means that sentences may be indefinitely lengthy and complex. Nevertheless, as should by now be clear, however complex they are, sentences and their constituents always have a well-defined meaning, structure, and function. To repeat a point from Chapter 2, if you satisfy yourself that your analysis gives each constituent a well-defined and recognisable meaning, structure and function, you should have little difficulty in analysing even the most complex sentences.

## Discussion of in-text exercises

I.

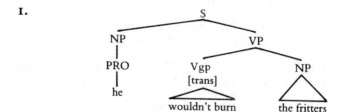

**2.**

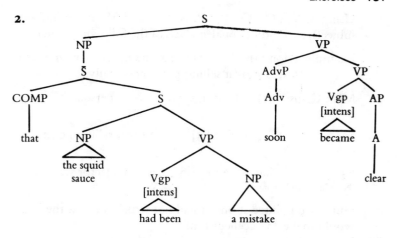

**3.**

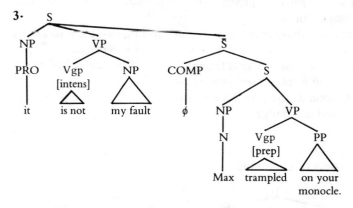

## Exercises

1. Give ABBREVIATED CLAUSAL ANALYSES of the following sentences. (c) and (d) contain two subordinate clauses each. Remember to check whether these are contained one within the other or whether they are independent of each other.

(a) They did not suspect they were being observed at all.

(b) That the ejector seat didn't work was quite forgotten.

(c) I don't think the fact that the moped has an ejector seat is a great selling point personally.

(d) Your suggestion that Max might refuse a second zabaglione just shows you don't know Max.

2. Using S, V, dO, iO, sP, oP, A, PC, and ES (for extraposed subject), give a functional analysis of the following sentences.

Example: I don't think the fact that the moped has an ejector seat is a great selling point personally.

Main Clause (S1):    I    don't think    S2    personally
                   S        V       dO       A

S2      :     $\phi$   [the fact S3]   is   a great selling point
(object)      comp      S      V      sP

S3           : that   the moped   has   an ejector seat
(N complement)   comp      S      V      dO

(a) Until you pointed it out, it had not struck me that the book would make an excellent film.

(b) I am slightly surprised that the producer knows anything about syntax.

(c) The fact that you endorse Omar's feeling that life is too short doesn't imply that you should get drunk every day.

(d) It appears that the chef thought he could slip away before the missing *bombes surprises* were noticed.

(e) As soon as the princess had ascended, I knew the palanquin would not budge.

## Discussion of exercises

1.(a)

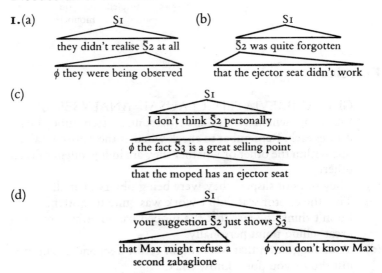

(b)

(c)

(d)

**2.**

(a)  S1  :  S2,  it  had not struck  me  S3
    Main    A    S     V      dO  ES

     S2  :  Until  you  pointed  it  out
          COMP  S    V    dO  PRT

     S3  :  that  the book  would make  an excellent film
          COMP  S     V        sP

(b)  S1  :  I  am  [slightly surprised S2]
    Main  S  V        sP

     S2  :  that  the producer  knows  anything about syntax
  COMP TO A  COMP    S      V        dO

(c)  S1  :  [the fact S2]  doesn't imply  S3
    Main        S      V     dO

     S2  :  that  you  endorse  [Omar's feeling S4]
  COMP TO N  COMP  S    V        dO

     S3  :  that  you  should get  drunk  every day
          COMP  S    V     sP     A

     S4  :  that  life  is  too short
  COMP TO N  COMP  S  V    sP

(d)  S1  :  It  appears  S2
    Main  S    V     ES

     S2  :  ∅  the chef  thought  S3
          COMP  S     V    dO

     S3  :  that  he  could slip away  S4
          COMP  S    V      A

     S4  :  before  the missing *bombes surprises*  were noticed
          COMP        S        V

(e)  S1  :  S2  I  knew  S3
    Main  A  S  V   dO

     S2  :  As soon as  the princess  had ascended
          COMP      S       V

     S3  :  ∅  the palanquin  would not budge
          COMP  S       V

# CHAPTER 9

# WH-Clauses

In Chapter 1 I used replacement by a single word to show that a sequence of words should be analysed as a constituent. As I pointed out there, WH-words (*who, what, which, whose, why, when, where, how*) can be used in this way. For example, in [1]

> [1] Vince is bringing Violetta's icon to Athens.

we can replace *Vince* with *who* (as in [2]), *Violetta's icon* with *what* [3], *Violetta's* with *whose* or *which* [4], and *to Athens* with *where* [5]:

> [2] Who is bringing Violetta's icon to Athens?
> [3] Vince is bringing what to Athens?
> [4] Vince is bringing $\left\{ \begin{matrix} \text{whose} \\ \text{which} \end{matrix} \right\}$ icon to Athens?
> [5] Vince is bringing Violetta's icon where?

Similarly, *by plane* could be replaced by *how*, *on Tuesday* could be replaced by *when*, *for restoration* and *so that it can be restored* could be replaced by *why*.

**Clauses that include a WH-word are called WH-CLAUSES. WH-words can appear in MAIN CLAUSES and in SUBORDINATE CLAUSES.** [2]–[5], of course, are main clauses; they are therefore **MAIN WH-CLAUSES.** As you can see, replacing a constituent in a main clause with a WH-word has the effect of turning it into a (WH)-**QUESTION**. I shall begin by describing WH-QUESTIONS (i.e. main WH-clauses) and then discuss subordinate WH-clauses and their functions.

## WH-questions

As you know, [3] has the alternative form, [6]:

> [6] What is Vince bringing to Athens?

What are the corresponding alternative forms for [4] and [5]?

[7] $\left\{ \begin{array}{l} \text{Which} \\ \text{Whose} \end{array} \right\}$ icon is Vince bringing to Athens?

[8] Where is Vince bringing Violetta's icon?

[6]–[8] differ from their corresponding forms in [3]–[5] in two ways. Before reading further, you might like to identify for yourself exactly in what two ways [6]–[8] differ from [3]–[5].

---

In the first place, [6]–[8] display **subject-auxiliary inversion**. In each case we have . . . *is Vince bringing* . . . rather than . . . *Vince is bringing* . . . . In this respect, standard WH-questions resemble *yes/no* questions, which also display subject-auxiliary inversion (see Chapter 6).

Secondly, notice that in [6]–[8] the WH-word has been displaced from whatever position it had in [3]–[5] to the front of the sentence. In the last chapter, I mentioned that WH-clauses display a distortion from the kind of sentence structure encountered in previous chapters. In mentioning a distortion, I was referring to **the displacement of the WH-expression to the front of the sentence. This phenomenon is called WH-FRONTING.**

**When a WH-expression appears at the front of a clause (even a main clause as in [6]–[8] above) it is represented as occupying the same position as the COMPLEMENTISER** *that.* To accommodate the complementiser we must use the S-bar (S̄) notation introduced in the last chapter. [6]–[8], then, have the (abbreviated) representations [9]–[11]:

[9]

[10]

[11]

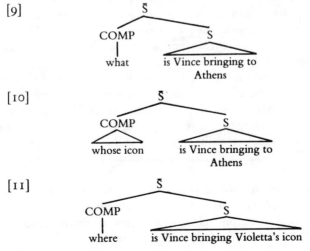

We have seen that [3]–[5] have alternative forms that display both subject-auxiliary inversion and WH-fronting. But what about [2]? [2] itself is the only possible form of that particular question. How exactly does [2] differ from [3]/[6], [4]/[7], and [5]/[8], and why? Well, notice that in [2] I used the WH-word to replace the subject. As subject, the WH-word appears at the beginning of the sentence anyway. The question is: **should we represent this WH-word as being in the subject position or should we represent it as being fronted into the complementiser position?** (In other words, does [2] display WH-fronting, like [6]–[8], or not?)

There are two good reasons for saying that the WH-word in [2] should be represented as fronted into the complementiser position, as in [12]:

[12]

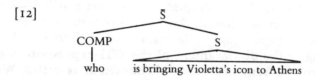

Firstly, it allows us to treat all WH-questions in the same way; that is, it allows us to say that **without exception, WH-expressions that appear at the front of clauses are represented as occupying the complementiser position.** The only difference in the case of [2] is that WH-fronting does not result in a change of word-order.

Secondly, representing the *who* of [2] as being in the COMP position, rather than in the original subject position, allows us to explain why [2] does not display subject-auxiliary inversion: since *who* is not in subject position (but in the COMP position), and since therefore there is nothing in the subject position, it seems reasonable to say that you can't have subject-auxiliary inversion, for there is nothing for the auxiliary to invert with.

In summary, then, [2] is different from [6]–[8] but not as different as you might at first have thought. Unlike [6]–[8], it does not display subject-auxiliary inversion but, like [6]–[8] it does display WH-fronting, though this does not give rise to a change of word-order.

From the discussion so far it is clear that there is an obvious difference between *that* as a complementiser and any WH-expression as a complementiser. You saw in the last chapter that, while *that* serves to introduce the clause, it plays no part in the structure of the clause that it introduces. If you ignore the complementiser *that* in [13], for example,

[13]

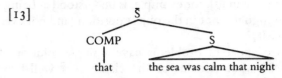

you can see that the S itself is complete. By contrast, in WH-clauses, **the WH-expression not only serves to introduce the clause, it actually has a function in the structure of the clause that it introduces.** This is most clearly seen in [9], [10], and [12], because the WH-expression functions as an OBLIGATORY element in the structure of the clause. If you ignore the WH complementiser, the S itself is clearly seen to be incomplete:

[14] *Is Vince bringing to Athens?
        (S of [9] and [10] – direct object missing)
[15] *Is bringing Violetta's icon to Athens?
        (S of [12] – subject missing).

It is perhaps less clear that, ignoring the WH-expression in COMP position, there is a constituent missing in the S of [11].

[16] Is Vince bringing Violetta's icon? (S of [11])

This is because the missing constituent (which has been fronted to the COMP position) functions as an OPTIONAL adverbial. Being optional, its absence from the S does not give the same impression of incompleteness. Nevertheless, *where* in [11] must still be interpreted as having a function in the S that follows it, like the other WH-elements.

Before reading further, do Exercise 1 at the end of the chapter.

Now, you may remember that in the last chapter I defined a CLAUSE as a constituent that could be analysed as having a well-formed SENTENCE structure. To be well-formed, a clause containing the active transitive verb *bring* requires a direct object NP to complement the verb. But there IS no direct object NP in [14]. And there is no subject in [15]. So can these Ss really be described as having a well-formed sentence structure, when they quite clearly have a constituent missing from them?

A related question arises in connection with the understood functions of the WH-expressions in COMP position. I have defined functions like 'subject' and 'object' in terms of particular positions in phrase-markers. How can we represent the fact that the WH-expression in [9], for example, is understood as being the object even though it is not in the object position (and not even in the actual S itself)?

These two apparent problems have a single solution. We CAN represent what remains of the clause as a well-formed constituent belonging to the category S provided we make provision for the missing constituent. In [9], for example, provided we make provision for a direct object NP slot, we can indeed analyse *Is Vince bringing to Athens* as a well-formed constituent having the structure of a sentence. And, provided we interpret the WH-expression in the COMP position as corresponding to that direct object NP slot, we can indeed capture the fact that *what* is understood as the object of *bring*. This can be achieved by using the zero symbol ($\phi$) under the direct object NP node. (Recall that I used the zero symbol in Chapter 6 to represent the gap left by the displacement of the auxiliary in clauses exhibiting subject-auxiliary inversion.)

So what does the full phrase-marker representation of a WH-question such as [17] look like?

[17] What will Vince be bringing?

To begin with, it would be a good idea to remind yourself of the structure of a possible (full-clause) answer to [17], [18] for example. Draw the phrase-marker.

[18] Vince will be bringing the icon.

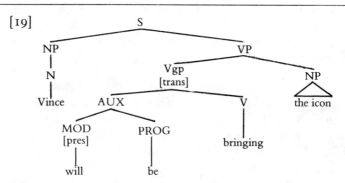

As you know, [17] displays subject-auxiliary inversion. If you just invert the subject and auxiliary in [19], you will get a *yes/no* question. Draw the phrase-marker of that *yes/no* question.

[20]

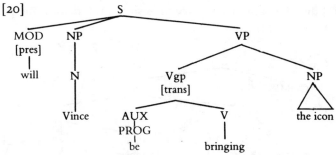

If we now replace the direct object NP, *the icon*, with the WH-word *what* and front it to the complementiser position (using S̄), this will leave a GAP under the direct object NP node, represented by φ, as in [21]:

[21]

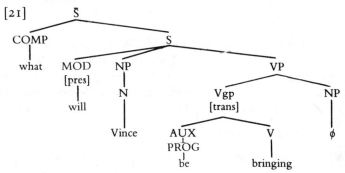

[21], then, is the full phrase-marker representation of the WH-question in [17].

**All WH-clauses, whether main or subordinate, will contain an empty constituent (or, a GAP) represented by the zero symbol. The WH-expression in the COMP position is always interpreted as functioning as if it occupied the position in which that zero symbol appears.**

Now try a phrase-marker representation of [22].

[22] What have you put the fritters in?

First, you need to establish the function of the WH-constituent. This is easily done by noting that [22] corresponds to [23]:

[23] You have put the fritters in what?

*What* clearly functions as the NP complement of the preposition *in*, within a PP. So a full representation of [22] will include a PP with a Noun Phrase missing (an NP gap). In addition, of course,

[22] displays subject-auxiliary inversion. [24], then, is the phrase-marker for [22].

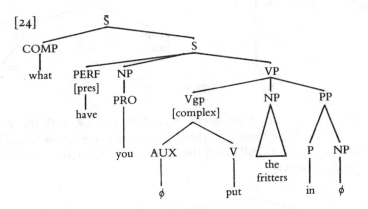

It is worth noting that when the WH-expression functions as the complement of a preposition within a PP (as in [22]/[23]), we have the option of fronting just the WH-word (as above) or, in more formal contexts, fronting the whole Prepositional Phrase containing the WH-word. Thus, a very formal version of [22] is:

[25] In what have you put the fritters?

What would you suggest as the representation of [26]?

[26] To whom did you speak?

Since the whole PP has been fronted, we need a PP gap in the S.

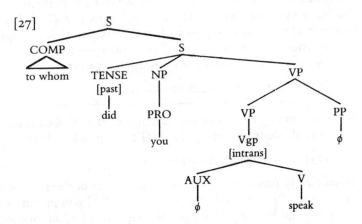

You may have noticed, too, that where the WH-word functions as a DETERMINER in an NP, as in *whose icon* and *which icon*, it is not possible to front just the WH-word, as in [28]; the whole NP must be fronted, as in [29]:

[28] *Whose is Vince bringing icon?
[29] Whose icon is Vince bringing?

See also *What colour is it?* and *What height is he?* Draw the phrase-marker for [29]. (Given as Discussion 1 at the end of the chapter.)

In addition, when the WH-word *how* functions as a DEGREE ADVERB in an AP or an AdvP, again the whole AP/AdvP must be fronted, not just the WH-word.

[30] [How often] do they go wrong?
(Compare: They go wrong too/very often)
[31] [How tall] is Max?
[32] [How quickly] can you do it?

Give the phrase-marker of [31]. (Given as Discussion 2.) You may find it useful to compare [31] with [75] in Chapter 6 (page 132).

To conclude this brief survey of WH-questions, a word about *where*, *when*, *how*, and *why*. Generally these are adverbs (and Adverb Phrases). But, as you saw in Exercise 1 above, they can be used to replace not only AdvPs but also PPs and subordinate clauses when these function as ADVERBIALS. When these words appear fronted in the COMP position, the Ss that follow them should be represented as having an empty AdvP slot. Give the phrase-marker of [33]. (Given as Discussion 3.)

[33] Where did you hide the monocle?

There are a couple of exceptions to this. In Exercise 1(e) *how* replaced *perfectly healthy* – an AP functioning as subject-predicative. (e) should be represented as having an empty AP slot. Secondly, recall that *put* has been sub-categorised as complex transitive, taking a direct object NP and an obligatory PP as object-predicative. In [34], then,

[34] Where did you put the monocle?

the S should be represented as having an empty PP slot, rather than an empty AdvP slot.

## Subordinate WH-clauses

The main point of the discussion so far is that all WH-clauses, whether main or subordinate, are introduced by a WH-expression in the COMP position, and this WH-expression corresponds to a gap of the appropriate category within the clause itself.

The one structural difference between MAIN WH-clauses and SUBORDINATE WH-clauses is that **only MAIN clauses exhibit subject-auxiliary inversion**. As you have seen, subject-auxiliary inversion is standardly required in the formation of a question. Only main clauses, therefore, can be used to ask questions as such. In the rest of this chapter, I consider just two main types of subordinate WH-clause. One type, without actually being a question, is used to report or mention questions that could be asked; these are called SUBORDINATE INTERROGATIVE CLAUSES. The other type has nothing to do with questions; these function as modifiers and are called RELATIVE CLAUSES.

## Relative clauses

Relative clauses function as modifiers. Though they can modify a variety of categories, I shall concentrate on their modifying functions within NP. Here are examples of NPs containing relative clauses.

[35] All the trampolines which I have bought
[36] The muggins who lent you a fiver
[37] A friend whose car we borrowed
[38] The usher who I showed my ticket to last night
[39] The place where you dropped the ice-cream

Identify the WH-(relative) clauses in each of those NPs.

[35a]  which I have bought
[36a]  who lent you a fiver
[37a]  whose car we borrowed
[38a]  who I showed my ticket to last night
[39a]  where you dropped the ice-cream

As you can see, these relative clauses have the same structure as WH-questions, except that they do not exhibit subject-auxiliary inversion. (Compare them with the WH-questions *which have I bought?, who lent you a fiver?, whose car did we borrow?* . . .) Having considered the structure of WH-questions in the last section, you should have no difficulty in analysing the structure of these relative clauses. First state the function of each of the WH-expressions in [35a]–[39a].

Then draw the phrase-markers of [35a] and [36a], using the triangle notation for NPs and Vgps.

[35a] *which* = direct object. [36a] *who* = subject. [37a] *whose car* = direct object. [38a] *who* = complement of preposition (*to*). [39a] *where* = adverbial.

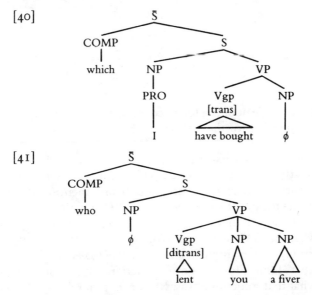

Just as with the corresponding WH-question, the function of *which* in the complementiser position in [40] is represented by the fact that there is an empty NP position in the complementation of the transitive verb *buy*: in other words, it functions as direct object. In [41], although there is no change of word-order, the WH-word is (as usual) represented as fronted to the complementiser position, leaving an empty subject NP in the clause itself. Note the lack of subject-auxiliary inversion in [40] and [41].

The relative clauses in [35]–[39] are all modifiers of the N within NOM. As POST-modifiers, they occupy the same position in NP structure as the PP and AP post-modifiers considered in

Chapter 7. You now have enough information to give a complete phrase-marker analysis of the NP in [37] (*a friend whose car we borrowed*).

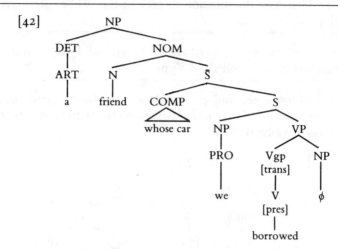

[42]

Using the triangle notation for all constituent NPs and Vgps, draw the phrase-marker for the NP [38] – given as Discussion 4.

Relative clauses like those in [35]–[39] are used to specify more exactly which trampolines, which muggins, which friend, which usher, and which place, are being mentioned. What distinguishes the use of a WH-word in a WH-question from its use in a relative clause is that when you ask a WH-question you do not know what the WH-word stands for (after all, that is why you ask the question). For example in asking *what did John jump onto?* you know that John jumped onto something but you want to know what that something was. By contrast, in relative clauses, it is quite clear what the WH-word stands for. It stands for the noun which is functioning as the head of the NP. In [42], for example, the possessive determiner *whose* stands for *a friend's*. When WH-words function in this way (introducing relative clauses as modifiers in NPs), they are called RELATIVE PRONOUNS. The relative clause in [42], then, corresponds with the full sentence *we borrowed a friend's car*. Give the full sentences that correspond to the other relative clauses in [35]–[39].

[43] I have bought some trampolines. [35]

[44] Some muggins lent you a fiver. [36]
[45] I showed my ticket to an usher last night. [38]
[46] You dropped the ice cream in some place. [39]

Before reading further, try Exercise 2 at the end of the chapter.

## *That* as a relative pronoun

A peculiarity of the kind of relative clause exemplified in [35]–[39] is that the WH relative pronoun can be replaced by THE RELATIVE PRONOUN *that*, e.g.

[47] The muggins *that* lent you a fiver
[48] All the trampolines *that* I bought.

This can lead to a confusion between NPs containing a relative clause introduced by the relative pronoun *that* and NPs containing the noun complement *that*-clauses discussed in the last chapter (e.g. *the fact that Mars is uninhabited*). How you would explain which is which in the following sentences?

[49] The news that she had given John shocked them all.
[50] The news that she had given John a good kick shocked them all.

*That*, as a relative pronoun introducing a relative clause, has a function in the structure of the clause that follows it; we should therefore expect the clause to be incomplete, to exhibit a gap corresponding to *that*. With the noun complement clause, on the other hand, *that* plays no part in the structure of the clause, so we expect the clause to be complete in itself. It is clear that the clause in the subject NP of [49] is missing a direct object (S = *she had given John*, which corresponds to *she had given John some news*). In [49], then, *that* is a relative pronoun introducing a relative clause. The clause in the subject NP of [50], on the other hand, is clearly complete (*she had given him a good kick*). It is therefore a noun complement clause. Notice that the RELATIVE CLAUSE [49] tells us something about the news but not what the news was. The NOUN COMPLEMENT CLAUSE [50] actually tells us what the news was.

## Omission of the relative pronoun

Note that it is possible to omit the relative pronoun altogether. Thus, corresponding to [35], [38], and [39], [51]–[53] are all possible:

[51] All the trampolines ⌃ I bought
[52] The usher ⌃ I showed my ticket to
[53] The place ⌃ you dropped the ice-cream.

There are two circumstances in which this omission of the WH-word in COMP is not possible. (a) When the relative pronoun functions as the subject of the clause that it introduces [55] as a form of [54] is impossible:

[54] The muggins who lent you a fiver lent me a tenner.
[55] *The muggins lent you a fiver lent me a tenner.

(b) Nor is it possible to omit the WH-word in COMP when other elements have been fronted with it:

[56] A friend whose car we borrowed is on the phone.
[57] *A friend car we borrowed is on the phone.

Relative clauses with the relative pronoun omitted from COMP will be represented as usual, but with the zero symbol in COMP.

## Restrictive vs non-restrictive relative clauses

All the relative clauses considered so far are described as RESTRICTIVE. The other kind of relative clause is described as NON-RESTRICTIVE (or APPOSITIVE). **The difference between restrictive and non-restrictive relative clauses lies not in their internal structure (which is identical) but in the way these clauses relate to the head noun within the overall NP.** In the examples that follow, all the subject NPs contain relative clauses. In the (a) examples, they are RESTRICTIVE, in the (b) examples NON-RESTRICTIVE.

[58a] The history books which I've read are very tatty.
[58b] The history books, which I've read, are very tatty.
[59a] The dogs which have rabies are dangerous.
[59b] The dogs, which have rabies, are dangerous.

As you can see, in writing, non-restrictives are distinguished from restrictives by being marked off by commas. The difference in function between the two types of relative clause can be brought out more clearly by showing that certain relative clauses can only be used non-restrictively in certain contexts:

[60a] *The dogs which are mammals must be treated with care.
[60b] The dogs, which are mammals, must be treated with care.
[61a] *Triangles which have three sides have interesting properties.
[61b] Triangles, which have three sides, have interesting properties.

The oddity of [60a] and [61a] arises from the fact that restrictive relative clauses are, as already mentioned, used to specify more exactly which things are being talked about. For example in [58a] the relative clause tells us which of the history books are tatty; **the restrictive relative clause serves to pick out a restricted set of history books, namely those that the speaker has read.** But the relative clauses in [60] and [61] cannot be used to pick out a restricted (more highly specified) set of dogs or triangles, since all dogs are mammals, and all triangles are three-sided, anyway. [60a] and [61a] suggests that it is possible to find dogs that are not mammals and triangles that are not three-sided. Of course, there is nothing to stop us adding the INCIDENTAL INFORMATION that dogs are mammals or that triangles have three sides – and this is precisely what the NON-RESTRICTIVE relative clause allows us to do (as in [60b] and [61b]). **A non-restrictive relative clause serves to add extra information, without restricting the set of things (*triangles, dogs, books* . . .) that is referred to by the NP in which the clause appears.**

To compare [59a] and [b]: [59a], with the restrictive relative clause, does not imply that all the dogs are dangerous – only a restricted set of the dogs (the rabied ones) are said to be dangerous. But [59b], with the non-restrictive relative clause, does imply that all the dogs are dangerous, adding the extra information that they also have rabies.

The representation of NPs containing a RESTRICTIVE relative clause has already been given. For ease of reference, that in [58a] is given here as [62].

[62]

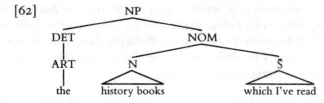

How a NON-RESTRICTIVE relative clause fits into NP structure is not so clear. Notice, however, that in [62] the determiner is a sister of *history books that I've read.* That is to say, the restrictive relative clause falls within the scope of the determining function of the definite article. If you omit *which I've read* you actually change the set of history books that is being mentioned. Now, in [58b] (with the non-restrictive), it is clear that the set of history books being mentioned is established perfectly well without the aid of the relative clause. Omit the non-restrictive relative clause, and you are left with the same set of history books. This suggests that the sequence *the history books* should be considered as an NP in its own right – with the (non-restrictive) relative clause just adding extra information about whatever the phrase *the history books* refers to. For the non-restrictive relative, then, I shall adopt the analysis given in [63]. Compare it with [62].

[63]

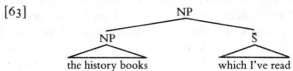

In other words, a non-restrictive relative clause modifies not the N within the NOM (as does a restrictive), but an independently complete NP, within another, higher, NP. On this analysis, the non-restrictive relative clauses fall outside the scope of the determining function of the definite article.

Before reading further, do Exercise 3 at the end of the chapter.

---

Two further points of difference between restrictive and non-restrictive relative clauses are that **in non-restrictives the relative pronoun cannot take the form of *that*, and it cannot be omitted.**

In this brief review of relative clauses, I have mentioned only relative clauses that appear in the structure of NPs. You should note, though, that non-restrictive relative clauses may modify other categories, including S (as in [64]) and PP [65]:

[64] *Lomax argued for trampolines*, which surprised me.

[65] Hedda got over the wall *with the aid of a trampoline*, which seems to me the most sensible way of doing it.

## Subordinate interrogative clauses

The following sentences all contain subordinate interrogative clauses.

[66] Martha was asking why he wore it on his foot.

[67] How he would fare on the trapeze preoccupied him.

[68] It is my affair what I wear at night.

[69] Marcel was not certain who he had invited.

[70] The most immediate problem is where we should hide these fritters.

[71] The little matter of who is going to pay for all this has yet to be resolved.

All these subordinate interrogative clauses have functions that are familiar to you from previous chapters. First, identify each subordinate clause and state its function in the structure of its superordinate clause; then state the function of the WH-expression within each subordinate clause.

---

[66a] why he wore it on his foot = dO (why = adverbial)

[67a] how he would fare on the trapeze = S (how = adverbial)

[68a] what I wear at night = ES (what = dO)

[69a] who he had invited = complement of adjective (who = dO)

[70a] where we should hide these fritters = sP (where = adverbial)

[71a] who is going to pay for all this = complement of prep (who = S)

As already mentioned, these subordinate interrogative clauses have the same STRUCTURE as WH-questions (but without subject-auxiliary inversion) and they have the same range of FUNCTIONS as the *that* clauses discussed in the last chapter. They can, in addition, function as the complement of a preposition within PP (as in [71]). Like *that* clauses, when functioning as subject or object, subordinate interrogative clauses are dominated by an NP node.

Using the triangle notation for all Vgps, PPs, and simple NPs (that is, NPs that do not include clauses), draw phrase-markers for [67], [68], and [69]. Leave yourself plenty of space.

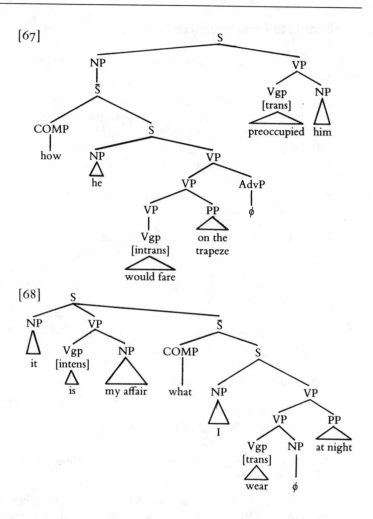

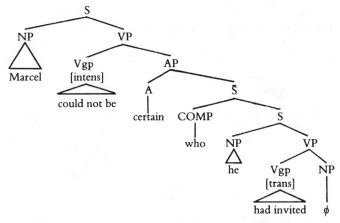

I will conclude the chapter by looking at a different type of subordinate interrogative clause. We have seen that subordinate interrogative clauses correspond in a straightforward way to (main clause) WH-questions. What about *yes/no* questions? Are there subordinate clauses that correspond to these? The answer is 'yes'. **Subordinate *yes/no* interrogative clauses are introduced by whether.** Here are some examples:

[72]   Max enquired whether Martha had seen his collection.
[73]   It is immaterial whether he's a juggler or a clown.
[74]   Whether you go or stay is your decision.

Such clauses have the same range of functions that other subordinate interrogative clauses have. In [72], it functions as direct object; in [73] as extraposed subject; in [74] as subject.

As regards their internal structure, though, they differ from the subordinate interrogative clauses that correspond to WH-questions. Can you see how?

Although *whether* looks like a WH-word, it resembles the complementiser *that* (Chapter 9) more than it resembles the WH-complementisers considered in this chapter: it is not fronted from within the clause that it introduces and it plays no part in the structure of that clause, which is complete in itself.

## Discussion of in-text exercises

**1.**

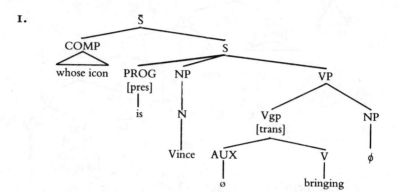

**2.**

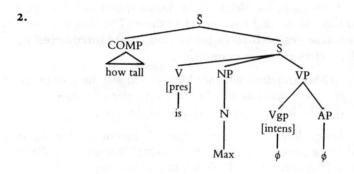

**3.**

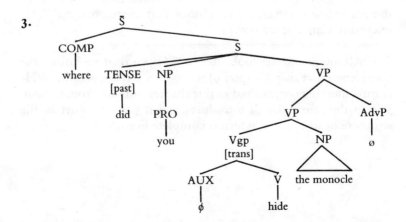

4.

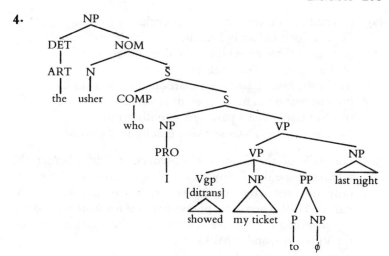

## Exercises

1.  First identify the function of the italicised constituent in the following sentences. Then, replacing that constituent by an appropriate WH-word, give the WH-question that results (with subject-auxiliary inversion where necessary and WH-fronting).

(a) We shall feed the cat *smoked salmon* today.
(b) He got to London *by hitching*.
(c) *The man at the front* called out.
(d) A recidivist is *a persistent offender*.
(e) You are *extremely healthy*.
(f) Tessa pocketed the fried egg *because it was too greasy to eat*.
(g) You have hidden the monocle *in the butter*.
(h) You said Roland had sent *a pork-pie* to the general.
(i) You said *Roland* had sent a pork-pie to the general.

2.  For each of the following sentences, embed the (i) sentence as a relative clause in an NP of the (ii) sentence, giving the sentence that results. For example, (i) and (ii) would yield (iii):
    (i) You mislaid some stilton last Christmas.
    (ii) The stilton has just strolled into the bedroom.
    (iii) The stilton which you mislaid last Christmas has just strolled into the bedroom.

(a)  (i) I had been trying to extract a cork.
     (ii) The cork suddenly launched itself at Widmerpool.
(b)  (i) Some officer issued this ridiculous order.
     (ii) I am going to override the officer.
(c)  (i) Crusoe said he had been marooned on an island.
     (ii) The island has never been discovered.
(d)  (i) I had borrowed a passenger's toothbrush.
     (ii) The passenger was seething quietly in the corner.

3.   For each of the following sentences, decide whether the
     relative clause that follows it could be (a) only restrictive, (b)
     only non-restrictive or (c) either, when included in the
     italicised NP. Then draw phrase-markers for sentences (a) and
     (b) including the relative clauses. (Use the triangle notation
     for Vgps, PPs, and SIMPLE NPs.)

(a)  *Napoleon Bonaparte* died in exile.
        who inaugurated the penal code
(b)  I haven't owned *a pig* in my life.
        which could fly
(c)  I prefer *cats (i)* to *cats (ii)*.
       (i)  which have stripes
       (ii) which have spots
(d)  *The acrobat* ate ravenously.
        who I had just hired
(e)  *The source of the Nile* was discovered by Speke.
        which I have visited
(f)  I would pit my dog against *any dog*.
        which has three legs

4.   The following sentences are all ambiguous. Explain the
     ambiguity first in words and then by drawing distinct phrase-
     markers for each interpretation. Abbreviate the phrase-
     markers as far as possible (but not so far as to obscure the
     distinction between the two interpretations).
(a)  I'd forgotten how bad beer smells.
(b)  The suggestion that Max has prepared for you should not be
     taken seriously.
(c)  When did you say he should go?

5.   Give Abbreviated Clausal Analyses of the following sen-
     tences. Against each subordinate clause, state what type of
     clause it is and its function. Example: *the history books, which
     I've read, are very tatty.*

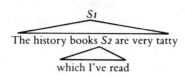

The history books *S2* are very tatty

which I've read

S2: Non-restrictive relative clause, modifier of *the history books*.

(a) I had never met a Lama who could speak English until I went to Tibet.
(b) Why Max didn't refute the suggestion that strange things had been happening in the greenhouse is a mystery.
(c) The acrobat, who is injured, is anxious that the high-wire should be strengthened before the animals are allowed on it again.
(d) Marcel often wondered whether Gilberte ever asked Swann what the boy she'd seen in the garden was called.

## Discussion of exercises

1. (a) What shall we feed the cat today?
(b) How did he get to London?
(c) Who called out?
(d) What is a recidivist?
(e) How are you?
(f) Why did Tessa pocket the fried egg?
(g) Where have you hidden the monocle?
(h) What did you say Roland had sent to the general?
(i) Who did you say had sent a pork-pie to the general?

Notice that in (h) and (i) a WH-word has been displaced from within a subordinate clause to the front of the main clause; it is the main clause subject and auxiliary, however, which are always inverted.

2. (a) The cork that I had been trying to extract suddenly launched itself at Widmerpool.
(b) I am going to override the officer who issued this ridiculous order.
(c) The island on which Crusoe said he had been marooned has never been discovered. (Or: The island which Crusoe said he had been marooned on . . .)
(d) The passenger whose toothbrush I had borrowed was seething quietly in the corner.

**3.** (a) Non-restrictive only. Since *Napoleon Bonaparte*, a proper name, already uniquely identifies a particular individual, it is impossible to restrict the range of reference of this NP any further.

(b) Restrictive only. If we included the clause as non-restrictive, the whole sentence would be equivalent to *I have never owned a pig in my life and a pig could fly*, which hardly makes sense. Notice that, in the context of this (negative) sentence, the expression *a pig* does not pick out a particular individual pig; only if it did pick out a particular individual pig could you then add the incidental information about that pig that it could fly. Notice, too, that when the relative clause is included as restrictive (as indeed it must), (b) could be uttered truthfully by a pig-owner.

(c) (i) and (ii) must both be restrictive. If either or both of them were non-restrictive, the resulting sentence would be contradictory, as indeed (c) is without the relative clauses.

(d) Both restrictive and non-restrictive are possible.

(e) Non-restrictive only. Like *Napoleon Bonaparte, the source of the Nile* already uniquely identifies a fully specified entity.

(f) As in (b) the expression *any dog* does not pick out a particular dog, so one cannot add the incidental (but very particular) information about having only three legs. With the relative clause included as non-restrictive, the sentence would be equivalent to *I would pit my dog against any dog and any dog has three legs!* With the relative clause included as restrictive, on the other hand, the sentence much more reasonably asserts that having only three legs is a condition that any dog must meet if it is to race the speaker's dog.

(a)

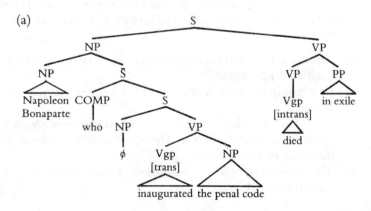

(b)

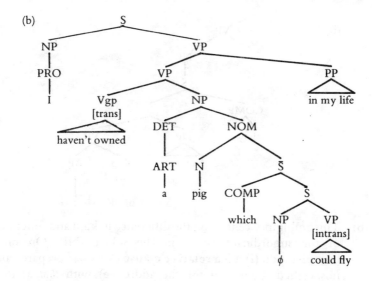

**4.**(a) In Chapter 1, I mentioned the ambiguity of *Hazeltine asked how old Sam was*. Sentence (a) exhibits exactly the same kind of ambiguity. On one interpretation (i), *how bad* forms a constituent, with *how* modifying *bad*; *how* functions as a degree adverb and the whole phrase *how bad* has been fronted into the COMP position. On the other interpretation (ii), *bad* and *beer* form a constituent; *how* functions as subject-predicative and has been fronted alone to the COMP position.

(i)

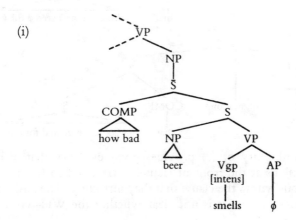

(ii)

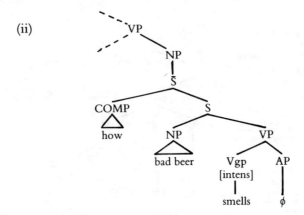

(b) This ambiguity centres on the difference in kind and function of the subordinate clause in the subject NP. On one interpretation **(i)** it is **a relative clause** (Max had prepared an unspecified suggestion for the addressee) with *that* as the relative pronoun fronted from within the clause. On the other interpretation **(ii)**, *that* plays no part in the structure of the subordinate clause; this is **a noun complement *that*–clause** (the suggestion WAS that Max had prepared for the addressee).

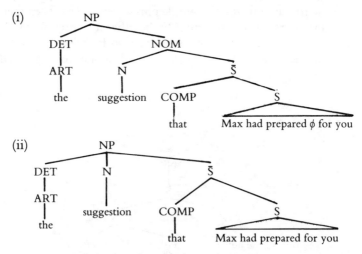

(c) The ambiguity of (c) provides good evidence that WH–expressions at the front of clauses correspond to functional positions within the clause that they introduce. The ambiguity arises because it is not clear whether the WH–word in complementiser position has a function in the MAIN clause (the *say* clause) or the SUBORDINATE clause (the *go* clause) of (c) i.e. with (c) one may be concerned with when the saying took place (i) or with when the going should take place (ii):

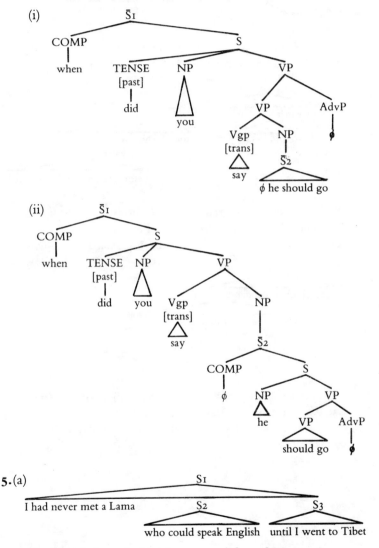

(i)

(ii)

5.(a)

S2: Restrictive relative clause, modifier of *Lama*.
S3: Adverbial clause.

(b)

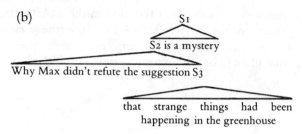

S2: WH-interrogative clause, subject of S1.
S3: *That* clause, complement of N (*suggestion*).

(c)

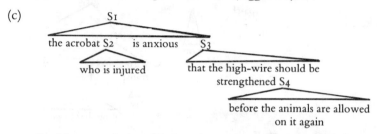

S2: Non-restrictive relative clause, modifier of *the acrobat*.
S3: *That* clause, complement of adjective (*anxious*).
S4: Adverbial clause in S3, modifying *should be strengthened*.

(d)

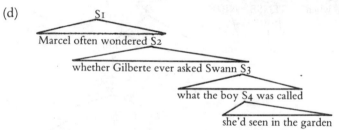

S2: *Yes/no* interrogative clause, direct object of *wonder*.
S3: WH-interrogative clause, direct object of *ask*.
S4: Restrictive relative clause (with relative pronoun omitted), modifier of *boy*.

# CHAPTER 10

# Non-Finite Clauses

I conclude this survey of English constituent types and their functions by looking at the different types of NON-FINITE CLAUSE. **A non-finite clause is one that contains a non-finite Verb Group.** The difference between a finite and non-finite Verb Group was introduced in Chapter 6: a finite Verb Group is one in which the first verb carries tense; in a non-finite Verb Group, there is no tense.

**Main clauses are always finite.** In other words, the Verb Group in a main clause always contains a tensed verb. **Non-finite clauses, therefore, can only be subordinate.**

I shall look first at the form of non-finite clauses and then at their functions. As far as their form is concerned, non-finite clauses can be grouped into four main types, corresponding to the four main types of (non-finite) Verb Group. Before looking at these Verb Groups, however, a general point about the form of non-finite clauses should be made at the outset.

Not only do non-finite clauses lack tense in the Verb Group, they may also lack one or more major elements of structure. As often as not, non-finite clauses omit the subject, for example. A non-finite clause lacks an element either (i) when that element can be understood as being identical to an element in the SUPERordinate clause, or (ii) when what it would refer to is so general and indefinite that there is no need to specify it. Consider [1] and [2]:

[1] Hedda loves *trampolining late at night*.
[2] *Trampolining late at night* is anti-social.

The italicised sequence is a subordinate non-finite clause, functioning as a verb-complement in [1] and as subject in [2]. In addition to lacking tense in the Verb Group (*trampolining*), the non-finite clause lacks a subject. In [1], the subordinate clause subject is understood as being identical to the subject of the main clause:

*Hedda.* Since this is understood, the subordinate clause subject can (and indeed must) be omitted. In [2], on the other hand, the subject is omitted for the second of the above reasons. [2] is used to assert that, generally, trampolining late at night is anti-social, no matter who does it; it would be beside the point to specify a particular subject. For whichever of these two reasons an element is omitted, the zero symbol should be used, as in previous chapters.

I will introduce here a convenient short-hand term for 'omitted because it is understood as being identical to some element in the superordinate clause'. **When an element is omitted in a subordinate clause because it is understood as being identical to some element in the superordinate clause, I shall say that the element in the superordinate clause CONTROLS (or IS THE CONTROLLER OF) the omitted element.** So, a simpler way of expressing the idea that Hedda must be understood as the subject of the subordinate clause in example [1] above is to say that the (omitted) subject of the subordinate clause is CONTROLLED by the main clause subject (i.e. *Hedda*). By contrast, in [2] the (omitted) subordinate clause subject does not have a controller in the main clause. This is why its interpretation is so general and indefinite. So, **in contrast to the CONTROLLED subject gap in [1], the subject gap in [2] can be described as FREE.**

Try Exercise 1 at the end of the Chapter before reading further.

---

## The non-finite Verb Group

Since what distinguishes a non-finite verb group from a finite one is the lack of tense in the first verb of the group, **the four types of non-finite verb group are classified according to the (untensed) form taken by that first verb.**

There are two types of INFINITIVE Vgp: (1) **THE BARE INFINITIVE** (which is always simple) and (2) **THE TO-INFINITIVE** (which can be complex); and two types of PARTICIPLE Vgp (3) **THE PASSIVE PARTICIPLE** (always simple) and (4) **THE -*ING* PARTICIPLE** (which can be complex).

## 1. The bare infinitive Verb Group

This consists of just the (untensed) stem of the verb. It is called the 'bare' infinitive because it lacks the infinitive particle *to*. Examples of sentences containing bare infinitive clauses are:

[3] She made him [*darn* her socks].
[4] All you have to do is [*squeeze* the trigger slowly].

To distinguish these non-finite forms from the simple present tense forms (as seen in *I darn her socks every other week*) I shall use the feature [− tense], to be read as 'minus tense', on the Verb node, as in [5]:

[5]

This feature will appear in all non-finite Vgps.

## 2. *to*-infinitive Verb Groups

These may be simple or complex. [6] contains a *to*-infinitive clause with a simple Vgp. In [7]–[9] the groups are complex.

[6] I'd much prefer [*to watch* the film in peace].
[7] He is thought [*to be hiding* in Brazil].
[8] I couldn't bear [*to be beaten* by a six year old].
[9] [For Max *to have been beaten*] is barely conceivable.

Following the INFINITIVE PARTICLE *to*, the verb has the basic stem form (as in the bare infinitive). In the simple Vgp, I shall analyse the infinitive particle itself as the sole representative of an untensed auxiliary element, and the AUX node will carry the [− tense] feature.

[10]

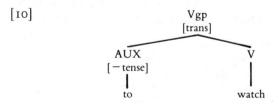

All the auxiliary possibilities introduced in Chapter 6 are possibilities in the *to*-infinitive Vgp, with one important exception: since non-finite Vgps lack tense, and since modals are always

tensed, **modals do not appear in any kind of non-finite Vgp.**
What would you suggest as the phrase-markers of the non-finite
Vgps in [7] and [9]?

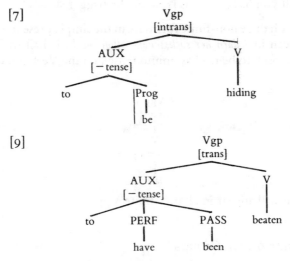

As [6]–[9] illustrate, *to*-infinitive clauses may appear with or
without an explicit subject (in [9], *Max* is the subject).

## 3. Passive participle Verb Groups

Like the bare infinitive, these can only be simple. As the label
suggests, they contrast with the bare infinitive (which is active) in
having a passive meaning. Here are some examples:

[11] [the palanquin *loaded*], we took a rest.
[12] [*loaded* to capacity], the palanquin lurched on its way.
[13] I found [Lydia's spatula *driven* into the cream caramel].

These simple Verb Groups will be distinguished from bare
infinitives by the feature [passive] and from (finite) past tense forms
by [ − tense].

[14]

Recall that PASSIVE in a Vgp affects the clause as a whole. Only verbs that can take objects in the active voice (i.e. monotransitive, ditransitive, and complex transitive verbs) can appear in the passive, since the choice of passive entails turning an object into subject. In [11] and [13] this subject is present (*the palanquin* and *Lydia's spatula*), but in [12] it is empty, controlled by (i.e. understood as identical to) the subject of the main clause (*the palanquin* again).

## 4. -*ing* participle Verb Groups

In common with *to* infinitive Vgps, these can be complex. They have the same structure except that, instead of the first verb being preceded by *to*, it takes the *-ing* affix. For example:

| *TO* INFINITIVE | *-ING* PARTICIPLE |
|---|---|
| to postpone | postponing |
| to have postponed | having postponed |
| to be postponed | being postponed |
| to have been postponed | having been postponed |

Here are some examples:

[15]  [*Getting up* before dawn every day] was hell.

[16]  [The microphone *having been switched off*], Murtlock spoke almost too frankly.

[17]  [*Having been switched off*], the microphone was forgotten.

Since *-ing* participle Vgps can be complex, I shall consistently analyse them with an auxiliary constituent bearing a [−tense] feature. In the simple *-ing* participle Vgp ([18] below), this auxiliary constituent will be empty.

[18]

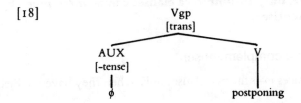

[19]

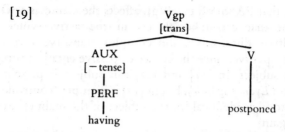

Notice that I have called these non-finite Vgps '-*ing* participle' rather than 'progressive participle'. While the participles discussed under (iii) clearly are related to the passive, non-finite -*ing* participles cannot be correlated with the progressive. The reason for this is that there are verbs (called STATIVE verbs) which cannot take progressive aspect ([20] and [21]) and yet do appear in non-finite -*ing* participle clauses ([22] and [23]):

[20] *I am knowing the Beethoven trios intimately.
[21] *I am owning this mangrove swamp.
[22] [Knowing the Beethoven trios intimately] helps a lot.
[23] [Owning this mangrove swamp] means nothing to me.

The perfect auxiliary *have* is also a stative verb (in other words, progressive *be* cannot precede perfect *have*):

[24] *Buster is having sold the mangrove swamp.

and it too can appear in -*ing* participle clauses:

[25] [Having sold the swamp], Buster slung his hook.

So much, then, for the form of the non-finite Verb Group itself. The next section deals with the form of the non-finite clause as a whole.

## Complementisers and non-finite clauses

There are two kinds of complementiser for non–finite clauses: (i) **for** and (ii) the **WH complementisers**. Of the four types of non-finite clause, **only *to*-infinitive clauses can be introduced by a complementiser.**

### (i) *For* as a complementiser

*For* introduces *to*-infinitive clauses only when they have a subject, as in

[26] [For Angelo to get all the blame] seems rather unfair.

[27] Bertram is anxious [for the clowns to get on with the job].

As a complementiser, *for* is not found in any other circumstance. In Chapter 8 I noted that the complementiser *that* is frequently optional. With minor exceptions, *for* differs in being either obligatory or impossible, depending on the function of the clause that it introduces. In all functions except that of complement of a Vgp, *for* is obligatory with *to*-infinitive clauses with explicit subject; when such clauses function as complement to a Vgp, however, *for* is impossible:

[28a] The magician expected [the rabbits to disappear].

[28b] *The magician expected [**for** the rabbits to disappear].

Since the presence/absence of the complementiser *for* is not a matter of choice, I shall employ the S-bar (S̄) and COMP nodes only when the complementiser is actually present. Here, then, is the representation of the subordinate clause in [26]:

[29]

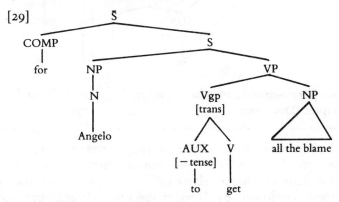

The subordinate clause in [28a], on the other hand, should be represented without S̄ and COMP.

## (ii) WH complementisers

Finite subordinate interrogative clauses were discussed in Chapter 9. Here I am concerned with their non-finite counterparts, infinitive interrogative clauses. This is the only other kind of non-infinite clause that requires a complementiser (a WH-expression) and hence the S̄ notation. As [30]–[32] illustrate, such clauses are always *to*-infinitive and always lack a subject.

[30]   He told me [where to put it] in no uncertain terms.
[31]   Orsini has already decided [who to vote for].
[32]   Louis was wondering [whether to support the Pope].

The subordinate clauses in [30] and [31] correspond to WH-questions in which, as seen in Chapter 9, the WH-expression in complementiser position corresponds to a gap in the clause itself. One might say that the WH-expression in the COMP CONTROLS the interpretation of the gap. In the subordinate clause of [30], then, there are two gaps – a subject gap (controlled by *me* in the main clause) and a PP gap (controlled by *where*).

[33]

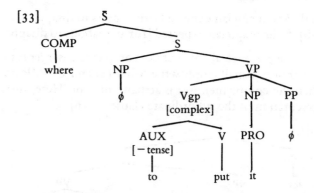

The phrase-marker of *who to vote for* is given at the end of the chapter (Discussion 1).

The subordinate clause in [32] corresponds to a *yes/no* question. As mentioned at the end of Chapter 9, *whether* is not fronted from within the clause itself, so that, apart from the absent subject (controlled by *Louis* in the main clause), the clause is complete. The phrase-marker of *whether to support the Pope* is given at the end of the chapter (Discussion 2).

All other non-finite clauses, in which there is no possibility of a complementiser, will be represented without S̄ or COMP. *to watch the film in peace*, for example, has [34] as its representation.

[34]

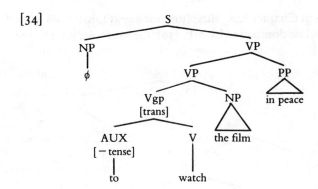

## The functions of non-finite clauses

In the rest of this chapter I list the major functions of the various types of non-finite clause, functions which will be familiar to you from previous chapters. Occasionally it has been necessary to make comments on potential problems, but I have kept these to a minimum. Complementation of the Vgp by non-finite clause requires more discussion, and this has been reserved until the end.

(i)    subject
(ii)   complement of A within AP
(iii)  complement of P within PP
(iv)   adverbial
(v)    postmodifier within NP
(vi)   complement of N within NP
(vii)  complement of Vgp within VP

### (i) Subject

This function can be filled by -*ing* participle clauses with explicit subject [35] and without [36], by WH *to*-infinitive clauses [37], and by non-WH *to*-infinitive clauses with explicit subject [38] and without [39].

> [35] [Oscar attempting the double somersault] should amuse you.
> [36] [Stripping wallpaper] is a wretched business.
> [37] [What to do with the fritters] is still undecided.
> [38] [For Oscar to attempt it] would be madness.
> [39] [To confess immediately] would be best.

As in Chapter 8, a clause functioning as subject (whether S̄ or S) should be dominated by NP. [36], for example, is represented as in [40]:

[40]

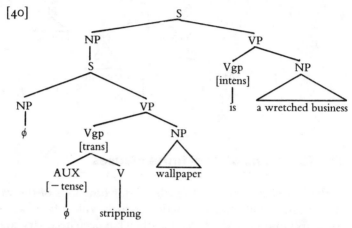

Most clauses that function as subject can appear as EXTRAPOSED SUBJECTS – leaving the empty expletive *it* in the subject NP position. What are the extraposed versions of [36]–[39]?

---

[41] It's a wretched business stripping wallpaper.
[42] It's still undecided what to do with the fritters.
[43] It would be madness for Oscar to attempt it.
[44] It would be best to confess immediately.

-*ing* participle clauses that have subjects are ungrammatical in extraposed position.

[45] *It should amuse you Oscar attempting the somersault.

However, with a comma between the main clause and the subordinate clause, [45] is grammatical. In that case, though, it illustrates another construction (not considered in this book) in which the clause is added as an afterthought to explain the reference of *it* in subject position.

## (ii) Complement of A within AP

-*ing* participle clauses without explicit subject and *to*-infinitive clauses with or without explicit subject can have this function. The clause is represented as a sister of the adjective. The participle clause is exemplified in [46], with the AP bracketed and the complement clause in italics.

[46]   He was [slow *getting up*]

    [busy
    [slow
    [late

There are several types of adjective complementation by *to*-infinitive clause. Here I shall distinguish just two main types. These are exemplified by [47] and [48].

[47]   Max is [reluctant *to try your cooking*].
[48]   That piano would be [impossible *for me to move*].

In [47], with *reluctant*, *Max* (the main clause subject) controls the (omitted) subordinate clause SUBJECT, Notice, by contrast, that if we omit the subject of the subordinate clause (*me*) in [48],

[49]   That piano would be [impossible *to move*]

the missing subject is not controlled by the main clause subject (*the piano*). Instead, omission of the subordinate clause subject has the generalising effect associated with a FREE gap. This is because, with adjectives like *impossible*, the main clause subject always controls the omitted subordinate clause OBJECT. Notice that, while the subordinate clause in [47] has an explicit direct object (*your cooking*), if you try and supply an explicit object in [48]/[49], you get an ungrammatical sentence:

[50]   *That piano is [impossible *(for me) to move the organ*]

The same explanation applies: the subordinate clause already has its direct object, an empty one controlled by the main clause subject, *the piano*.

In fact, there are sentences corresponding to [48]/[49] in which *the piano* explicitly appears as the object of the infinitive subordinate clause:

[51]   *(for me) to move that piano*   would be   impossible
              S               V        sP
[52]   It   would be   impossible   *(for me) to move that piano*
     S   V      sP           ES

With adjectives like *reluctant*, then, it is the omitted SUBJECT of the complement clause that is controlled by the main clause subject. Other such adjectives are *anxious, eager, hesitant, (un)willing, furious, happy, liable, quick.* With adjectives like *impossible*, on the other hand, it is the OBJECT of the complement clause that is controlled by the main clause subject. Other adjectives that pattern like *impossible* in this way are *easy, hard, difficult, tough, tiresome, boring, enjoyable, delicious.*

Try Exercise 2 at the end of the chapter.

---

### (iii)  Complement of P within PP

Only *-ing* participle clauses (with or without explicit subject) can occur as the complement of a preposition within PP. In the examples that follow, I illustrate (bracketed) PPs consisting of P + *-ing* participle clause in a variety of functions.

[53]  Maria disposed of the car [by *driving it over a cliff*]. (PP as adverbial)

[54]  [With *the troglodytes approaching*], Argon capitulated. (PP as adverbial)

[55]  This was the result [of *Maria having watched too much TV*]. (PP as modifier of N)

[56]  He was hopeless [at *writing letters*]. (PP as complement of A)

[53] is represented in [57].

[57]

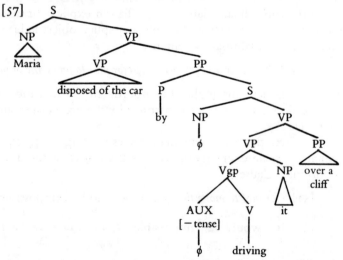

The phrase-marker for [56] is given at the end of the chapter (Discussion 3).

## (iv) Adverbial

In (iii) you saw that non-finite clauses can function as the complement of a preposition in a PP functioning as an adverbial. Non-finite clauses can also function as adverbials in their own right. With the exception of bare infinitive clauses, all types of non-finite clause (with and without explicit subject) can function as adverbials. The subject is omitted only if it is controlled by the SUBJECT of the superordinate clause.

[58] *The count having invited us to the castle*, we accepted.

[59] *Having furnished ourselves with garlic*, we set off.

[60] We hung around several hours *for the count to appear*.

[61] We helped ourselves to the wine *to relieve the boredom*.

[62] *The wine finished*, we dozed fitfully in our chairs.

[63] We returned, *disappointed by our evening*.

[63] is represented in [64].

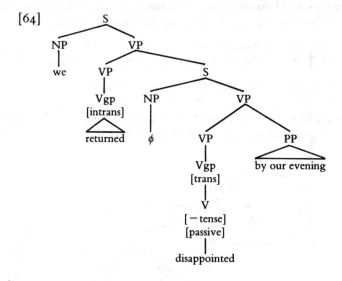

## (v) Post-modifier within NP

*to*-infinitive clauses with explicit subject [65] or without [66], *-ing* participle clauses (without explicit subject) [67], and passive participle clauses (without explicit subject) [68] can all function as modifiers in NP (bracketed in the examples below).

[65] [A book *for you to review*] is in the post.

[66] [The instrument *to use here*] is a No. 10 scalpel.
[67] There are no WCs on [the train *now leaving Platform 10*].
[68] [A cat *fed on smoked salmon*] will start demanding champagne.

Within all such clauses, there will be at least one missing element and this will be controlled by the head of the NP (*book, instrument, train, cat*). In participle clauses – [67] and [68] – it is always the subject. In infinitive clauses, this gap can be an object (as in [65] and [66] above), the subject (as in [69] and [70]) or the complement of a preposition (as in [71]):

[69] Cesare Borgia was [the first man *to be threatened with excommunication by his own father*].
[70] Max seems [the most likely person *to succeed*].
[71] Boswell found him [a difficult walker *to keep up with*].

**Non-finite clauses functioning as modifiers in NPs correspond to finite relative clauses.** For example, the relevant NP in [66] corresponds to [72] and that in [68] to [73].

[72] The instrument that one should use here.
[73] A cat which has been fed on smoked salmon.

Draw the phrase-marker of the subject NP in [66].

---

The clause in this NP contains two gaps. A FREE (uncontrolled) subject gap, and an object gap controlled by the head of the NP.

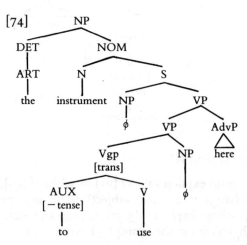

The structure of [69]–[71] raises an interesting question.

Notice that they contain both pre- and post-modification. In the corresponding finite relative clauses, it is clearly seen that these modifiers are not independent of each other. For example:

[75] The person who is most likely to succeed.
[76] A walker who was difficult to keep up with.

In each of these, the infinitive clause functions as the complement of the adjective (*likely/difficult*), within an AP.

In terms of its SYNTACTIC CONSTITUENTS [77] seems an appropriate analysis of the relevant NP in [70]:

[77]

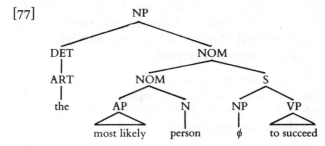

In [77] *most likely* forms a (NOM) constituent with *person*. Yet, [70] corresponds in MEANING to [75] in which *most likely* forms a constituent, not with *person*, but with *to succeed*. In short, while [77] may be justified in purely syntactic terms, it may well not be the most appropriate representation from the point of view of its meaning. Throughout this book, I have made the assumption that syntax and semantics always agree, in other words, that an appropriate representation of the constituents of a phrase will always accord with what we understand that phrase to mean. This is reasonable as a guiding principle, but, as these examples (and current work in linguistics) illustrate, it remains to be established as a fact.

Since non-finite clauses with a modifying function within NP correspond to relative clauses, it is reasonable to ask whether the restrictive/non-restrictive distinction is applicable in their case. The examples shown above are certainly all restrictive – and as such have been represented, within NOM, as sisters of the head noun. In the following examples

[78] The train, approaching the tunnel, slowed down.
[79] The cat, fed on smoked salmon for three weeks, started demanding champagne.

the non-finite clauses could well be analysed as non-restrictive modifiers corresponding to the (non-restrictive) relative clauses in [80] and [81]:

[80] The train, which was approaching the tunnel, slowed down.

[81] The cat, which had been fed on smoked salmon for three weeks, started demanding champagne.

As non-restrictive modifiers within the NP, they would be represented as sisters of the NP within a higher NP.

On the other hand, however, if someone wished to claim that these non-finite clauses really functioned as ADVERBIALS, this would be difficult to disprove. Compare them with the adverbial clauses in [58]–[63] above. Notice, too, that they have the characteristic mobility of adverbials:

[82] Approaching the tunnel, the train slowed down.

[83] The train slowed down, approaching the tunnel.

[84] Fed on smoked salmon for three weeks, the cat started demanding champagne.

## (vi)   Complement of N within NP

In Chapter 8 complementation of nouns by finite *that* clause was introduced. Complementation of nouns by non-finite clauses is much less common. I mention this function of non-finite clauses here only to distinguish it from the post-modifying function considered under (v) above. Only *to*-infinitive clauses are permitted in this function, with explicit subject [85] and without [86].

[85] [No appeal *for us to come*] will be ignored.

[86] [His ability *to think straight*] was severely impaired by his experience in the dogs home.

Other examples are *attempts to pervert the course of justice* and *your proposal to bring the dogs*.

As with finite noun complement clauses (Chapter 8), the complement clause relates to the head noun in exactly the same way as it would to a verb (*your proposal to bring the dogs* is the NP version of *you proposed to bring the dogs*). See the next section on Complement of the Vgp. Non-finite noun complement clauses can be distinguished from non-finite post-modifying clauses by noting that the complement clauses do not correspond to relative clauses (which are modifiers). In contrast to post-modifying clauses (which do have finite relative clause counterparts), they can be complete (as in [85]), and even when incomplete (as in all the other examples) the gaps are not controlled by the head noun. The analysis of the subject NP of [86] is given as Discussion 4 at the end of the chapter.

## (vii) Complement of the Verb (Group)

As mentioned earlier in this chapter, complementation of the Verb (Group) by non-finite clause requires more discussion. The presentation that follows is intended to give just an initial impression of this rich and sometimes controversial area of English grammar.

Since Chapter 4 we have operated with a useful six-way sub-categorisation of verbs which has the effect of assigning more specific syntactic functions to their complements (direct and indirect object, subject- and object-predicative, prepositional complement). It is not clear, however, that this sub-categorisation (and the functions associated with it) is wholly appropriate in cases of complementation by non-finite clause. For example, if a verb takes a single NP as direct object – i.e. is a (mono)transitive verb – as in [87]

[87] I believed his story.

it is not always clear whether a non-finite clause complementing that verb (as in [88] and [89]) should be taken as direct object.

[88] I believe [William to have been in the garden].
[89] William is believed [to have been in the garden].

Furthermore, there are verbs (e.g. *condescend, hope, suppose*) which cannot take an NP as direct object (and hence are not (mono)transitive)

[90] *He $\left\{\begin{array}{l} \text{has condescended} \\ \text{hoped} \end{array}\right\}$ the decoration of the ceiling

but CAN take a non-finite clause in complementation:

[91] He $\left\{\begin{array}{l} \text{has condescended} \\ \text{hoped} \end{array}\right\}$ to decorate the ceiling.

Can we then analyse the non-finite clause as a direct object?
Again, *promise* and *ask* are ditransitive verbs:

```
         S      V        iO          dO
[92]  I   promised  Bjorn   my spaghetti machine
      She  asked     him     a question
```

This might lead us to analyse the sentences in [93] as ditransitive structures with indirect and direct objects:

```
        S      V        iO          dO
[93]  I   promised  [Astrid]  [to wear the wig upside down]
      I   asked     [Herzog]  [to make no comment]
```

So far, so good. There are good reasons, though, for analysing the complementation of *force* and *dare* as having the same constituent structure as that of *promise* and *ask*.

$$[94] \quad I \left\{ \begin{array}{l} \text{dared} \\ \text{forced} \end{array} \right\} \text{[Astrid] [to wear the wig upside down]}$$

Yet neither *dare* nor *force* can take two NPs in complementation (i.e. they are not obviously ditransitive verbs) – and it is anyway not obvious that *Astrid* in [94] is understood in the way we understand indirect objects.

Rather than give further examples of specific problems to do with the functions, I will mention here a more general consideration. As regards their complementation by clauses, verbs really need to be sub-categorised in a way that is quite independent of the sub-categorisation employed so far. A fully detailed and explicit sub-categorisation would need to sub-categorise a verb for at least the following:

(i)    whether it takes a clause in complementation;
(ii)   if so, whether the clause can be finite or non-finite;
(iii)  if the clause can be non-finite, which of the four types of non-finite clause are permitted;
(iv)   whether or not the verb allows a NP to intervene between it and the non-finite verb;
(v)    if so, whether that NP functions as its object or as the subject of the non-finite clause;
(vi)   when there is a gap in the non-finite clause, what element controls the gap.

Clearly, answering these questions in a systematic manner for a representative sample of the several thousand English verbs would be an ambitious exercise by any standards and well beyond the scope of this chapter. But notice that it would result in a sub-categorisation of verbs rather different from that employed so far, one that is independent of the more specific functions dO, iO, sP, oP. This is not to say that there is no correspondence between verb complementation by non-finite clause and other kinds of verb complementation discussed in previous chapters; there is, as we saw with *promise* and *ask* above. As a further example, consider complements of *be* as in [95] and [96].

[95] The noise you can hear is [Tessa slurping her coffee].
[96] All he ever did was [clean his ears and lounge about].

These clearly parallel SUBJECT-PREDICATIVES in function, but they (and other types of non-finite complement of *be*) are the only examples that I would care to offer as being indisputable cases of this.

So, when a non-finite clause complements a Verb Group, I shall not attempt to assign it a more specific function (dO, iO, sP, oP) in terms of the sub-categorisation of the verb that it complements. This means that when a Vgp is complemented by a non-finite clause, the sub-categorisation feature employed so far can be dispensed with. As with all verb-complements, non-finite clauses will be represented as sisters of the Vgp within VP. The clauses will not be dominated by an NP node.

When a verb is complemented just by a non-finite clause WITHOUT SUBJECT, it suffices to note that only *to*-infinitive and *-ing* participles clauses are admitted, and that the subject gap in the non-finite clause is always controlled by the superordinate subject. Examples are

[97] I remember [dropping it out of the window].
[98] We appear [to have hit the jackpot].

[98], for example, will have the following representation.

[99]

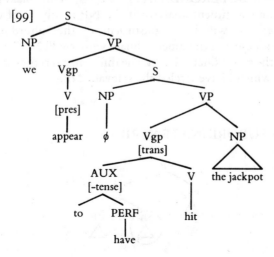

Matters are not quite so straightforward, however, when an NP intervenes between the superordinate verb and the non-finite verb of the subordinate clause. In [100]–[109], these NPs are italicised.

Vgp + NP + *to*-infinitive.

[100] I'd prefer *the butler* to taste it first.
[101] She encouraged *Muldoon* to buy her diamonds.
[102] Machiavelli believed *Cesare* to be The Ideal Prince.
[103] I'd like *the Right Honourable Member* to try it for a week.

Vgp + NP + *-ing* participle.

[104] I've heard *Victoria and Albert* playing that duet.
[105] I caught *the clowns* helping the elephants on to the trapeze.

Vgp + NP + bare infinitive.

[106] Marcel made *Celeste* peel him a grape.
[107] He watched *Matilda* polish off the toast.

Vgp + NP + passive participle.

[108] They found *the icon* buried in the wall.
[109] She kept *Raleigh* imprisoned in the tower.

The principal question raised by these is whether the italicised NP is (I) the SUBJECT of the SUBORDINATE verb or (II) the OBJECT of the SUPERORDINATE VERB. This makes a difference to the constituent analysis: if the NP is subject of the subordinate verb, it will be a constituent of the subordinate clause, but if it is object of the superordinate verb it will NOT be a constituent of the subordinate clause. The difference is represented by I and II, in which I have circled the relevant NP.

(I)

SUBJECT OF SUBORDINATE VERB

[110]

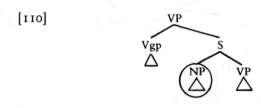

(II)
## OBJECT OF SUPERORDINATE VERB

[111]

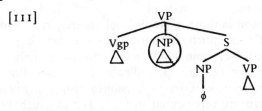

This uncertainty about the function of such NPs arises for three reasons.

(i) When functioning as complements of a Vgp, non-finite clauses only very rarely allow a complementiser. *Prefer* is almost the only verb in British English to do so (and then only for some speakers):

[112] I'd prefer [for the butler to taste it].

Since the function of the complementiser is to introduce the subordinate clause, it very clearly marks the division between superordinate and subordinate clause. In [112] (and [100] above), then, *the butler* falls squarely into the SUBordinate clause – as subject. In the (much more usual) absence of a complementiser, however, no such clue as to the function of the NP is provided.

(ii) If you replace the italicised NPs in [100]–[109] by pronouns, those pronouns must appear in their ACCUSATIVE form: *them, him, her (me, us)*. This might appear to indicate that these NPs function as objects and not as subjects, and hence that they are part of the SUPERordinate clause, not the SUBordinate clause. Against this, however, it could be (and has been) argued that subjects of NON-FINITE verbs just do appear in the accusative, and the following sentences would seem to support this view:

[113] [For *him* to attempt it] is ludicrous.
[114] [*Him* attempting it] is difficult to imagine.

Here the pronouns are clearly functioning as subjects of the subordinate clause and they appear in their accusative form.

(iii) The fact that the NP is understood as the subject of the non-finite verb does not help us, either. This fact can be explained in either of two ways. EITHER: the NP is understood as the subject of the subordinate clause because it actually is the subject; OR: while the NP actually is the object of the superordinate clause, it

CONTROLS the empty subject of the subordinate clause (i.e. the subordinate subject is understood as being identical to the superordinate object).

Structures such as those in [100]–[109] are subject to widely varying analyses – and much discussion. The one point of general agreement is that they cannot all receive the same analysis: it depends on the verb in the superordinate clause. But different grammatical theories make different decisions as to how many sub-categories of verb are represented in [100]–[109], which verbs belong to which sub-categories, and even as to what considerations are relevant in deciding these questions.

For the purposes of this chapter, I shall divide verbs taking non-finite clause complements into just two sub-categories: **sub-category (I), in which the verbs have just ONE complement: a full non-finite clause WITH EXPLICIT SUBJECT; and sub-category (II), in which the verbs have TWO complements: an OBJECT Noun Phrase AND a non-finite clause WITH EMPTY SUBJECT.** See diagrams (I) and (II) above. Some examples are listed below.

(I)  Vgp + [NP + VP]
        s      s

assume, believe, consider, claim, desire, dread, expect, feel, find, hate, hear, imagine, know, like, love, observe, prefer, prove, regret, see, suppose, think, watch . . .

(II)  Vgp + NP + [Ø VP]
            s    s

advise, ask, beg, coax, compel, dare, encourage, forbid, force, promise, persuade, urge . . .

At this point, you may be asking yourself how one is supposed to distinguish between these. The following closing comments should help in this.

A verb should be assigned to sub-category (I) unless there are compelling reasons for doing otherwise (and assigning it to sub-category (II)). What would count as a compelling reason for assigning a verb to (II) rather than (I)? Well, clauses denote things like events, facts, states of affairs, ideas, propositions. You can assume, believe, expect, see, consider, or prove an event, fact, state of affairs, proposition, or idea. Accordingly, *assume, believe, expect, see, consider, prove* and similar verbs belong to sub-category (I), taking just a clause (with explicit subject) as complement. By contrast, you cannot advise, coax, force, persuade, or tempt any of those kinds of things. It is reasonable, then, not to assign *advise, coax, force, persuade* to sub-category (I), but to assign them to sub-category (II), as taking not just a clause but also a separate NP object.

In fact, the verbs in (II) normally require an ANIMATE Noun Phrase object. This observation can be useful in testing the sub-category of a verb. Consider [115]

[115]  The rock moved.

[115] expresses something which can be believed without making any special assumptions about the rock, in contrast to [116]

[116]  I persuaded the rock

which requires rather special assumptions, for example, the fairy-tale assumption that the rock has a mind. While [115] shows that no special assumptions are required for *the rock* to be SUBJECT of *move*, [116] shows that special assumptions are required for it to be OBJECT of *persuade*. Consider now [117], where the syntactic function of *the rock* is in question:

[117]  I persuaded the rock to move.

This requires just those special assumptions about the rock that [116] requires – indicating that *the rock* should be taken not as the subject of *move* (as in [115]) but as the object of *persuade* (as in [116]). By this test, then, *persuade* is demonstrated to belong in sub-category (II).

Since *expect* belongs to (I) and *persuade* belongs to (II), [118] and [119]

[118]  She expected the bear to dance a tango.
[119]  She persuaded the bear to dance a tango.

have different representations, [118] as in [120], which conforms to [110] above, and [119] as in [121], which conforms to [111] above.

[120]

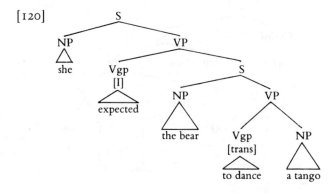

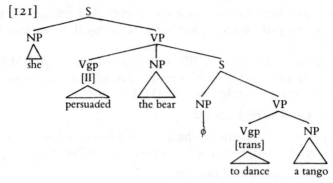

With just one verb, *promise*, there is an even more compelling reason for assigning it to sub-category (II) rather than (I). In the light of the discussion of CONTROL in this chapter, can you identify the reason?

---

With all the other verbs listed under sub-category (II), the empty subject of the subordinate clause is controlled by the OBJECT of the superordinate clause. For example, in [121] above the empty subject is understood to be *the bear*. It is this that may cause confusion in deciding the function of the NP – see the discussion under (iii) on page 231). But with *promise*, the empty subject of the subordinate clause is not controlled by the superordinate clause object but by the superordinate clause subject. Compare *promise* and *beg* (which both belong to II) in Exercise I at the end of the chapter. Since *Bill* cannot even be understood as the subject of *give* it must be taken as the object of *promise*.

## Discussion of in-text exercises

I.

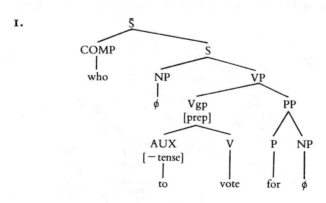

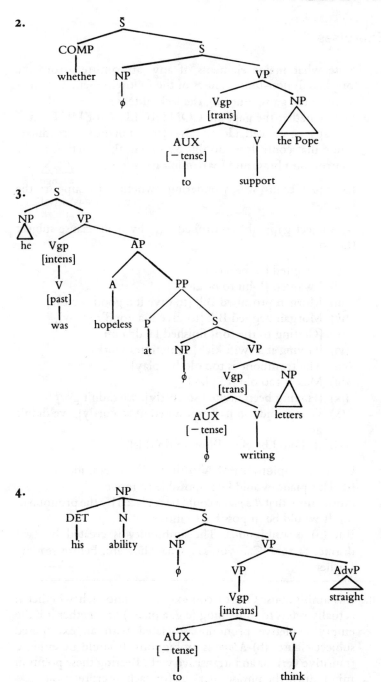

**2.**

```
                    S̄
         COMP              S
       whether       NP           VP
                      |      Vgp        NP
                      ∅    [trans]       △
                                       the Pope
                        AUX      V
                      [−tense]
                         |       |
                         to    support
```

**3.**

```
              S
      NP            VP
      △     Vgp            AP
      he  [intens]     A         PP
             V      hopeless  P           S
           [past]             |     NP         VP
             |                at    |      Vgp      NP
            was                     ∅    [trans]    △
                                                  letters
                                      AUX       V
                                    [−tense]
                                       |        |
                                       ∅      writing
```

**4.**

```
                    NP
       DET      N            S
       his   ability   NP              VP
                        |        VP              AdvP
                        ∅      Vgp                 △
                             [intrans]           straight
                               AUX       V
                             [−tense]
                                |        |
                                to      think
```

## Exercises

1. (a) State what major elements, if any, are omitted from the (bracketed) non-finite clauses of the following sentences (i.e. identify the gaps, ignoring the lack of tense);
   (b) State whether the gaps are CONTROLLED or FREE;
   (c) If a gap is controlled, identify the element in the superordinate clause that controls it (do this by giving the function of the controlling phrase and by naming it).

   Example: Louis was wondering [whether to support the Pope].

   (a) Subject gap   (b) controlled   (c) by main clause subject (*Louis*)

   (i) I wanted [to be alone].
   (ii) I wanted [John to be alone].
   (iii) Morgan promised Bill [to give it a good review].
   (iv) Morgan begged Bill [to give it a good review].
   (v) [Getting to the top] finished Hedda off.
   (vi) [Giving it a swift kick] sometimes works.
   (vii) The trombone is too old [to play].
   (viii) Max is too old [to play].
   (ix) [Having been invited so curtly], we didn't go.
   (x) [The mandarin having invited us so curtly], we didn't go.
   (xi) It should be clear [how to do this].

2. Under **Complement of A within AP**, we considered
   (i) This piano would be impossible to move.
   Notice now that *the piano* could be replaced by the pronoun *it*:
   (ii) It would be impossible to move.
   But (ii) is ambiguous. The ambiguity is created by two distinct factors. Can you say what they are, before reading further?

   ---

   (a) *it* is ambiguous. Out of context, we cannot tell whether *it* actually refers to something (e.g. a piano) or whether it is the empty expletive pronoun associated with an extraposed subject clause. (b) *Move* is ambiguous. It could be either a transitive verb or an intransitive verb. Bearing these points in mind, draw the phrase-markers for each interpretation.

3. Assign each of the following verbs to sub-category (I) or (II). You will find this easier if you invent sentences of the form [NP – finite Vgp – NP – non-finite Vgp . . .], taking into account the concluding comments of this chapter.

*mean, teach, understand, want, tell, imagine, order, warn.*

4. (a) Draw abbreviated clausal analyses of the following sentences (they all contain more than one subordinate clause);
(b) indicate the omission of major elements by the zero symbol;
(c) against each clause state its function; (d) if it is non-finite, state what type it is. (v) and (vi), being quite complex, will require careful analysis.

Example: Having shaved your head, you can report to the make-up man.

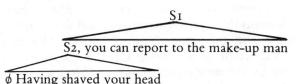

S₁

S₂, you can report to the make-up man

∮ Having shaved your head

S₂: Adverbial: perfect -*ing* participle clause.

(i) The Doge appears to have been eager to join the Crusade.
(ii) The first chef to be informed of it congratulated Melvin on having rescued the steaks.
(iii) Having been taught by Mozart himself, Max knew the quintet to be beyond his capacities.
(iv) Plans to recover the vehicles abandoned during the night are now being drawn up.
(v) I distinctly recall Mr Mills suggesting that to allow elephants on to the trapeze would be to court disaster.
(vi) Andrews heard Davis ask Bill whether being drawn to play against Borg in the first round would affect his chances.

## Discussion of exercises

1.  (i) (a) Subject  (b) controlled  (c) main clause subject (*I*).
    (ii) No gaps.
    (iii) (a) Subject  (b) controlled  (c) main clause subject (*Morgan*).

   (iv) (a) Subject   (b) controlled   (c) main clause object
        (*Bill*).
    (v) (a) Subject   (b) controlled   (c) main clause object
        (*Hedda*).
   (vi) (a) Subject   (b) free.
  (vii) (a) Subject (free) and object   (b) controlled   (c) main
        clause subject (*the trombone*).
 (viii) (a) Subject   (b) controlled   (c) main clause subject
        (*Max*).
   (ix) (a) Subject   (b) controlled   (c) main clause subject
        (*we*).
    (x) No gaps.
   (xi) (a) Subject   (b) free.

**2.**   When *it* actually refers to something (e.g. a piano), the clause
    complements the adjective (*impossible*) and the verb must be
    transitive, with the (omitted) object controlled by the main
    clause subject (*it* or *the piano*). On this interpretation the
    sentence has the same representation as (i) has, see (a) below.
    On the other interpretation, *it* is the empty expletive
    pronoun, and the clause must be analysed as an extraposed
    subject, and (ii) would be equivalent to *to move would be
    impossible*. On this interpretation, *move* is intransitive. See (b)
    below. Notice that the expletive pronoun, being empty,
    cannot control any element in the subordinate clause.

(a)

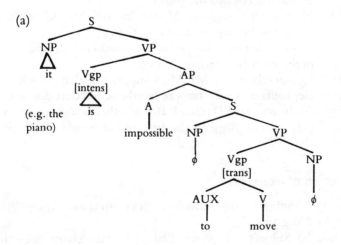

(b)

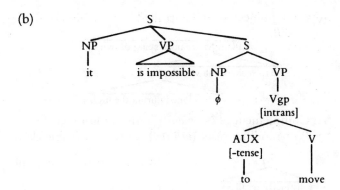

**3.** (I): *mean, understand, want, imagine.*
(II): *teach, tell, order, warn.*

**4.** (i)

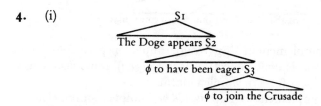

S2: Complement of Vgp (*appears*), perfect *to*-infin. clause.
S3: Complement of A (*eager*), simple *to*-infin. clause.

(ii)

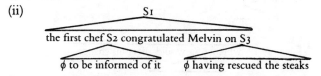

S2: Post-modifier of N (*chef*), passive *to*-infin. clause.
S3: Complement of P (*on*), perfect *-ing* participle clause.

(iii)

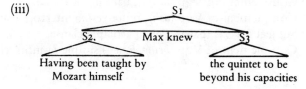

S2: Adverbial, perfect passive *-ing* participle clause.
S3: Complement of Vgp (*knew*), simple *to*-infin. clause.

(iv)

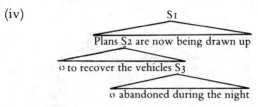

S2: Complement of N (*plans*), simple *to*-infin. clause.
S3: Post-modifier of N (*vehicles*), passive participle clause.

(v)

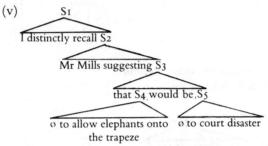

S2: Complement of Vgp (*recall*), simple *-ing* participle clause.
S3: Complement (object) of Vgp (*suggest*), finite *that*-clause.
S4: Subject (of S3), simple *to*-infin. clause.
S5: Complement to Vgp (*would be*), simple *to*-infin. clause.

vi)

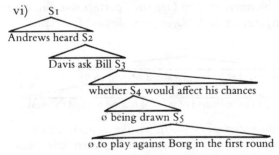

S2: Complement of Vgp (*heard*), bare infin. clause.
S3: Complement of Vgp (*ask*), finite *yes/no* interrog. clause.
S4: Subject (of S3), passive *-ing* participle clause.
S5: Complement of Vgp (*being drawn*) simple *to*-infin. clause.

# CHAPTER 11

# Languages, Sentences, and Grammars

This concluding chapter is concerned with the general background to, and ultimate purpose of, the kind of analysis you have encountered in previous chapters, rather than with extending that analysis.

## Languages

I will begin by considering a very general question:

[1] What is a language?

How do you begin to think about this? The question seems so general as to be almost empty of content. How one goes about answering such a question depends very much on one's reasons for asking it in the first place. It would not be far from the truth to say that one could really understand the question only in the light of particular answers to it. Different thinkers about language have answered it in their different ways and, in doing so, have given the question a different significance.

A natural answer often given is

[2] A language is a system of communication.

Expanding that answer (deciding e.g. what we meant by 'system' and 'communication', and what it is about the system that permits communication) and exploring its implications would open up one avenue of thought about language, and a perfectly valid one. But other answers are possible. My purpose in considering the question in [1] is to raise certain questions about the kind of analysis you have encountered in previous chapters, and to put that analysis into a general context. In order to do this, I will consider the following answer:

[3] A language is a set of sentences.

I hope, by the end of this chapter, to have shown that this less obvious answer opens up an interesting and fruitful way of thinking about language. It is, very briefly, the answer proposed by Noam Chomsky, Professor of Linguistics at The Massachusetts Institute of Technology. It has had a profound effect on the development of language study over the last thirty years or so. Taken out of context, it would probably make little sense. But, considered carefully, this answer has quite specific implications for how languages are to be described, and raises in turn further questions which are felt to be of central significance for language study.

Before considering these implications, however, we need to compare this account with what is perhaps a more common idea of what a language is. If a language really is a set of sentences, it follows that **DIFFERENT languages are distinguished by being made up of DIFFERENT sets of sentences.** Two people will speak exactly the same language if (and only if) the set of sentences in each of their languages are exactly the same. A consequence of this is that, almost certainly, no two people speak EXACTLY the same language.

By way of illustration of this, consider again [4]

[4] Max put the car in the garage and Bill did so in the lay-by.

If I had inadvertently said this, I would consider it a mistake on my part and, given the opportunity, I would want to correct myself. So, for me, [4] is not a (grammatical) sentence of my language. In fact, there is a measure of agreement among English speakers that [4] is not a sentence of their language. But suppose we do find someone who could use [4] without any feeling that there is something wrong with it. Then, for that person, [4] IS a sentence of his or her language. Now, if a language is a set of sentences, that person and I must be said to speak slightly different languages, different to the extent that the set of (grammatical) sentences that constitutes his or her language includes [4] whereas the set of sentences that constitutes my language excludes [4].

When I say that this other speaker and I speak 'slightly' different languages, I am assuming for the purposes of the discussion that she and I agree about the other sentences mentioned in this book, disagreeing only about this sentence [4]. But wait a moment. If all the (grammatical) sentences mentioned in this book are sentences of this other speaker's language, doesn't that mean that this other speaker speaks what is known as *English*? And don't I, as author of this book, speak English too? And English, after all, is a language. Surely, then, we speak the same language: English.

This conclusion appears to contradict the idea that a language is a set of sentences and that particular languages are distinguished by consisting of different sets of sentences. English is normally regarded as a language, yet by the definition of a language given in [3], speakers of English are characterised as speaking more or less different languages. Do speakers of English speak the same language or don't they?

This last question is really a matter for us to decide, because it amounts to this: should we use the expression 'a language' in a way that allows us to say that English is a language, the common language of its speakers (this is a decision to abandon [3] altogether), or should we use that expression in a way that obliges us to say that strictly speaking, English is not a language itself, but a gigantic collection of largely overlapping languages? Answer [3] encourages this second use.

There is nothing to stop us using the expression 'a language' in both of these ways. In fact, we normally do use it in both ways. It depends on the context in which one is using it. Clearly, by comparison with French (or, the gigantic collection of overlapping languages that go to make up what is known as French) English is an identifiable language (in the first sense above), absolutely distinct from the French language. Well-known phrases and sayings apart, there are no sentences of English in the set of French sentences, and vice-versa: there is no overlap.

But within what is known as English, you know as well as I that there are differences. Geordies, Glaswegians, Londoners, Californians, Belfastians, Jamaicans, Canberrans, Sidneyans speak differently. And this is not simply a matter of accent. Each and every Geordie, Glaswegian, Californian (etc.) has a language and each of these languages can be described as a set of sentences. These sets are known to differ to a greater or lesser degree. I'll give just two small examples. [5] is a grammatical sentence of the language spoken by most Geordies:

[5] You can't do it, can't you not?

but not of the languages spoken by, for example, Jamaicans, Californians, or Glaswegians. Conversely, [6]

[6] Did you eat yet?

is a grammatical sentence of the language of Californians (and most U.S. languages) but not, for example, of Geordies, Jamaicans, or Londoners.

The discussion so far suggests that it is not in fact such a calamity to conclude that, **in one useful sense of the expression 'a language', English is not a language (but a collection of overlapping languages).**

Indeed, there is almost no limit to the variety within English we may recognise if it suits our purpose. I have mentioned general variation associated with geographical differences. I could also have mentioned variation associated with age differences, educational, social, and political differences, and I would still have said nothing about linguistic variation across time, variation caused by the fact that languages change through the centuries. In one perfectly good sense of 'a language', we, Shakespeare, Chaucer, and the Gawain poet have different languages. In another perfectly good sense, it is all the same language. Amid all the variety, we cannot lose sight of the common ground, the overlap between the varieties. It is this overlap that justifies the label 'the English language' (and the use of the word 'English' in the title of this book) and it is this that enables its speakers, with more or less success, to communicate with each other.

Linguistic variation, however, is a study in its own right (sometimes called socio-linguistics, or dialectology) and is not the topic of this book. I shall continue to assume, safely I believe, that the sentences and structures analysed in this book fall within the common ground, forming a central part of the language of its readers. Let us now consider some more specific consequences of [3] for the description of languages.


## Describing languages

**If a language is a set of sentences, then the job of describing a language consists in indicating, for every sequence of words, whether or not that sequence counts as a grammatical sentence of the language.**

The idea that a language is a set of sentences suggests to many people encountering it for the first time that you should be able to gather all the sentences of a language together, make a list of them, and say 'This is the complete language'. And certainly, if you can make a list of all the sentences of a language, [3] suggests a very easy way to go about DESCRIBING a language: to give a fully explicit and comprehensive description of a language, all that is required is to draw up such a list, one that includes all the word sequences that are grammatical sentences of the language and excludes all word sequences that are not.

Imagine, if you can, a language in which there are just TEN SENTENCES. We could call this language 'Justen'. If a language is a set of sentences, we have only to list those ten sentences in order to have an explicit and comprehensive description of Justen. By consulting that list we could be able to tell immediately what was, and what was not, Justen.

How realistic is this? Can you really imagine a proper language in which you could say just ten things? I doubt whether such a 'language' properly deserves the name. 'Code' would perhaps be a more appropriate description. So, that account of what a language is works well enough for Justen, but Justen is altogether unreal. Should we, then, reject that account?

Well, if you share the feeling that [3], as a definition of what a language is, makes it appear as though all languages are as simple as Justen, then you probably do want to reject it. However, this is probably because the definition suggests to you that a language has to be a fairly small set of sentences, small enough at least to make a list of and put a number on. But there is nothing in the idea that a language is a set of sentences to suggest that it has to have any limit on it. A set of things can be indefinitely large. Indeed, there is no reason why a set of things should even be finite. For example, numbers form a set of things, and this set is infinite: there is no largest number. What about the set of SENTENCES that form a language?

We have agreed that Justen is unreal. But how unreal is it? If your language does not contain just ten sentences, how many does it contain? Five hundred? Five thousand? Five million . . .? Could you, in fact, put a number on it?

In asking this question, I am not asking how many sentences you have actually used and understood so far in your life. Nor am I asking how many you will have used and understood by the time you die. Rather, **the question concerns the number of word sequences that you would accept as being sentences of your language, available for your use whether or not you actually get to make use of them.** Now, if what we are concerned with is not the number you will actually use in your lifetime but the number that are in principle AVAILABLE for use, we come closest to the truth in saying that there is no finite number of sentences in your language. **You speak an infinite language.**

There are well-known ways of demonstrating this. Consider, for example, a single word of your language, the word *and*. We can be perfectly confident that Justen does not include any word having the same function as *and*. How can we be so sure of this? Well, if Justen included this word it would, quite simply, be an infinite language. Adding this one word to that ten-sentence language changes it, at a stroke, into an infinite language. One of the functions of *and* is to join any two or more sentences together to form another, co-ordinate, sentence. Say we number the sentences of the original Justen, S1 to S10. With the addition of *and* a whole new language opens up, one that includes the following four sentences:

(i) [S1 and S2]   (ii) [S2, S3, and S4]   (iii) [S10, S9, S8, and
   s       s            s        s            s         s
S3]   (iv)   [ [S7 and S6] and [S5 and S10] and [S9 and S10] ]
   s      Ss          s       s         s       s             s S

and an infinity of further sentences.

Your language includes *and*. There is no sentence of which you could say 'This is the longest sentence in my language'. For any sentence that you care to think of, however long, it is always possible to create another, longer, sentence by co-ordinating a further clause within it.

Of course, *and* is not the only device that allows you to elaborate the length and complexity of your sentences. Another, encountered in Chapter 9, is the relative clause. Think of the nursery rhyme 'This is the house that Jack built'. Here's the last sentence: *This is the farmer sowing his corn that kept the cock that crowed in the morn that woke the priest all shaven and shorn that married the man all tattered and torn that kissed the maiden all forlorn that milked the cow with the crumpled horn that tossed the dog that chased the cat that killed the rat that ate the malt that lay in the house that Jack built.*

Each new sentence of the rhyme is created by subordinating the previous sentence as a relative clause functioning as a modifier in a newly-introduced NP. This could go on for ever. The fact that it doesn't go on longer has nothing to do with the language itself but with boredom, exhaustion, hunger and, finally, mortality.

Before I continue, let me summarise the last two most

important points. (1) In contrast to the artificial example of Justen, NATURAL languages (the languages which, in the words of the phrase, we learn at our mother's knee) are INFINITE. (2) The infinity of natural languages does not in any way conflict with the idea that a language is a set of sentences; sets can be infinite and a language can be defined as an infinite set of sentences.

## Describing infinite languages

But now we have a new question, and it is this: how do you describe an infinite set of sentences? If it is the purpose of a language description to indicate which are, and which are not, the grammatical sentences of a language, how to you do this when the language is infinite?

Clearly, we must abandon the idea of listing. Just as you cannot list the infinity of numbers, so you cannot list an infinity of sentences. The significance of [3] as an answer to the question 'What is a language?' is that it forces you to state explicitly which are the grammatical sentences of the language and which are not – and to do this for an INFINITE set of sentences and non-sentences. Since listing is out, [3] forces us to find an alternative principle on which to base our descriptions.

I shall approach the alternative that seems to be required by the preceding remarks by comparing the two artificial languages considered above, Justen and the language that consists of the ten sentences of Justen augmented by *and*. We can call this second language 'Justenand'. I have shown that nothing is easier than the complete description of Justen: because it is a finite language, we merely list its ten sentences. But we can't do this for Justenand. Before reading further, ask yourself whether it is possible to give a complete description of Justenand and, if so, how you would go about doing so. Remember, in asking for a complete description of Justenand, I want to know categorically, for any sequence I care to think of, whether it is a sentence of the language or not.

---

If you have thought about this, you will have realised that Justenand, infinite though it is, is still a very rudimentary language. It is not only possible to describe this language in its entirety, it is not even very difficult. The description will fall into two parts. The first part must be the original list of ten sentences. To account for the infinity of other sentences which have become possibilities because of the addition of *and*, something different is required. What we need, for the second part, is an EXPLICIT STATEMENT to the effect that **a sentence of Justenand may consist of any other two or more sentences of Justenand joined by *and*.** This statement tells us that, given that S1 and S2 are sentences of Justenand, then there is another Justenand sentence (call it S11) having the form:

And, since S11 has been defined by the statement as being a grammatical sentence of Justenand, we know by the same token that S12 is one too:

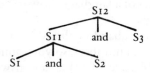

and so on *ad infinitum*.

By means of the statement in the second part of the description, we have given a complete description of Justenand without resorting to an infinite and hence uncompletable list. We have, in fact, provided a finite description of an infinite set of sentences. Although a list is included in the full description (and it is this list that makes Justenand hardly less artificial than Justen), that list has been supplemented by something quite different, namely a RULE. For that is what the above statement is, a rule for forming the infinity of Justenand sentences. **It is by means of RULES that we can give FINITE descriptions of INFINITE sets of sentences.**

This difference between List and Rule is of central importance in language study. The very idea of 'sentence' as you and I understand it is bound up with the notion of 'rule'. To see this, think about Justen again. This toy language is probably more different from your own language than you realise. In particular, it is not even clear that what we have been calling its 'sentences' bear any relation at all to the things that you call sentences in your language.

In explanation of this, remember that, since Justen is a finite 'language', it is actually possible to identify its 'sentences' by numbers. Indeed, the speakers of this so-called language could themselves identify their ten sentences by number. The only problem with this idea is that whereas the numbers are infinite, Justen has only ten sentences. But, if it is unlikely that numbers would be used, there is nothing to prevent these speakers having NAMES for their ten sentences. S1 could be *Oink*, S2 *Woops*, S3 *Umph*, S4 *Whack* and so on. Given that there are only ten sentences in the language, the speakers of Justen could convey everything that the language was capable of conveying by means of such names.

Now do you see how different Justen is from your language? Names are SIMPLE words. They do not have syntactic structure. In other words, a language that could consist of names alone has no need of, indeed cannot be said to have, hierarchical structure, syntactic categories, or syntactic functions. In a word, it would have no syntax. Even the distinction between 'sentence' and 'word' would be meaningless. Rules would have no part to play in the description of such a language. Not only can we list the 'sentences' of this language, we must list them if we want to describe it.

By contrast, sentence-listing plays no part either in the description of your language or in the way you use that language. You do not have a list of ready-made sentences in your head. If you did, the language would have to be finite; your head, after all, has a finite capacity. Furthermore, if you could hold them all in your head, as prepackaged sentences, there would be no need for them to be complex, i.e. there would be no need for them to have structure. If knowing a natural language could be a matter of remembering sentences as such, why bother with COMPLEX things like sentences at all? It would be easier to remember simple names, and more efficient.[1]

Instead, you have to CONSTRUCT your sentences as and when the need arises. And it is the fact that you do construct sentences on the spot that enables you to utter any of an infinite number of sentences, appropriate to an infinite variety of situations. Knowing a natural language, then, does not consist in having an inventory of sentences in your head, but in knowing HOW to construct the sentences. But, and this is the important point, in order to know how to construct the grammatical sentences of a natural language, you have to know in very general terms what counts as a grammatical sentence of the language,

---

1. Jorge Luis Borges, in 'Funes the Memorious' (*Labyrinths*, Penguin books) has written an interesting story on the effects of an infallible memory on a person's language.

in other words, what it is that makes a sentence grammatical or ungrammatical.

When it comes to describing languages, we can take our cue from this. Our ultimate task in describing a language is still to specify what the grammatical sentences of the language are. But we cannot expect to do this directly. What we can and must do is specify what it is that makes a sequence of words grammatical or ungrammatical. This amounts to saying that, **in order to describe a particular language, you have to give a general definition of the concept 'grammatical sentence' for that language**. It is by reference to this general definition that we can state, for each of an infinity of word-sequences, whether it is a grammatical sentence or not. This will be done, not by consulting a sentence-list, but by PREDICTION. The general definition forces us to make predictions about word-sequences we had never even thought about or encountered before. This in turn means that, in describing an infinite language, we cannot say that a particular sequence of words is not a grammatical sentence of the language without simultaneously explaining why it isn't.

This was not done for Justen. In just listing the 'grammatical sentences' of Justen, we did not define what it was for something to be a Justen sentence. This, as we saw, was not necessary. In fact, it is not even possible. The idea of 'knowing how to construct a sentence' is completely inappropriate in the context of Justen. In the first place, you can only CONSTRUCT something if that thing is COMPLEX, has structure. But the sentences of Justen are perfectly simple. In the second place, you can only 'know how to construct' the things in a set by knowing general principles that apply to them. And this entails knowing not only what distinguishes them from each other but what they have in common. But only complex things (things that have parts) can have something in common and yet be different. Totally simple things can only be absolutely the same (identical) or absolutely different.

If an English-speaking 'speaker' of Justen were to point out that we had overlooked the existence of an eleventh 'sentence', all we could do would be to shrug our shoulders and add it to the list. We would have learnt nothing more about what it was to be a Justen sentence. There is no way we could have PREDICTED or EXPLAINED its existence because we have no general idea (or definition) of what counts as a Justen sentence in the first place.

We have a better general idea of what counts as a Justenand sentence, though, and this is expressed in the general statement (the rule) that formed the second part of its description. That rule gives a partial definition of what it is for something to be a grammatical sentence of Justenand. It is only partial, since we still don't have any definition that covers the original ten sentences. But provided those ten sentences are the only original sentences, we are in a position to make an infinite number of predictions about what is and what is not a sentence of Justenand. Furthermore, that statement has resulted in a partial DESCRIPTION of Justenand sentences – see the phrase-markers on page 248. It is only partial because we have not described sentences 1–10. And we have given a (partial) EXPLANATION of why ungrammatical 'sentences' of Justenand are ungrammatical: they are ungrammatical because they deviate from the general principle outlined in that statement.

## Grammars

At the risk of repetitiveness, I shall summarise what seems to have emerged so far. The discussion of Justen is neatly and more generally summarised in the following statement:

[9] A finite language is its own grammar.

I have not used the term 'grammar' before in this chapter. Instead, I have talked about language description. But this is what a grammar is, the description of a language. In the terms established so far, then, **the function of the grammar of a language is to specify which word sequences are, and which are not, in the infinite set of its sentences.**

Justen illustrates [9] as follows: If a language is a set of sentences, then Justen IS exactly those ten 'sentences'. A grammar describes a language. But, as we have seen, the grammar of Justen IS the list of those ten sentences. The ten sentences of Justen, then, constitute both the grammar itself and the language itself. It is in this sense that Justen, being a finite language, is its own grammar.

It's an odd sort of grammar, though, that doesn't specify any kind of syntax for its language – one far removed from our ordinary conception of what a grammar is. And this is pretty well what is said in [9]. Essentially, there is no real grammar of Justen. In view of our conclusion that Justen cannot seriously be considered as a language, this is not surprising.

By contrast, the discussion of natural languages and their grammars can be summarised as follows.

1. A natural language is an INFINITE set of sentences.

2. The description of a language (the GRAMMAR of a language) states which are, and which are not, in the infinite set of its sentences.

3. It is the COMPLEXITY of natural language sentences (the fact that they have structure) that makes it possible to construct an INFINITY of sentences, and it is the infinity of natural languages that makes a GENERAL DEFINITION of 'sentence' necessary in order to achieve what is described in 2 above.

4. Equally, it is the fact that the sentences of a natural language are complex that allows each different sentence to have more or less in COMMON with every other different sentence.

5. And it is the fact that the sentences of a language do have more or less in common with every other different sentence that makes it possible to state GENERAL PRINCIPLES (to FORMULATE RULES) about them.

6. The COMPLEXITY of natural language sentences, then, makes a general definition of sentence both possible and necessary.

7. In conclusion, the ideal envisioned here is that a GRAMMAR is the description of a language by means of a DEFINITION OF 'SENTENCE' in that language. The definition takes the form of A SET OF RULES. The definition automatically has three interrelated functions (i) to make an infinite number of PREDICTIONS about what is and is not in the set of sentences of a language, (ii) to give DESCRIPTIONS of the grammatical sentences, and (iii) to give EXPLANATIONS of the ungrammaticality of the ungrammatical 'sentences' (the non-sentences). These three functions are interrelated in the sense that, for an infinite number of sentences, it is impossible to do any one of these without doing the other two.

## Grammars and sentence analysis

How do these very general considerations relate to the analyses discussed in previous chapters? You might be forgiven if at some point in your reading of those chapters you had asked yourself whether phrase-markers were the be-all and end-all of syntax. You might be forgiven for thinking 'OK, so now I know how to draw a plausible phrase-marker. Where does this lead me? Where do we go from here?'

We have seen what phrase-markers can do. They provide explicit descriptions of sentences in terms of category, function, and constituency. Descriptions of sentences, whether given in the form of phrase-markers or some equivalent notation (e.g. labelled brackets), are an important and indispensible part of language-description. They are not by any means the whole story. Your reading of this chapter should have given you an idea of what phrase-markers, in themselves, cannot do.

For example, you know that [10] is not a (grammatical) sentence of your language.

[10] *Stream a beside sunbathed Sam.

Nothing I have said so far in this book, however, prevents us assigning [10] a phrase-marker, [11] for example:

[11]

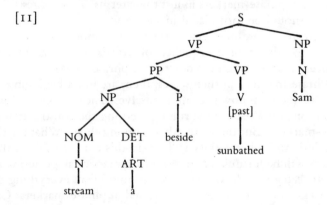

Indeed, there is nothing that obliges us to give it that phrase-marker even.

I have suggested that, to describe a natural language, a definition is required of what it is to be a (grammatical) sentence of the language. And I have suggested that such a definition would, automatically and simultaneously, PREDICT which are the grammatical sentences and which are not, DESCRIBE the grammatical sentences, and EXPLAIN the ungrammatical sentences. In other words, if you wish to PREDICT that [10] is not a grammatical S in your language, that *Stream a beside sunbathed* is not a grammatical VP, that *stream a beside* is not a grammatical PP, that *stream a* is not a grammatical NP, you must explain why not, and, in order to explain why not, you must describe (by means of rules) what does count as a grammatical S, or VP, or PP, or NP . . . in your language.

While phrase-markers DESCRIBE sentences, they do not, in themselves, give an indication of what it is to be a sentence; hence they do not, in themselves, make any PREDICTIONS, or give any EXPLANATIONS.

Ultimately, then, we must make the connection between the phrase-markers on the one hand and, on the other, the RULES that constitute the definition of what it is to be a grammatical sentence.

This is a natural connection to make. It is clear from the discussion of this chapter that the rules of the grammar must be expressed in terms of syntactic categories and how they are structured into sentences. After all, it is the COMPLEXITY of natural language sentences (i.e. all that we understand by their having STRUCTURE) that makes such rules both possible and necessary. And the description given in previous chapters are expressed in phrase-markers in just these terms. This suggests that the rules should be formulated in such a way that they, in some sense, create phrase-markers as their descriptions of sentences, so that, in admitting a sequence of words as a grammatical sentence, the rules assign it a descriptive phrase-marker.

Phrase-markers, in themselves, then, are just a beginning. A variety of questions now present themselves. The most general and obvious one is: What are the rules governing the construction of phrase-markers? But there are others, among them: What are the best rules? And what counts as 'best' in this context? Given that the rules will be formulated in terms of syntactic categories, what syntactic categories do we need to recognise? Can everything we want to say about sentences be expressed in phrase-markers? Can everything we want to say about each sentence be expressed in a single phrase-marker?

Of course, it will have occurred to you that, although no explicit mention was made of rules in the preceding chapters, the analyses suggested there are not just arbitrary; in suggesting them, I have been guided IMPLICITLY by general principles. In asking 'What are the rules?' then, we are concerned with laying bare those general principles, with making them fully EXPLICIT, and with whether those are the best general principles available.

Such questions, and the thinking that leads up to them, open up the prospect of a rich and extremely ambitious method of language description. When a grammar is conceived of in the terms outlined in this chapter, it is called a GENERATIVE GRAMMAR. In the section on Further Reading that follows, I briefly discuss more detailed introductions to the enterprise of generative grammar. Here I have been concerned to give an idea of the kind of thinking that gives rise to that enterprise, and to place the phrase-marker descriptions within a more general context. Of course, a conclusion that consists of questions like those above is something of a cliff-hanger. If you feel this, I have at least succeeded in whetting your appetite.

Finally, why bother? Why is it so important to formulate the rules of natural languages in a fully explicit manner? After all, we all speak one language or another without bother. Why not leave it at that?

There are two related answers to this. The first takes us back to comments made in the introduction. It is precisely the fact that we all speak a language without bother that gives this enterprise its interest and importance. There is a sense in which you know the rules of your language. This must be so, since you are capable of making an infinite number of judgements as to what is and what is not a grammatical sentence of your language. But the sense in which you know these rules is different from the sense in which you know the rules of chess, know how to read music, make zabaglione, or drive a car. You know the rules of your language IMPLICITLY, as if by instinct. The job of the generative grammarian of a language is to describe what its speakers implicitly and instinctively know about that language, in other words, to make EXPLICIT what it is that speakers know in knowing their language.

Secondly, the discussion above might have given the impression that the grammarian first of all decides what the most appropriate descriptions of sentences are and then goes to work on the rules that govern the construction of those descriptions. It is not quite like this, however. There is no guarantee that, when we attempt to state the rules in the best possible way and as explicitly as possible, we will not want to revise our ideas as to what the best descriptions are. If anything is guaranteed, the opposite of this is: it is by attempting to formulate a systematic and fully explicit set of rules for a language that we can expect to gain new insights into its structure, new insights, that is, into what it is that a speaker knows in knowing that language.

# A Final Exercise

Discuss as fully as possible the difference between the following (a) and (b) examples, and draw phrase-markers that differentiate them. Answers are not provided but, if you need some clues, relevant chapters of the book are cited against each example. (NB. The differences between (a) and (b) in 14 and 15 pose problems for the description offered in this book. What are the problems?)

**1.**(a) Max is shaving.                    Ch. 4 (and 6)
  (b) Max is surprising.

**2.**(a) John left this message.          Ch. 5 (and 4)
  (b) John left this morning.

**3.**(a) Albert looked up the shaft.                    Ch. 5
  (b) Albert looked up the answer.

**4.**(a) They considered him unfair.          Ch. 4 and 5
  (b) They considered him unfairly.

**5.**(a) Max keeps ducks on his farm.          Ch. 4 and 5
  (b) Max keeps wolves off his farm.

**6.**(a) Max submitted in the Spring.          Ch. 4 and 5
  (b) Max submitted to my demands.

**7.**(a) Sebastian was drunk by midnight.          Ch. 6 (and 4)
  (b) The wine was drunk by midnight.

**8.**(a) John is taking things too far.          Ch. 6 and 10
  (b) This is taking things too far!

**9.**(a) Flying planes is dangerous.          Ch. 7 and 10
  (b) Flying planes are dangerous.

**10.**(a) I would hate John to go.                    Ch. 10
  (b) I would advise John to go.

**11.**(a) John is eager to leave.                Ch. 10
    (b) John is difficult to leave.

**12.**(a) He doesn't need to have a bath.      Ch. 6 (and 10)
    (b) He needn't have a bath.

**13.**(a) Who is a celebrity?               Ch. 9
    (b) What is a celebrity?

**14.**(a) They treated him with aspirin.      Ch. 4 and 5
    (b) They treated him with contempt.

**15.**(a) The number of elephants is getting larger.      Ch. 7
    (b) A number of elephants are getting larger.

**16.**(a) Jo will finish the last drink.      Ch. 5
    (b) Jo will finish the drink last.

**17.**(a) This will make the thicker juice.      Ch.4
    (b) This will make the juice thicker.

**18.**(a) It is positive she'll be charged.      Ch. 8
    (b) Dogberry is positive she'll be charged.

**19.**(a) They asked him when to leave.      Ch. 10
    (b) They asked him when leaving.

**20.**(a) That fact that I communicated with Mona      Ch. 8 and 9
      is irrelevant.
    (b) The fact that I communicated to Mona is irrelevant.

**21.**(a) Purvis has made a little jam.      Ch. 7
    (b) Purvis has made a little mistake.

**22.**(a) Coco has made many patients happy with      Chs. 4 and 7
      their lot.
    (b) Coco has met many patients happy with
      their lot.

**23.**(a) Interestingly enough, Creon didn't speak.      Ch. 5
    (b) Creon didn't speak interestingly enough.

**24.**(a) These are contributions to the fund from
      unknown sources.      Ch. 7
    (b) These are contributions to the fund for Ethiopia.

# Further Reading

There are many texts available on both linguistics and the description of the English language. The following is a brief discussion of a small selection of those which are appropriate as further reading in connection with the present text.

**Quirk and Greenbaum's** *University Grammar of English* **(UGE)** is a condensed version of the famous *Grammar of Contemporary English* (GCE), a standard reference work on English grammar. It is the only contemporary work to offer a comprehensive description of English sentences, with much more detail than is offered in the present text. The description given in the present text is in part based on that of UGE – in particular, the verb sub-categorisation outlined in Chapter 4 is that of UGE.

There are points of difference, however. Most generally, the present text emphasises constituency and its representation; in UGE there is little discussion of constituency. On a more detailed level, UGE allows for obligatory adverbials, whereas in the present text it has been convenient to make it part of the definition of an adverbial that it is optional. There are also some minor differences of terminology, the most salient being the use of the term 'Verb Phrase'. In UGE 'Verb Phrase' is used to refer to what in the present text is called the 'Verb Group'; and what in the present text is called the 'Verb Phrase' is called 'Predicate' in UGE.

The reader should consult UGE or GCE on several important constructions which are not dealt with in the present text, for example: (1) Nominal Relative Clauses (also known as Free Relative Clauses) – UGE: Ch. 11; (2) Apposition – UGE: Ch. 9; (3) Gerunds (also known as Gerundive Nominalisations–) UGE: Ch. 4.9–.12; (4) Imperative sentences – UGE: Ch. 7, where they are called 'commands'; (5) Existential *there* sentences – UGE: Ch. 14.

Particularly appropriate as further reading in connection with the present text is **Huddleston's *Introduction to the Grammar of English***, which offers a more wide-ranging and more detailed discussion of English syntactic structures and the linguistic concepts used in their description. Descriptive complexities which are either ignored or merely alluded to in the present text are there given more attention. There is a useful bibliography of items accessible to the intermediate student.

Apart from the assumption of some correlation between constituent structure and meaning in the present text, little has been said about meaning. This was particularly marked in discussion of the Verb Group. **Leech's *Meaning and the English Verb*** is a good short introduction. **Palmer's *The English Verb*** is a more comprehensive work on the form, function, and meaning of English verbal forms.

In Chapter 11 I introduced the idea of generative grammar. In this connection, two books are useful. **Radford's *Transformational Syntax*** is relevant in several respects. Like the present text, it takes constituency (and its representation in the form of phrase-markers) as the leading idea in syntax. Chapter 1 is an account of how Chomsky (mentioned in Chapter 11 here) views the general aims of language study. Chapter 2 is concerned with structure and how structural descriptions can be generated by rules. Having read the present text, the reader should have no difficulty in tackling this. At the end of that chapter, the reader is invited to compare six different analyses of English verbal elements, mentioned as being controversial in Chapter 6 above. The rest of the book is an introduction to Chomsky's theory of generative grammar as it applies to English. Of particular relevance is the discussion of Chomsky's approach to complementation of the Verb by non-finite clause in the later chapters (discussed in Chapter 10 above).

A good general introduction to the enterprise of generative grammar is **Smith and Wilson's *Modern Linguistics.*** This discusses not only syntax in generative grammar but phonology, semantics, and linguistic theory generally. It is tough in places.

Finally a word must be said about competing linguistic theories and how they apply to the descriptions in the present text. The last two books mentioned fall within the framework of a particular theory of generative grammar, transformational generative grammar. The central claim of transformational grammar is that, in describing the sentences of a language, it is impossible to express everything that needs to be expressed about each sentence within a single phrase-marker. The claim is that several phrase-markers are required to describe a sentence properly. The theory proposes that one kind of rule be used to create an initial phrase-marker (these are called Phrase Structure Rules) and another kind of rule (called Transformational Rules) be used to relate phrase-markers to other phrase-markers. The description of each sentence, then, consists of several phrase-markers related to each other by transformational rules.

Although this theory has been the most widely accepted over the last thirty years or so, its central claim is now being seriously questioned, in particular by proponents of the generative theory called Generalised Phrase Structure Grammar. The claim of this theory is that the sentences of a language can be described by means of Phrase Structure rules without the aid of Transformational rules, in a single phrase-marker.

As mentioned, the last two texts deal with Transformational Generative Grammar. But I do not see the present text as preparing the ground solely for that theory. As far as I am aware, the question of whether transformations are a necessary part of linguistic description has been left completely open by the discussion of the previous chapters. I would have liked to recommend a textbook in Generalised Phrase Structure Grammar, which is equally compatible with the assumptions of the present text, but no such book exists yet.

Huddleston, R. (1984) *Introduction to the Grammar of English*. Cambridge University Press.

Leech, G. N. (1971) *Meaning and the English Verb*. Longman.

Palmer, F. R. (1974) *The English Verb*. Longman.

Quirk, R. and S. Greenbaum (1973) *A University Grammar of English*. Longman.

Quirk, R., S. Greenbaum, G. Leech, and J. Svartvik (1972) *A Grammar of Contemporary English*. Longman.

Radford, A. (1981) *Transformational Syntax – A student's guide to Chomsky's Extended Standard Theory*. Cambridge University Press.

Smith, N. V. and D. Wilson (1979) *Modern Linguistics – The results of Chomsky's revolution*. Pelican.

# Index